NICK COHEN is a columnist for the *Observer*. He also writes for *Standpoint*, the *Spectator* and many other titles. He is the author of *Cruel Britannia: Reports on the Sinister and the Preposterous*, *Pretty Straight Guys*, *What's Left?: How the Left Lost its Way* and *Waiting for the Etonians: Reports from the Sickbed of Liberal England*. He lives in London.

## Also by Nick Cohen

*Cruel Britannia: Reports on the Sinister and the Preposterous*
*Pretty Straight Guys*
*What's Left?: How the Left Lost its Way*
*Waiting for the Etonians:*
*Reports from the Sickbed of Liberal England*

# NICK COHEN

# *You Can't Read This Book*

## Censorship in an Age of Freedom

**FOURTH ESTATE • London**

First published in Great Britain in 2012 by
Fourth Estate
An imprint of HarperCollins*Publishers*
1 London Bridge Street
London SE1 9GF
www.4thestate.co.uk

This revised edition published by Fourth Estate 2013

A catalogue record for this book is
available from the British Library

ISBN 978-0-00-751850-0

Typeset in Minion by G&M Designs Limited,
Raunds, Northamptonshire

Printed by CPI Group (UK) Ltd, Croydon CR0 4YY

**MIX**
Paper from
responsible sources
FSC™ C007454

*For Christopher Hitchens*
*(1949–2011)*

# CONTENTS

*There is an all-out confrontation between the ironic and the literal mind: between every kind of commissar and inquisitor and bureaucrat and those who know that, whatever the role of social and political forces, ideas and books have to be formulated and written by individuals.*

CHRISTOPHER HITCHENS

# INTRODUCTION

Do you believe in freedom of speech?

Really, are you sure?

You may say you do. It's the sort of thing that everyone says. Just as everyone says they have a sense of humour, especially when they don't. You will certainly have had serious men and women assure you that freedom of speech is inevitable whether you believe in it or not. In the late twentieth century states, courts, private companies and public bureaucracies confined information, their argument runs. If it spread beyond those with 'a need to know', the authorities of the nation state, whether a dictatorship or a democracy, could imprison or fine the leaker. The threat of punishment was enough to deter newspapers from publishing or television stations from broadcasting.

That manageable world has gone for good. If one person living in a court's jurisdiction breaks an injunction, a judge can punish him. But how can a judge punish a thousand, ten thousand, a hundred thousand on Twitter or Facebook? If a court in New Delhi, Copenhagen or London bans the publication of embarrassing information, sites outside the jurisdiction of the Indian, Danish or British courts can publish it on the Web, and everyone with access to a computer in India, Denmark or Britain can read it, along with billions of others.

If the Web has a soul, then a loathing for censorship stirs it. The Streisand effect – first named in 2005 after the star tried to sue a photographer for publishing pictures of her Malibu mansion, and succeeded only in directing hundreds of thousands of viewers to his website – is a real phenomenon. Label a report 'confidential' and it becomes as desirable as forbidden fruit. Once a whistleblower leaks it, you can guarantee that the Web will broadcast its contents, regardless of whether they are interesting or not.

Optimists about the liberating potential of technology can find many reasons to be euphoric. The Net has no borders. National laws cannot contain it. Attempts to press down on the free circulation of information in one country just push it into other countries. The ability of users to copy, link and draw others into their campaigns had stripped censors of their power.

On this cheerful reading, we live in a new world where information is liquid. Wall it in, and it will seep through the brickwork. 'An old way of doing things is dying; a new one is being born,' announced a US cyber activist. 'The Age of Transparency is here.'

So it appeared. WikiLeaks became the new age's journalistic phenomenon, as it dumped masses of confidential information onto the Web about the American war in Afghanistan and the American war in Iraq and the American prison at Guantánamo Bay and the American State Department. America, the most powerful country in the world, could not stop it. WikiLeaks was based in Sweden, beyond America's control, although everyone in America with access to the Net could read what it published.

The new technologies justified their revolutionary possibilities by playing a part in the Arab Spring of 2010–11. In Syria and Libya, they allowed the victims of closed societies to talk to the rest of the world. In Egypt, Facebook became a means of organising revolutionary protest. The Arab dictators knew the arts of torture and repression well. They could break the bodies and the will of their traditional opponents. They could not cope with the mobilisations of the young the Web allowed, because they had never experienced anything like them before.

The promise of the Net inspired politicians as well as activists. After the fall of the Berlin Wall, optimistic leaders and intellectuals believed that history was over and that any society that wanted to be wealthy had to embrace liberal capitalism. In the early 2010s, optimists switched from political to technological determinism. They predicted that genocides would become impossible when all it would take to stop an atrocity would be for witnesses to alert the conscience of humanity by uploading videos from their iPhones to YouTube. They warned dictators who censored that they were imperilling economic growth by stopping their businesses accessing the sources of knowledge they needed to compete in a global market. Any society that wanted to be wealthy had to embrace freedom of speech.

With tyrannies tumbling and computing power guaranteeing the triumph of liberal values, why write a book on censorship?

I am all for liberal optimism, and hope a new world is being born. Before euphoria carries us away, however, consider the following scenarios.

• A young novelist from a Muslim family writes a fictional account of his struggles with his religious identity. He describes religion as a fairy tale and mocks the prohibitions of the Koran he was taught as a child as bigoted and preposterous. His writing shows that he does not regard the life of Muhammad as exemplary. Quite the reverse, in fact. If word of his work seeped out in Pakistan, the courts would charge him with blasphemy, a 'crime' that carries the death sentence. In Iran or Saudi Arabia, the authorities would arrest him, and maybe kill him too. In India, they would confine themselves to charging him with 'outraging religious feelings'. In most Western states, prosecutors would not charge him, but he would receive the worst punishment the world can inflict on a writer other than depriving him of his life or liberty: no one would publish his work. He would find that although American and European countries do not have blasphemy laws that protect Islam, or in most cases Christianity, the threat of violent reprisals against Western publishers and authors is enough to enforce extra-legal censorship that no parliament or court has authorised.

- An African feminist comes to Holland and denounces its tolerance of the abuse of women in ethnic and religious minorities. Newspaper editors and television producers cannot get enough of her fresh and controversial voice. After religious fanatics murder one of her supporters and threaten to murder her, their mood changes. Intellectuals say she is an 'Enlightenment fundamentalist' who is as intolerant and extreme as the religious fanatics she opposes. Politicians and newspaper columnists complain about the cost to the taxpayer of her police protection and accuse her of bringing rancour to their previously harmonious multi-cultural society. No one bans her books, but her work inspires no imitators. She becomes a leader without followers. Women, who were prepared to support her arguments, look at the treatment she received, and put down their pens.

- The editor of a Danish newspaper wonders why comedians, who boast of their willingness to 'transgress boundaries' and 'speak truth to power', will mock Jesus but not Muhammad. He invites Danish cartoonists to satirise the Prophet. Most respond by satirising the editor. It makes no difference. They still have to spend the rest of their lives under police protection.

- Two bankers, one from New York and one from London, meet for lunch and discuss an issue that has troubled them both. Not one of the great newspapers that cover high finance saw the crash of 2008 coming. Nor did bloggers make it their business to find out about the risks their banks were running. The Net was as clueless as the 'dead tree' press. Insiders knew that the lust for bonuses and the pressure to accede to management demands for quick profits could have catastrophic consequences. But the information had never leaked. The two bankers discuss writing a joint article for the *Financial Times* or the *Wall Street Journal* exposing the continuing failure to address the structural problems in Western banking. They think that their intervention could improve public debate, but dismiss the idea as too dangerous. They know that if they speak out, their banks will fire them and they will never work in banking again. No other bank will want people marked as troublemakers on its 'team'.

- A British newspaper reporter moves from the politics to the business desk. She resolves to start digging into the backgrounds of the Russian oligarchs who have set up home in London. She has criticised British politicians without fear of the consequences for years, but her editor turns pale when she talks about using the same tactics against plutocrats. The smallest factual mistake or unsupportable innuendo could lead to a libel action that could cost the paper a million pounds, 'and we don't have a million pounds'. She ploughs on, and produces an article that is so heavily cut and rewritten by the in-house lawyers no one can understand it. 'I want a thousand words on trends in fashion retailing by lunchtime,' the editor says when she starts work the next day.

- A member of the Central Committee of the Chinese Communist Party reads a speech by Hillary Clinton. 'When countries curtail Internet freedom, they place limits on their economic future. Their young people don't have full access to the conversations and debates happening in the world or exposure to the kind of free enquiry that spurs people to question old ways and invent new ones. Barring criticism of officials makes governments more susceptible to corruption, which creates economic distortions with long-term effects. Freedom of thought and the level playing field made possible by the rule of law are part of what fuels innovation economies.' The old communist is a man who has trained himself never to show his emotions in case they reveal weaknesses to his rivals in the party. But he thinks of China's booming economy and America's fiscal and trade deficits, and for the first time in years he throws back his head and roars with laughter.

What follows is an examination of how censorship in its clerical, economic and political forms works in practice. It is a history of the controversies of our times, and an argument that free speech is better than suppression in almost all circumstances. I hope that I will have convinced you by the end that the limits on free speech – for there are always limits – should be few, and that the law must refuse to implement them if there is a hint of a public interest in allowing debate to continue unimpeded.

My subject is censorship that hurts, not spin or the unstoppable desire of partisan newspapers, broadcasters and bloggers to preach to the converted and dismiss or ignore news their audiences do not wish to hear. I accept that press officers' manipulation of information is an attempt to limit and control. But manipulation becomes censorship only on those occasions when the law punishes those who expose the spin. I agree too that editorial suppression is a type of censorship, because it ensures that readers rarely find a good word about trade unions in a right-wing newspaper, or a sympathetic article about Israel in a left-wing journal. The effects are trivial, because those readers who do not wish to be spoon-fed opinions can find contrary views elsewhere, and a journalist who does not like the party line of one media organisation can choose to move to another.

True censorship removes choice. It menaces and issues commands that few can ignore. Write a freethinking novel, and religious terrorists will come to assassinate you. Tell the world about your employers' incompetence, and they will deprive you of your livelihood. Criticise a pharmaceutical corporation or an association of 'alternative health' quacks and they will seek to bankrupt you in the English courts. Speak out in a dictatorship, and the secret police will escort you to jail.

The invention of the Net, like all communications revolutions before it, is having and will have profound effects – which I do not seek to belittle. Its effect on the ability of the strong and the violent to impose their views is less marked than optimists imagine, because they fail to understand the difference between *total* control and *effective* control. Everyone who wants to suppress information would like to remove all trace of it. But when total power eludes them, they seek to impose limits. It may irk a Russian oligarch that readers can find accounts of his mafia past somewhere on the Web, or infuriate the Chinese, Iranian and Belarusian regimes that dissident sites escape their controls. But they are not threatened unless people can act on the information. Action requires something more than an anonymous post somewhere in cyberspace. It requires the right to campaign and argue in public. As we have seen in the Middle East, in dictatorships it can require the courage to risk your life in a revolution.

Censorship's main role is to restrict the scope for action. If religious terror ensures that every mainstream broadcaster is frightened of lampooning Islam's founding myths, or if the citizens of a dictatorship know that they will be arrested if they challenge their leaders' abuses of power, then censors are exercising effective control by punishing those who challenge them and bullying their contemporaries into silence.

'You can be a famous poisoner or a successful poisoner,' runs the old joke, 'but you can't be both.' The same applies to censors. Ninety-nine per cent of successful censorship is hidden from view. Even when brave men and women speak out, the chilling effect of the punishments their opponents inflict on them silences others. Those who might have added weight to their arguments and built a campaign for change look at the political or religious violence, or at the threat of dismissal from work, or at the penalties overbearing judges impose, and walk away.

Technology can change the rules, but it cannot change the game. Freedom always has to be fought for, because it is rooted in cultures, laws and constitutions, not in microchips and search engines, and is protected by institutions that are obliged to defend it. The struggle for freedom of speech is at root a political struggle, not least because the powerful can use new technologies as effectively as the weak – often more effectively. Today's techno-utopianism is at best irritating and at worst a dangerous distraction, because it offers the comforting illusion that we can escape the need to fight against reactionary and unjust governments, enterprises and movements with the click of a mouse. When the first edition of this book came out, an otherwise kind critic bemoaned my failure to understand that the Web brought the dissident enemies of the Putin regime in from the fringe and allowed them to challenge the kleptocracy. 'The great boon of the Web is that distinctions between the mainstream and the esoteric crumble,' he said. 'How can Cohen not see that?'

One year on, and the protests against the Russian state's rigging of elections are over, and Putin is still in power. I wish it were otherwise, but contrary to the shallow views of Net utopians, technology cannot ensure progress. When it comes, progress in human affairs does not advance in a straight line. It bends and swerves; and sometimes it retreats. Today's debates assume that we are living in a better and more open world than our repressed ancestors. The most striking counter-argument against modern complacency is to begin by looking at that most contentious and dangerous of forces, and observe that we were freer to challenge religions that claimed dominion over men's minds and women's bodies thirty years ago than we are now.

In 1988, Salman Rushdie for one thought that a writer could criticise religious bigotry without running the risk that fanatics would murder him and everyone who worked with him, just for telling a story.

# PART ONE

# *God*

*I cannot praise a fugitive and cloistered virtue,
unexercised & unbreathed, that never sallies out and
sees her adversary, but slinks out of the race, where
that immortal garland is to be run for.*

JOHN MILTON, 1644

# ONE

# 'Kill the Blasphemer'

*It would be absurd to think a book could cause riots. That would be a strange view of the world.*

SALMAN RUSHDIE, 1988

Of course it was blasphemous. A book that challenges theocracy is blasphemous by definition. Not just because it questions the divine provenance of a sacred text – Did God speak to Moses? Inspire the gospels? Send the archangel Gabriel to instruct Muhammad on how to live and what to worship? – but because it criticises the bigotries the sacred text instructs the faithful to hold. By this measure, any book worth reading is blasphemous to some degree, and *The Satanic Verses* was well worth reading.

To say that Salman Rushdie did not know his novel would cause 'offence' is not true in the narrow sense of the word. He and his publishers never imagined the viciousness of the reaction, but just before the book was published in 1988, he sent a draft to the Palestinian intellectual Edward Said. Rushdie wanted Said's opinion because he thought his new novel 'may upset some of the faithful'. Indeed it did, but in the late twentieth century, no honest writer abandoned his or her book because it might upset a powerful lobby. Lackeys working for a plutocrat's newspaper or propagandists serving a state or corporate bureaucracy guarded their tongues and self-censored, but not artists and intellectuals in free countries.

Rushdie was writing in one of the most optimistic times in history. The advances in political, sexual and intellectual freedoms were unparalleled. It seemed that decent men and women needed only to raise their angry voices for tyrants to totter and fall. First in the fascistic dictatorships of Spain, Portugal and Greece in the 1970s, then in the military dictatorships of South America in the 1980s, and from 1989 to 1991 in the Soviet Union, Eastern Europe and apartheid South Africa, hundreds of millions of people saw their oppressors admit defeat and embrace liberal democracy.

Those who fought on the side of liberty did not worry about offending the religious or challenging cultures. Forty years ago a campaigner against state-enforced racism knew that supporters of apartheid came from a white supremacist culture with deep roots in the 'communities' of Dutch and English Africans. Their clerics provided a religious justification for racism by instructing them that blacks were the heirs of Ham, whom God had condemned to be 'the servants of servants' because of a curse – vindictive even by the standards of the Abrahamic religions – that Noah placed on Ham's son Canaan. (Ham had had the temerity to gaze on a sleeping Noah when he was naked and drunk, and laugh at him. God therefore damned his line in perpetuity.) The opponents of oppression did not say that they must 'respect Afrikaans culture', however. They did not say that it was Afrikaanophobic to be judgemental about religion, or explain that it was imperialist to criticise the beliefs of 'the other'. If a religion was oppressive or a culture repugnant, one had a duty to offend it.

The liberal resurgence, which brought down so many tyrannies, was also an attack on the beliefs and values of the old democracies. The 1960s generation brought an end to the deference shown to democratic leaders and established institutions.

Many found its irreverence shocking, but no matter. The job of artists, intellectuals and journalists became to satirise and expose; to be the transgressive and edgy critics of authority. They did not confine themselves to politics. Cultural constraints, backed by religious authority, collapsed under the pressure of the second wave of feminism, the sexual revolution and the movements for racial and homosexual emancipation. The revolution in private life was greater than the revolution in politics. Old fences that had seemed fixed by God or custom for eternity fell as surely as the Berlin Wall.

Struggling to encapsulate in a paragraph how the cultural revolution of the second half of the twentieth century had torn up family structures and prejudices, the British Marxist historian Eric Hobsbawm settled on an account from a baffled film critic of the plot of Pedro Almodóvar's 1987 *Law of Desire*.

> In the film Carmen Maura plays a man who's had a transsexual operation and, due to an unhappy love affair with his/her father, has given up on men to have a lesbian, I guess, relationship with a woman, who is played by a famous Madrid transvestite.

It was easy to mock. But laughter ought to have been stifled by the knowledge that within living memory transsexuals, transvestites, gays and lesbians had not been subjects that writers and directors could cover sympathetically, or on occasion at all. Their release from traditional morality reflected the release of wider society from sexual prejudice.

That release offended religious and social conservatives who thought a woman's place was in the home, sexual licence a sin and homosexuality a crime against nature. Although the fashion for relativism was growing in Western universities in the 1980s, leftish academics did not say we had no right to offend the cultures of racists, misogynists and homophobes, and demand that we 'respect' their 'equally valid' contributions to a diverse society. Even they knew that reform is impossible without challenging established cultures. Challenge involves offence. Stop offending, and the world stands still.

Salman Rushdie was a man of his time, who would never have understood the notion that you should think twice before offending the powerful. *Midnight's Children*, the 1981 novel that made him famous, was an account of how the ideals of independent India, which Nehru announced as the chimes of midnight struck on 14–15 August 1947, degenerated into the tyranny of Indira Gandhi's state of emergency. Its successor, *Shame*, dissected the brutalities of military and religious tyranny in Pakistan. By the time he began *The Satanic Verses* Rushdie was the literary conscience of the subcontinent. He deplored the cruelties of post-colonialism, while never forgetting the cruelties of the colonists. It was not a surprise that after looking at post-partition India and Pakistan, he turned his attention to Islam. He had been born into a secular Muslim family in Bombay. He had studied the Koran at Cambridge University, as a literary text written by men rather than God's creation. The Islamic Revolution in Iran, which brought the Ayatollah Khomeini to power in 1979, had pushed religious conservatism to the centre of politics. Rushdie would no more treat religious authority uncritically than he would treat secular authority uncritically. If he had, he would have committed a real offence against the intellectual standards of his day.

## A God of Bullies

Rushdie's title declared his intention. According to a contested religious tradition, the satanic verses were the lines the devil tricked Muhammad into believing were the words of God as he struggled to convert the pagan people of Mecca to Islam. Satan suggested that Muhammad tell the Meccans he would compromise his harsh new religion and allow Mecca's pagan goddesses

Al-Lat, Al-'Uzzá and Manāt to intercede with God on their behalf. The biographers of the Prophet claimed that the angel Gabriel chastised Muhammad for allowing Satan to deceive him. Mortified, the Prophet took back the satanic words and returned to uncompromising monotheism.

To modern and not so modern eyes, the episode raises pertinent questions about how believers can consider a sacred text to be the inerrant word of a god or gods when the devil or anyone else can insert their thoughts into it. The cases of the Koran, Old Testament and New Testament gave them excellent grounds for scepticism, because the texts were not prepared until decades after the supposed revelations. Rushdie endorsed scepticism by showing how well the Koran suited the prejudices of early medieval Arabia, and threw in the oppression of women for good measure.

Al-Lat, Al-'Uzzá and Manāt were goddesses, and Islam, like Judaism and Christianity, was determined to wipe out the goddess cults of the ancient world and replace them with the rule of a stern and unbending patriarch. It is worth mentioning Christianity and Judaism at this point, because although everyone who raises the subject of sexism and religion in the post-Rushdie world concentrates on Islam's attitude to women, liberalism's task of knocking misogyny out of the other mainstream religions is not over. As late as 2010, a modest proposal to allow women to become bishops with the same powers as their male counterparts pushed the Church of England close to schism. In any other area of public life, the suggestion that male employees could refuse to serve a woman boss would be greeted with derision. To a large faction within the supposedly modern and moderate Church of England, sexism remained God's will, and equality of opportunity an offence against the divine order. At about the same time as Anglicans were displaying their prejudices, gangs of Orthodox Jews were forming themselves into 'chastity squads'. They beat divorced women in Jerusalem for breaking religious law by walking out in the company of married men, and asked the courts to uphold men's 'right' to force Orthodox women to sit at the back of buses – an unconscious homage to the segregation of blacks and whites in the old American South.

Rushdie was touching therefore on a theme that was close to being universal. While there always have been and always will be men who wish to dominate women, the peculiar iniquity of religion is to turn misogyny into a part of the divine order: to make sexism a virtue and equality a sin.

The authors of a recent study of religious oppression dispensed with the circumlocutions of modern commentators, and put the case for an unembarrassed critique of religion plainly. They considered how Sharia adultery laws state that a raped woman must face the next-to-impossible task of providing four male witnesses to substantiate her allegation or be convicted of adultery; how when rapists leave Pakistani women pregnant courts take the bulge in their bellies as evidence against them; how in Nigeria, Sharia courts not only punish raped women for adultery but order an extra punishment of a whipping for making false accusations against 'innocent' men; how in the United States, the fundamentalist Church of Latter Day Saints gives teenagers to old men in arranged marriages and tells them they must submit to their wishes; and how the theocratic Saudi Arabian state stops women walking unaccompanied in the street, driving a car and speaking to men outside the family. Then – after drawing a deep breath – they asked, 'Does God hate women?'

Well, what can one say? Religious authorities and conservative clerics worship a wretchedly cruel unjust vindictive executioner of a God. They worship a God of ten-year-old boys, a God of playground bullies, a God of rapists, of gangs, of pimps. They worship – despite rhetoric about justice and compassion – a

God who sides with the strong against the weak, a God who cheers for privilege and punishes egalitarianism. They worship a God who is a male and who gangs up with other males against women. They worship a thug. They worship a God who thinks little girls should be married to grown men. They worship a God who looks on in approval when a grown man rapes a child because he is 'married' to her. They worship a God who thinks a woman should receive eighty lashes with a whip because her hair wasn't completely covered. They worship a God who is pleased when three brothers hack their sisters to death with axes because one of them married without their father's permission.

Although the authors looked at the abuse of children by the Catholic Church, and prejudice in Jewish, American Baptist and Mormon sects, most of their examples came from Islam and Hinduism. That is not a sign of prejudice on their part. Any writer tackling religious oppression has to accept that liberalism tempered the misogyny of mainstream Christianity and Judaism in the rich world after centuries of struggle, but left the poor world largely untouched. Christianity and Judaism are not 'better' than Islam and Hinduism. Free-thinkers have just made a better job of containing their prejudices and cruelties.

Rushdie's Muhammad does not always pretend that religious ordinances come from heaven. As he considers the Meccans' demand that their goddesses should be allowed to argue with his male god, he is no longer a prophet seeking to understand divine commands, but a politician weighing the options. The pagans of Mecca will accept his new religion in return for him allowing them to keep their old goddesses. That's the bargain. That's the offer on the table. God's will has nothing to do with it. Nor do the tricks of Satan. If Paris is worth a mass, is Mecca worth a goddess, or two, or three?

'I've been offered a deal,' he shouts, but his followers will have none of it. Like so many leaders, Rushdie's Muhammad is trapped by the fanaticism of disciples who deny him space for compromise. They had believed that every word he said came from God via Gabriel. If they changed their story to suit political pressures, they would become a laughing stock. Why should anyone trust them if they diluted their absolute faith and accepted that God's commands were open to interpretation and negotiation? Why should they trust themselves?

'How long have we been reciting the creed you brought us?' asks one. 'There is no god but God. What are we if we abandon it now? This weakens us, renders us absurd. We cease to be dangerous. Nobody will ever take us seriously again.' In any case, a second disciple tells Muhammad, 'Lat, Mamnat, Uzza – they're all females! For pity's sake! Are we to have goddesses now? Those old cranes, herons and hags?'

Muhammad realises that if he compromises, he will lose his followers and with them his power base. The Meccans will have no reason to deal with him. He falls into a crisis of self-doubt, a scene Rushdie carries off with great pathos, although neither his religious detractors nor many of his secular admirers could admit it.

As the book went on, Rushdie provided his enemies with more ammunition by continuing in the feminist vein. Can a man who has so many wives under his control be the leader of a new faith, he asks. Or as Aisha, Muhammad's youngest wife, says in the novel, 'Your God certainly jumps to it when you need him to fix things up for you.' When Rushdie's Muhammad confronts free-thinking women, 'bang, out comes the rule book, the angel starts pouring out rules about what women mustn't do, he starts forcing them back into the docile attitudes the Prophet prefers, docile or maternal, walking three steps behind or sitting at home being wise and waxing their chins'.

To illustrate how you cannot have blasphemy until there is a religion to blaspheme against, Rushdie had the men of Mecca go to a brothel where the courtesans were named after the Prophet's wives. He tested the belief that the Koran was the sacred word of God by having a sceptic rewrite the Prophet's divine revelations. As I said, to those with the mentalities of heretic-hunters and witch-burners, *The Satanic Verses* was a blasphemous book, and no one could deny it. The single point that his supporters should have needed to make in his defence was that Salman Rushdie was born in democratic India and moved to democratic Britain. He was a free man in a free country, and could write what he damn well wanted.

Events were to prove that his supporters needed additional arguments.

The first was to emphasise that the best novelists do not produce agitprop.

*The Satanic Verses* is not just 'about' religion and the rights of women. It is a circus of magical realism, with sub-plots, dream sequences, fantasies, pastiches, sudden interruptions by the author, a bewildering number of characters, and a confusion of references to myths and to the news stories of the day. If you insist on nailing down its political message – and trust me, you will whack your thumb with the hammer many times before you do – you will discover that the novel is 'about' migrants from India to the West who, like Rushdie, are contending with their changing identities and their dissolving religious and cultural certainties.

The protagonists – Gibreel Farishta, a Bollywood movie star who plays Hindu gods in religious epics, and whose fans worship him as a god, and Saladin Chamcha, an actor who has left India and makes a living doing voiceovers for London advertising agencies – confront the pressures on the psyche migration brings. Somewhat prophetically given what was to happen next, the Anglicised Saladin tells his Indian mistress, who is trying to find what remains of India inside him:

'Well this is what is inside … An Indian translated into English-medium. When I attempt Hindustani these days, people look polite. This is me.' Caught in the aspic of his adopted language he had begun to hear in India's Babel an ominous warning: don't come back again. When you have stepped through the looking glass you step back at your peril. The mirror may cut you to shreds.

If people wanted reasons to find offence – and as we will see, there are people who are offended if you *don't* give them reasons to find offence – then the British police and immigration services might have issued death threats, because Rushdie showed them as racists and sadists. When the controversy broke and he needed police protection, supporters of law and order complained about the lack of 'respect' for the British state Rushdie had displayed in his writings. The cops, however, took his satire on the chin and went on to guard him from assassins. If you wanted to be fussy, you could also notice passages which showed that Asian shopkeepers in London were not always comradely soldiers joined with their Afro-Caribbean brothers in the struggle against white prejudice, as the anti-racist orthodoxy of the 1980s said they must be. Rushdie's Asian Londoners are contemptuous of the black youths they assume must be criminals. Britain's black community once again lived with the offence.

But, and here is the second large point, to go through *The Satanic Verses* with the squinting eye of a censor searching for thought crimes, or even to seek to see it in the round, as I have tried to do, is to blind yourself to the real reason why the fatwa against Salman Rushdie became the Dreyfus Affair of our age. That reason is as brutal now as it was then.

## Globalising Censorship (1)

Terror is why *The Satanic Verses* is still the novel that all modern arguments about the silencing of sceptical and liberal voices must deal with first. The terror unleashed by its opponents and the response of the inheritors of the liberal tradition to their enemies' demands for censorship and self-censorship. No terror, and *The Satanic Verses* would be one of several great works by a great novelist, rather than shorthand for a battle whose outcome defined what writers can and can't say.

Rushdie did not understand what he was fighting. 'The thing that is most disturbing is they are talking about a book which does not exist,' he said as the protests grew. 'The book which is worth killing people for and burning flags is not the book I wrote. The people who demonstrated in Pakistan and who were killed haven't actually read the book that I wrote because it isn't on sale there.' He had not grasped that reactionary mobs and those who seek to exploit them have a know-nothing pride in their ignorance. It was sufficient that clerical authorities said that the book was blasphemous, and could quote a passage or two to prove their case. The vast majority of religious fanatics who murdered or threatened to murder publishers, translators, booksellers and innocent bystanders did not want to read the book in the round, or to read it at all. Most would not have understood it if they had tried.

Their violence rolled around the world. The brutality of the reaction was beyond anything that Rushdie or his publishers anticipated or could have anticipated. Penguin released *The Satanic Verses* in 1988. Without pausing to consider its contents, President Rajiv Gandhi put it on India's proscribed list. The opposition MP who demanded that Gandhi ban the book had not read it either, but decided, 'I do not have to wade through a filthy drain to know what filth is.' Gandhi was frightened of communal riots and of losing the Muslim vote, and perhaps remembered how Rushdie had excoriated his mother, Indira, in *Midnight's Children*.

In India and Pakistan and later in Britain, Jamaat-e-Islami organised the protests. Its enmity was a compliment to Rushdie, for Jamaat's supporters were enemies any liberal should be proud to have. Jamaat's founder, Maulana Abu'l Ala Maududi, began agitating in British-occupied India in 1941, and had a good claim to be the first of the Islamists. He combined his version of a 'purified' Islam with European totalitarianism. From the communists he took the notion of the vanguard party, which would tell the masses what they wanted, regardless of whether the masses wanted it or not, and vague notions of a just future where all would be equal. From the Nazis, Jamaat, and its partners in the Arab Muslim Brotherhood, took the Jewish conspiracy theory. They explained that Muslims were weak because they were victims of the plots of sinister Jews, or 'Zionists', as they came to call them, who were everywhere seeking to undermine their faith and morals. Muslims would free themselves by building a caliphate, where the supreme ruler of a global empire would not be a Nazi führer or communist general secretary but a theocrat ruling with total power in accordance with Koran and Sharia.

After the British withdrew from India in 1947, leaving millions to die in the slaughters of partition, Jamaat supported the new Muslim state of Pakistan, which was split between its Bengali east wing and the Punjabi-dominated west. When the Bengalis of East Pakistan revolted against a system that made them second-class citizens, the Pakistani army's retaliation stunned a twentieth century that thought it had become inured to genocide. Jamaat aided the army's campaigns of mass murder and mass rape because it believed in the caliphate, and hence could not tolerate the secession of Bangladesh from Pakistan, because it broke Islamic unity. At the time this book went to press, Bangladeshi prosecutors were beginning war crime proceedings against Jamaat leaders they claimed were members of the paramilitary squads Pakistan recruited to help with killing.

Rushdie had already noticed that the Pakistani military dictatorship of the 1980s needed the Jamaatists to provide a religious cover for tyranny. 'This is how religions shore up dictators; by encircling them with words of power, words which the people are reluctant to see discredited, disenfranchised, mocked,' he said, as he gave Jamaat reasons to hate him as well.

The next countries to ban *The Satanic Verses* were Sudan, Bangladesh and apartheid South Africa. If you find the alliance of militant Islamists and white supremacists strange, then you have yet to learn that all the enemies of liberalism are the same. In its dying days, the regime tried to uphold the apartheid state by co-opting mixed-race and Asian South Africans into the system, the better to deny South Africa's black majority the vote. Most coloured and Asian South Africans refused to cooperate. But Islamists saw the chance to use apartheid's censorship laws against Rushdie. The left-wing *Weekly Mail* and the Congress of South African Writers had invited him to visit Johannesburg in 1988 to discuss the censorship of the opponents of white rule. Rushdie had to pull out because of death threats from Islamists. The white-skinned rulers learned they could now rely on brown-skinned religious extremists to intimidate a writer who was proposing to come to their country and denounce their regime.

Even before the Ayatollah Khomeini's fatwa, Rushdie had many enemies, but they were not dangerous enemies. The Indian government regularly banned books it thought might provoke communal violence. Jamaatists in Pakistan and white supremacists in South Africa had always threatened authors. An Anglo-Indian writer based in London had little to fear from them. Intellectuals who had made it to the West were beyond the reach of oppressive forces. They had a place of sanctuary.

The fatwa changed all that. It redrew the boundaries of the free world, shrinking its borders and erasing zones of disputation from the map of the liberal mind. It ensured that London, New York, Paris, Copenhagen and Amsterdam could no longer be places of safety for writers tackling religious themes.

Journalists throw around the word 'unprecedented' so carelessly and ceaselessly that we miss the new when it stares us in the face. Khomeini's incitement to murder was without precedent. Here was a head of state ordering the execution of the private citizens of foreign countries for writing and publishing a work of fiction. A grotesque regard for the forms of legality had accompanied previous outbreaks of state terrorism. Even Stalin forced his victims to confess at show trials so that when he murdered them, he did so with a kangaroo court's approval. No such concern with keeping up appearances inhibited Khomeini. On 14 February 1989, he said that the faithful must kill Rushdie and his publishers and 'execute them quickly, wherever they may find them, so that no one will dare insult Islam again. Whoever is killed in this path will be regarded as a martyr.' Just in case zealous assassins doubted that they would receive eternal life in paradise along with the services of seventy-two virgins, an Iranian foundation offered the earthly reward of $3 million.

There was not even a show trial. Khomeini did not listen to the religious scholars who said that as Rushdie was not a citizen of an Islamic state, he could not punish him for blasphemy or apostasy. And he took even less notice of the more substantial objections from secularists that no one had the right to order the murder of a writer for subjecting religion to imaginative scrutiny.

Far from making himself the object of repulsion, the Ayatollah's endorsement of state-sponsored murder won him many followers. After the death sentence, preachers whipped up mobs against Pakistani Christians in Islamabad. In Bombay, twelve died in battles with the police. A bomber murdered a security guard at the British Council offices in Karachi. In Dhaka, fifteen thousand people tried to break through police lines and ransack the British Council's library. In the United States, Islamists threatened bookstores and firebombers hit the offices of the *Riverdale Press*, a weekly paper in the Bronx, after it published an unexceptional editorial saying that the public had the right to read whatever novels it pleased.

In Britain, demonstrators in Bradford burned copies of *The Satanic Verses*. I doubt they had heard Heinrich Heine's line that 'Where they burn books, so too will they in the end burn human beings' – a condemnation from the German Enlightenment of the burning of the Koran by the Spanish Inquisition, ironically enough. Onlookers were entitled to wonder whether Heine was right, and Rushdie's British enemies would burn the human being in question if they could get hold of him. As in America and Europe, British bookshops withdrew the novel in the face of threats – two independent bookshops on the Charing Cross Road were bombed, as were Penguin bookshops and a department store. Police surrounded Penguin's head office with concrete barricades to stop suicide bombers crashing cars into the building. They X-rayed all packages for explosives and patrolled the perimeter with guard dogs. Meanwhile Special Branch officers moved their charge from safe house to safe house. Rushdie was at the beginning of a rolling programme of house arrest that was to deprive him of his liberty for years.

He had nowhere to run. If he had left Britain, no other country could have promised him safety. The global scale of the malice directed against him made him a refugee without the hope of asylum. Iranian or Pakistani writers who saw the violence in the West realised that if clerics issued fatwas against them in Tehran or Lahore, they could no longer expect to flee to a safe haven. If the controversy was raucous, if the media amplified the death threats, there would be nowhere on the planet to hide.

To justify their death threats and make the shocking seem reasonable, Rushdie's enemies aped the European fascists and communists of the twentieth century. Just as the Nazis said that the Germans were the victims of supernatural Jewish plots or the communists said that the proletariat was the target of the machinations of the treacherous bourgeoisie, so the Islamists told the faithful that they were being persecuted by a conspiracy of global reach and occult power. Ali Akbar Rafsanjani, the speaker of the Iranian parliament, declared that the West had been engaged in a cultural war from colonialism on to 'undermine the people's genuine Islamic morals'. Rushdie was at its forefront. He was the ideal undercover agent for Western intelligence, Rafsanjani announced – 'a person who seemingly comes from India and who apparently is separate from the Western world and who has a misleading name'. Rushdie was a white colonialist, hiding beneath a brown skin; a traitor hiding behind a Muslim name. The British secret service had paid him to betray the faithful, the Iranian theocracy explained as it added corruption to the list of charges against him. It gave him bribes, disguised as book advances, as it organised the assault on Islam by the cunning if curious means of a magical realist novel.

As with Nazism, the conspiracy theory needed Jews. The Iranian interior minister said that Zionists had 'direct involvement' in publishing the book. The Iranian president said that 'Zionist-controlled news agencies' had made Rushdie famous. In Syria, the Ba'athist dictatorship said that the novel was part of a plot to distract the world's attention from Israel's treatment of the Palestinians. In Pakistan, religious leaders talked of an 'American Jewish conspiracy'. Across the planet, the drums shuddered to the same beat: 'It's the Jews, it's the Jews, it's the Jews.'

The demonstrations against Rushdie were not confined to the poor world. The faithful marched in Bradford and London as well as Tehran and Lahore. They inspired a fear in the West that went almost unnoticed during the elation the 1989 revolutions in Eastern Europe produced.

Fear was a novel emotion for Western liberals, and I understand why they wanted to push it to the back of their minds. However much they talked about the bravery of the stands they were making, those in the West who campaigned against apartheid in southern Africa, and those, much fewer in number, who wanted to help the opponents of communism in Eastern Europe and the Soviet Union, had not had to put their lives on the line. They had not had to come to terms with the knowledge that the publication of a book or a cartoon, or the vigorous condemnation of an oppressive ideology, would place families, colleagues and themselves in danger. They had never felt the need to glance twice at dark doorways or listen for quickening footsteps coming up behind them in the street.

By the early 1990s, events seemed to have taught liberals that they could win without pain, in bloodless revolutions. After the fall of white South Africa and the break-up of the Soviet Union, fear appeared to be an unnecessary emotion. History's lesson was that dictatorships would collapse of their own accord without the usual wars and revolutionary terrors. Party hacks and secret policemen, who had never uttered a dissenting word in their lives, had of their own accord given up serving worthless ideologies and embraced the ideals of Western liberalism. 'The heroes of retreat', the German poet Hans Magnus Enzensberger, called them – Kadar, Suarez, Jaruzelski, Botha and above all Gorbachev: apparent 'yes men' who decided to say 'no' to the regimes they had promised to protect. Just like that, without anyone invading their countries or storming their palaces and holding guns to their heads. One day apartheid was there, the next Nelson Mandela was president of South Africa, and the world was granting him a status dangerously close to sainthood. For forty years the Iron Curtain had divided Europe, and then as if a magician had waved his wand, it vanished and tourists could gawp at what was left of the Berlin Wall, before going on to holiday in what had once been the forbidden territory of Eastern Europe.

Humanity had seen nothing on the scale of the bloodless revolutions of 1989 to 1991 before. Former enemies acknowledged their mistakes. They came to agree with our way of thinking without us having to risk our personal safety. The world lived through an age of miracles; but the trouble with witnessing miracles is that you come to expect more of them.

The tactless Rushdie spoilt the ecstatic mood. The reaction to his novel showed that history was not over. One enemy of liberalism was not coming round to our way of thinking, holding up its hands and admitting that we had been right all along. It asked questions of liberals that were close to home. Would they be able to defend their values, when their opponents were not Russian communists sending dissidents to Siberia, or right-wing dictators in faraway lands ordering the torture and murders of Latin American leftists, but fellow citizens who were threatening to kill novelists and bombing bookshops in the cities of the West? Would they defend free speech in murderous times? Or would they hold their tongues and accept that they must 'respect' views they knew to be false?

## RULES FOR CENSORS (1):

# *Demand a Respect You Don't Deserve*

Once again I ask, do you believe in freedom of speech?

And once more, are you sure?

Far be it from me to accuse you of living with illusions, but unless you are a tyrant or a lunatic – and the line between the two is thin – you will rarely speak your mind without a thought for the consequences. You would be friendless within a day if you put a belief in absolute freedom of speech into practice. If you propositioned complete strangers, or told them that they were fools, if you sat down at a meeting and announced that the woman next to you was ugly and the man next to her stank, you would run out of people willing to spend time in your company.

Humans are social primates, and socialising with the rest of our species requires a fair amount of routine self-censorship and outright lying, which we dignify with names such as 'tact', 'courtesy' and 'politeness'.

The appeal of censorship becomes evident when you consider whether you would be happy for others to say what they thought about you. Even if what they said was true – particularly if what they said was true – you would want to stop them saying that you were ugly, boring or smelly. You would expect them to lie to you, just as they would expect you to lie to them. Humans have a bias in favour of information that bolsters their prejudices and validates their choices. Above all, our species has a confirmation bias in favour of information that upholds our good opinion of ourselves. We want our status confirmed. We want others to lie to us so that we can lie to ourselves. We want to be respected.

As well as a provision for freedom of speech, most guarantees of basic liberties have a right to privacy sitting uneasily alongside them. It recognises that the full truth about an individual's life cannot be made public without crushing his or her autonomy. Under the pressure of exposure, his sense of who he was would change. He would become suspicious, fretful, harassed; he would be left exposed to gales of mockery and condemnation. In the interests of preventing a surveillance society, it is better that the state allows the citizen to live a lie. 'If you've nothing to hide, you have nothing to fear,' say authoritarians. But everyone has something to hide, and if there isn't a dirty secret, there is always something that your enemies can twist to make you look dirty.

Privacy was meant to offer the citizen protection against the over-mighty state. The emphasis on the right to a private life was an understandable and necessary reaction against the informers and spies the communist and fascist totalitarian regimes recruited to monitor daily life. But in the late twentieth century, at the same time as the *Satanic Verses* controversy began, judges began to adapt the law. Instead of stopping the secret service from tapping the phones or opening the mail of citizens, judges decided to stop the media revealing details of the private lives of wealthy celebrities and other public figures.

The privacy law they developed could not have been more different from traditional libel law. Libel is meant to protect the individual from the pain inflicted by malicious gossips who spread lies about him or her. Privacy protects against the pain that comes from hearing the truth broadcast. In libel, truth is an absolute defence. If writers and publishers can justify what they say, they may leave the court without punishment. In privacy cases, truth is not a defence but an irrelevance. The law intervenes not because the reports are false, but because they tell too much truth for the subject to cope with, and open him up to mockery, to pain ... to disrespect. Privacy rights allowed the wealthy to suppress criticisms, even though the criticisms were true. They could demand respect, even though they were not respectable.

The persecution of Rushdie appeared to follow the old precedents. Contemporaries looking for a parallel to Khomeini's gangsterish order for assassins to 'hit' him recalled the Vatican's order to take out Elizabeth I in the 1570s. They talked about the re-emergence of the Inquisition, or quoted Voltaire's pointed question, 'What to say to a man who tells you he prefers to obey God than to obey men, and who is consequently sure of entering the gates of Heaven by slitting your throat?'

The comparison with the past fails, because there is an unbridgeable gulf between today's religion and the religious ideas which persisted for most of history. Until the Enlightenment, maybe until the publication of *On the Origin of Species*, believers could reassure themselves that the wisest thinkers of their time believed that a divine order structured the universe. As late as the 1690s, a belief in science and magic could co-exist even in the great mind of Isaac Newton, who divided his days between trying to understand the laws of motion and trying to work out when the Book of Revelation foretold the 'great tribulation and the end of the world'. (He thought that God would wind us up in 2060, readers expecting to make it through the mid-twenty-first century should note.)

Charges of blasphemy and heresy were once like accusations of libel. The wretched sinner had sought to spread falsehoods against the true religion, which the faithful exposed. The Protestant divines of Elizabethan England and the papacy that confronted them fought over what kind of supernatural power ordered the world. But they agreed on the fundamental question that a supernatural power must order the world. The Catholic believed that if the Protestant converted to Catholicism he would find the truth. The Protestant believed the opposite. Now you have to be a very isolated believer to imagine that your religion, or any religion, can provide a comprehensive explanation of the world. When they study beyond a certain level, all believers learn that the most reliable theories of the origins of life have no need for the God of the Torah, the New Testament or the Koran. The most brilliant modern scientists have little in common with Newton. They are atheists, or believers in a remote God who is nothing like the capricious, interventionist deity of the holy books. The best thought has moved beyond religion. It is for this reason that religion, which once inspired man's most sublime creations, can no longer produce art, literature or philosophy of any worth; why it is impossible to imagine a new religious high culture.

If you go to the chapel at King's College, Cambridge – which was Salman Rushdie's college, as it happens – you will see one response to the loss of religious authority. The inheritors of the priests and stonemasons who sent arches soaring heavenwards to show their confidence in a divinely ordained universe are now modest people. Their information for visitors makes no pretence that the gospels are accurate accounts of Christ's life and teaching. Cambridge Anglicans stress that unknown hands wrote them long after Christ's death. They offer worshippers a celebration of tradition, symbolic truths and parables, not literal truths. Everywhere liberal Christians, Jews and Muslims follow the same example. They worship in a narrow religious sphere, which is cautious and a touch vapid, and do not try to force the rest of society to accept their views. For them there is a secular world informed by science, and there is their world of faith.

Religious fanatics appear to be opposed to the liberal modernists. They would never accept that their holy books could be anything other than the word of God. The philosopher Ernest Gellner wrote just after the fatwa that Westerners ought to rethink the assumption that industrialisation undermined religious belief. The post-Khomeini world was showing that the forward march of secularism was not inevitable. Islam 'demonstrates that it is possible to run a modern, or at any rate a modernising economy, reasonably permeated by the appropriate technological, educational and organisational principles *and* combine it with a strong, pervasive, powerfully internalised Muslim conviction and identification'.

The differences between religious fundamentalists and religious modernists are not as great as either imagine. Both want to keep religion in a separate sphere; it is just that the religious sphere of the fundamentalist is wider and the means used to protect it from scrutiny more neurotic and brutal. Trying to maintain a 'strong, pervasive, powerfully internalised' religious conviction in a world that can manage without religious explanations creates perpetual tensions, however. The effort required to resolve them is harder than Gellner believed. At some level, even murderous fanatics know that their ideologies are redundant. They are not the vanguard for a new age of piety, but reactionaries, who hope that if they indoctrinate and intimidate they can block out modernity. Their desires mock their hopes. The rifles they fire, the nuclear weapons they crave come from a technology that has no connection to their sacred texts.

To prevent defeat, religious extremists stop the sceptical, evidence-based approach of science moving into the religious sphere and asking hard questions about the validity of their holy books. Rushdie crossed the boundary, and asked modern questions about the evidence behind the story of the founding of Islam. His persecution was just as modern. Rather than representing a continuation of the persecutions of medieval inquisitors, who thought they were protecting the truth from its enemies, his tormentors were closer to celebrities' lawyers, who claim that their client's feelings would be hurt and their image tarnished by the discussion of unwelcome facts. Rushdie's critics were more concerned about the effect of his writings on the psyche of believers than whether what he had said was true. The charge they threw at him was that he had 'offended' the faithful by 'insulting' their religion. It was as if he had invaded their privacy.

I accept that the individual needs protection from the surveillance of an over-mighty state. I accept too that the judges will have to tackle the explosion of character assassination on the Net directed at private citizens. I find the use of privacy law to restrict the media's reporting of public figures far harder to justify. But if judges could be trusted with the power to prohibit, then I would accept too that people in the public eye need not be exposed to the scrutiny they receive in the United States. All of these acts of censorship, however, are protections for *individuals*. No honest jurisdiction can defend using censorship to protect ideological systems from the harm or offence of criticism. You must treat ideologies which mandate wars, and govern the sexual behaviour of men and women and, in their extreme forms, every aspect of life for hundreds of millions of people, with the utmost candour. For they are ideas that seek to dominate.

Politics is as much a part of the identity of the committed leftist, green or conservative as religion is a part of the identity of the committed Christian, Jew, Muslim or Hindu. When the political partisan's beliefs are insulted or ridiculed, he feels the 'offence' as deeply as any believer who has heard his god or prophet questioned. We do not, however, prohibit or restrict arguments about politics out of 'respect' for political ideologies, because we are a free society. We call societies that prohibit political arguments 'dictatorships', and know without needing to be told that the prohibiting is done to protect the ruling elite. If political or religious believers are offended to the core of their being by criticism, free countries must reply, 'Tough. Learn to live with it. We know that we tell white lies about many things. We accept that the truth can be suppressed on some occasions.

But religion and politics are too important and too dangerous to risk handling with kid gloves.'

Respect for religion is the opposite of religious tolerance, because it allows the intolerant to impose their will on others. The Virginia Statute for Religious Tolerance, written by Thomas Jefferson in 1776, highlighted the distinction in flowing prose:

> Be it enacted by General Assembly that no man shall be compelled to frequent or support any religious worship, place, or ministry whatsoever, nor shall be enforced, restrained, molested, or burthened in his body or goods, nor shall otherwise suffer on account of his religious opinions or belief, but that all men shall be free to profess, and by argument to maintain, their opinions in matters of Religion, and that the same shall in no wise diminish, enlarge or affect their civil capacities.

Salman Rushdie was not free to abandon and criticise the religion of his childhood. The Islamists said that if he – and by extension all other Muslims – changed his religion or decided that he was an atheist, he would face assassination for the 'crime' of apostasy. They wanted to make Rushdie 'suffer on account of his religious opinions'; to restrain, molest and burthen his body for his blasphemy, and to do the same to anyone, Muslim or not, who echoed his ideas. In his most compelling line, Jefferson concluded that 'all men shall be free to profess, and by argument to maintain, their opinions in matters of Religion'.

'Argument' was his key word. Religious toleration did not limit argument, but removed the sanctions of the state and the established Church that had stood in argument's way. It did not rule out appeals to logic, reason, imagination and sympathy – but gave them the space to breathe without the threat of punishment. Argument involves the true respect that comes from treating others as adults who can cope with challenging ideas and expecting them to treat you with a similar courtesy. The 'respect' demanded by Rushdie's enemies infantilised both the giver and the receiver, and suited religious reactionaries well. They had every interest in keeping their subject populations in a state of infantile ignorance, and in spreading the fear that all who thought about arguing with them would know that they risked becoming the next target.

# TWO

# *A Clash of Civilisations?*

*I see no way to secure liberalism by trying to put its core values beyond any but internal or consensual reasoning. The resulting slide into relativism leaves a disastrous parallel between 'liberalism for the liberals' and 'cannibalism for the cannibals'.*

MARTIN HOLLIS

Islamism is a movement of the radical religious right. Its borrowings from fascism include the anti-Jewish conspiracy theory and the anti-Freemason conspiracy theory. It places men above women. It worships martyrdom and the concomitant cult of death. You do not have to stare too long or too hard at its adherents to realise that they are liberalism's enemies. Yet the most jarring aspect of Khomeini's denunciations was that he and his supporters implied that Western liberals should regard them as brothers in the struggles to defend the wretched of the earth. They used the anti-imperialist language the political left employed when it castigated the machinations of the White House and the CIA, and the anti-racist language it employed when castigating white oppression.

With a devious inversion, they turned the freedom to speak and to criticise into instruments of coercion the strong inflicted on the weak. If you wanted to be a genuine liberal, if you wanted to be on the side of the weak in their battle with the strong, you must be against Rushdie. Of all the lies that surrounded the fatwa, this was not only the most noxious but also the most farcical.

Rushdie was a typical leftist of the 1980s. He supported all the old causes. He was a candid friend of the Nicaraguan revolution, and wrote in defence of the Palestinians. At first, he welcomed the overthrow of the Shah of Iran and the arrival of the Islamic revolution, although he changed his mind long before its admirers tried to kill him. In Britain, he was the first great novelist English literature had produced to confront the disorientation felt by migrants. By necessity, his subject and his own experience made him a tough and on occasion vituperative enemy of racism. In the early 1980s, he broadcast a blood-chilling description of Britain as an island saturated with chauvinism. Unlike the Germans, who had come through painful self-examination to 'purify German thought and the German language of the pollution of Nazism', the British had never come to terms with the evils of Empire, he told the liberal viewers of Channel 4, who were doubtless suitably guilt-ridden. 'British thought, British society has never been cleansed of the filth of imperialism. It's still there, breeding lice and vermin, waiting for unscrupulous people to exploit it for their own ends. British racism, of course, is not our problem. It's yours. We simply suffer from the effects of your problem. And until you, the whites, see that the issue is not integration, or harmony, or multi-culturalism, but simply facing up to and eradicating the prejudices within almost all of you, the citizens of your new and last Empire will be obliged to struggle against you.'

If Rushdie was an agent of the imperialists, he was operating under deep cover.

Assessing the response of liberals to the assault on liberalism and the attempts to murder one of their own is blighted by the old problem that we remember the best writers' work, because it survives and moulds the future's thinking, but forget the lesser journalists and authors who dominate debate at the time. The best left-wing writers of the 1980s understood that the left's commitment to freedom of speech was far from certain. They knew that it had its own foul history of fellow travelling with tyranny. Their noses sniffed the air to catch the first whiff of treachery. In *Culture of Complaint*, his dissection of the politicisation of the arts and humanities in the 1980s, Robert Hughes lacerated the universities for their failure to defend Rushdie. Academics were forever berating dead white males for their failure to conform to exacting modern standards, he said, but stayed silent as murderers threatened the basic standards of intellectual life. On American campuses, they held that if a man so much as looked around with a lustful eye, or called a young female a 'girl' instead of a 'woman', he was guilty of gross sexual impropriety. 'Abroad it was more or less OK for a cabal of regressive theocratic bigots to insist on the chador, to cut off thieves' hands and put out the eyes of offenders on TV, and to murder novelists as state policy. Oppression is what we do in the West. What they do in the Middle East is "their culture".' Leftists could not make a stand, because to their minds defending Rushdie would at some level mean giving aid and comfort to racists and strengthening the hand of the one enemy they could admit to having: the imperialist warmongers in Washington, DC.

Rushdie's friend Christopher Hitchens saw the centres of British cities clogged with men who wanted to pass blasphemy laws and give the police the power to control what free citizens could read. 'That this ultra-reactionary mobocracy was composed mainly of people with brown skins ought to have made no difference. In Pakistan, long familiar with the hysteria of Jamaat Islami and other religio-dictatorial gangs, it would have made no difference at all. But somehow, when staged in the streets and squares of Britain it did make a difference. A pronounced awkwardness was introduced into the atmosphere.'

Too many of his former comrades were dodging the issue by imagining a false moral equivalence, he said. Rushdie and his oppressors were to their minds equally guilty. They could not see that 'all of the deaths and injuries – *all of them* – from the mob scenes in Pakistan to the activities of the Iranian assassination squads were directly caused by Rushdie's enemies. None of the deaths – *none of them* – were caused by him, or by his friends and defenders. Yet you will notice the displacement tactic used by … the multicultural left which blamed the mayhem on an abstract construct – "the Rushdie Affair". I dimly understood at the time that this kind of post-modern "left" somehow in league with political Islam was something new. That this *trahison* would take a partly "multicultural form" was also something that was ceasing to surprise me.'

The Western leftists Hughes and Hitchens had in their sights were making the elementary howler of confusing ethnicity – which no one can change – with religions or political ideologies – which are systems of ideas that men and women ought to be free to accept or reject. As that howler now howls like a gale through liberal discourse, we had better take the time to explain why its assumptions are false before moving on.

When Serb extremists killed Bosnian Muslims because of their religion, their lethal religious prejudice was indeed akin to lethal racial prejudice. When employers from the old Protestant ascendancy in Northern Ireland refused Catholics jobs because they were Catholics, a comparison with colour bars against black workers in the old American South applied. When people said that a conspiracy of American Jews controlled American foreign policy, or that Muslim immigrants were imposing a jihadi theology on Europe, they were propagating racist conspiracy theories. Moral equivalence held in all these cases.

When supporters of Rushdie opposed the murder of authors, however, their ideals could not have been further from the dark fantasies of racial hatred. Islamists could call them 'Islamophobes' if they wanted, for they were indeed opposing reactionary Islamic doctrines, but they were doing so because they were liberals who wanted to show solidarity with liberals from the Muslim world, not because they were filled with an irrational loathing. When Catholic reactionaries accuse opponents of papal doctrine on contraception and abortion of 'anti-Catholicism', and when believers in a greater Israel accuse opponents of Israeli expansion into the West Bank of anti-Semitism, they too are palming a card from the bottom of the deck. They are trying to pass off rational morality as an irrational hatred.

In 1989, such confusions lay in the future. Hitchens and Hughes may have realised that an ominous shift was taking place, but most commentators at the time did not. Liberal opinion seemed to me and many others to reel from the threats of the extremists, collect itself and fight back.

## Liberalism's First (and Last) Stand

The staff and directors of Penguin, Rushdie's publishers, showed steadiness under fire. Led by Peter Mayer, the chief executive, they contemplated the consequences of withdrawing *The Satanic Verses*. Penguin would not suffer alone, they decided. Every other publisher putting out works that a demagogue could take offence at might become a target.

Mayer and his colleagues were living in fear. The sneering claim that they 'knew what they were doing' when they published *The Satanic Verses* was contradicted by their evident astonishment. As furious men plotted murder, they had to worry about keeping Rushdie from harm. They had to protect their buildings and shops in Britain, and their export offices all over the world. They had to agonise about their staff, most of whom did not realise that they were signing up to fight for freedom of speech when they signed on for mundane jobs. Despite what critics said against them, they had to and did worry about British Muslims, trying to integrate into a new culture. And when the heat was at its fiercest, they had to worry about protecting their own lives and the lives of their families.

They did not spend too much time thinking about Milton or Galileo, Mayer recalled, 'but I did think of books we and others had published that some Catholics probably did not like; other books that offended some Jews or evangelical Christians, or minorities who felt their beliefs, values or ethnicity had been treated negatively. And what of books that offend *majorities*, a subject I heard no one raise? Cease to publish those books, too, when someone raised a hand against them?' Workers in bookshops, who were neither well paid nor well protected, said that they must continue to stock it. Even bookshops Islamists bombed kept it under the counter when they reopened. The customer only had to ask.

The mediocrity of Rushdie's critics in the West strengthened the resolve of liberals. Most of his enemies came from the political right. American neo-cons, who a few years later would shout until they were hoarse about the threat of Islamism, were delighted that the dictatorial regimes and movements of the poor world were targeting a left-wing novelist. Whatever their politics, comfortable English intellectuals were equally incapable of seeing extremist blackmail for what it was. John le Carré, whose George Smiley seemed to understand that political freedom had to be defended, saw no similar case for a defence of religious freedom. There was 'no law in life or nature that says great religions may be insulted with impunity', he said, apparently unaware that the law of the land he lived in specifically protected its citizens from assassination. It was not that he supported the fatwa, of course. But his anger was directed at the writer, not the men who wanted the writer dead. 'When it came to the further exploitation of Rushdie's work in paperback form, I was more concerned about the girl at Penguin books who might get her hands blown off in the mailroom than I was about

Rushdie's royalties. Anyone who had wished to read the book by then had ample access to it.'

In one of his rare public interventions during his underground life, an icy Rushdie wrote from his secret address to say that le Carré was taking 'the philistine, reductionist, militant Islamist line that *The Satanic Verses* was no more than an insult', and that anyone 'who displeases philistine, reductionist, militant Islamist folk loses his right to live in safety. He says that he is more interested in safeguarding publishing staff than in my royalties. But it is precisely these people, my novel's publishers in some thirty countries, together with the staff of bookshops, who have most passionately supported and defended my right to publish. It is ignoble of le Carré to use them as an argument for censorship when they have so courageously stood up for freedom.'

The Tory historian Hugh Trevor-Roper, who wasted his time and talent in snobbish feuds, revelled in Rushdie's suffering. 'I wonder how Salman Rushdie is faring these days,' he mused, 'under the benevolent protection of British law and British police, about whom he has been so rude. Not too comfortably, I hope ... I would not shed a tear if some British Muslims, deploring his manners, should waylay him in a dark street and seek to improve them. If that should cause him thereafter to control his pen, society would benefit and literature would not suffer.' Roald Dahl said that Rushdie knew what he was doing, an assertion which was not true but allowed him to turn the blame from the potential murderers to their intended victim. 'This kind of sensationalism does indeed get an indifferent book on to the top of the bestseller list,' he continued, 'but to my mind it is a cheap way of doing it.'

The English establishment has a dictionary of insults for men and women who take on the futile task of making it feel guilty – 'chippy', 'bolshie', 'uppity', 'ungrateful' ... It directed them all at Rushdie.

I do not think I am reading too much into Dahl's accusation of cheapness or Trevor-Roper's hope that Islamists would beat manners into an author in a dark alley when I say that members of the traditional intelligentsia could not support Rushdie because in his success they could sense their decline. The Indian and South American magical realists of the 1980s foretold a time when great literature would not come from the world they knew. Rushdie was the master of the English language, their language. He came to literary London and took their prizes at the Booker awards. Reviewers in their serious newspapers praised him for his ability to draw from different cultures and ideas. The immigrant from a Muslim family, the most famous Indian in England, seemed interested in everyone except them. He did not describe the agonies of the English upper-middle class or the life and loves of Oxbridge dons, but the slums of London and the politics of the subcontinent, while never forgetting to remind the well-bred among his readers of the shame of British imperialism and the persistence of white racism.

Conservatives claimed that the slippery foreigner 'knew what he was doing'. Rushdie deliberately insulted Islam because he wanted to make money from the controversy, and then forced the taxpayer to meet the cost of his police protection. They made him into a figure from Tory fantasy: the highbrow scrounger, the champagne socialist, who collected his royalties while milking the public purse. When a snide Prince Charles joined the hostile chorus, Ian McEwan said that His Royal Highness's security cost far more, even though the prince 'had never written anything worth reading'. Understandably, Rushdie was more outraged than amused. It took him four years to write *The Satanic Verses*. Did his opponents not find it strange that a serious writer would spend a tenth of his life creating something as crude as an insult? But of course, his enemies could not accept that he was a serious writer, he said. In order to attack him and his work, it was necessary to paint him 'as a bad person, an apostate traitor, an unscrupulous seeker of fame and wealth, an opportunist whose work was without merit, who "attacked Islam" for his own personal gain. This was what was meant by the much-repeated phrase "He did it on purpose".

Those who have never believed in universal human rights described the persecution of Rushdie as the first manifestation in the West of a 'clash of civilisations'. We had 'our values' – human rights, freedom of speech – the Islamic world had theirs – fanatical blasphemy laws, the oppression of women – and never the twain would meet.

Rushdie's persecution and the reactions to it showed that from the beginning the clash-of-civilisations hypothesis was condescending and bovine. It flattered the West by ascribing to its leaders a virtue they did not possess. Hardly anyone in a position of authority was prepared to speak up for 'our' values. Religious leaders were as keen as upper-class intellectuals were on shutting up Rushdie. Immanuel Jakobovits, the then Chief Rabbi of Britain, said Penguin should not have published. Robert Runcie, the then Archbishop of Canterbury, proposed that the government extend England's blasphemy law to cover Islam. In these and similar statements from religious conservatives, you could see Christian and Jewish leaders sensing an opportunity. Maybe they could use the violence of Jamaat and the Khomeinists to create an ecumenical taboo that might protect all religions from criticism, even though those religions were incompatible, and their adherents had spent the best part of two millennia killing each other. If writers became frightened of taking on Islam, the reasoning ran, maybe they would keep away from Christianity and Judaism too.

The *Economist* looked at the trade unionism of the faithful and said, 'Rabbis, priests and mullahs are, it seems, uniting to restrain free speech, lest any member of their collective flock should have his feelings hurt … The Rushdie affair is showing not just that some Muslims do not understand the merits of free speech. It shows that many Western clerics do not either.'

Nor did many politicians in Margaret Thatcher's government and George Bush senior's administration understand either. 'The British government, the British people have no affection for this book,' said Britain's then Foreign Secretary, Geoffrey Howe. 'It compares Britain with Hitler's Germany.' Rushdie did not compare Britain with Nazi Germany, as it happens, and hundreds of thousands of British readers bought and enjoyed his novels. If these were forgettable mistakes from an ignorant man, Howe's next words proved fateful. 'We do not like that any more than people of the Muslim faith like the attacks on their faith.'

Western governments followed the same script. After anti-Rushdie riots in Islamabad, the US State Department said, 'The Embassy wishes to emphasise that the US government in no way associates itself with any activity that is in any sense offensive to Islam or any other religion.' Margaret Thatcher, adopting the royal 'we' as was her wont in her last days in power, said, 'We have known in our own religion people doing things which are deeply offensive to some of us. We feel it very much. And that is what is happening to Islam.' Thatcher's acolyte Norman Tebbit called Rushdie an 'outstanding villain', and asked, 'How many societies having been so treated by a foreigner accepted in their midst, could go so far to protect him from the consequences of his egotistical and self-opinionated attack on the religion into which he was born?'

From their different perspectives, Susan Sontag, one of Rushdie's most loyal defenders, Daniel Pipes, an American conservative, and, later, Kenan Malik, a British historian of the struggles for free speech, all noticed the dangers of London and Washington's stance. They were telling Muslim democrats, free-thinkers, feminists and liberals that human rights were Western rights, and not for brown-skinned people from a clashing 'civilisation'. You can call this cultural relativism, but 'racism' is a blunter and better word.

Consider the position of the West in 1989. It had looked upon Iran as a threat from the moment the ayatollahs took power in 1979. It had given air cover to Saddam Hussein's genocidal regime during the Iran–Iraq war because it thought that any enemy of Iran was better than none. Western politicians lectured their own Muslim citizens on the need to adapt to the Western way of life, but then assumed that all Muslims wanted to burn books and murder authors. Freedom of speech was a Western value, not a universal right. Muslims could not be expected to handle it.

The best in the Muslim world did not want Westerners to patronise them or protect them from dangerous books. They wanted the freedom to challenge theocracy and tradition. The bravest was the Egyptian novelist Naguib Mahfouz, winner of the Nobel Prize for Literature, who put his life on the line by condemning Khomeini as a terrorist. One hundred Arab intellectuals joined him when they came out in solidarity with Rushdie. One hundred and twenty-seven Iranians signed a declaration condemning the 'terrorist and liberty-cide methods' of the Islamic Republic.

The Rushdie affair was not a 'clash of civilisations' but a struggle for civilisation. On 27 May 1989, rival demonstrations in central London made the choice on offer clear to anyone willing to look. Thousands of anti-Rushdie protesters came to the capital. Malise Ruthven, author of one of the first accounts of the controversy, was shocked by the violence of their slogans. 'Rushdie is a devil'. 'Rushdie is a son of Satan'. 'Kill the bastard'. 'Jihad on Agnostics'. 'Devil Rushdie Wanted Dead or Alive'. One poster showed Rushdie, with devil's horns, hanging from a gallows. Another had his head on the body of a pig surrounded by the Star of David.

Shameless Labour MPs, who were prepared to court the ethnic vote by forgetting what liberal principles they had once possessed, addressed them. Ranged against them in Parliament Square were two counter-demonstrations. Skinheads from the neo-fascist National Front were hanging around on the fringes, looking for a fight. Meanwhile, in the lawn in the centre of the square, a small band of Asian women who ran hostels for battered wives and safe houses for the victims of misogyny staged a protest of their own.

'Here to doubt/Here to stay/Muslim leaders won't have their way,' they chanted. The police had to protect them from the Asian religious demonstrators, who hated them for not being submissive, and from the British neo-fascist demonstrators, who hated them for not being white. The women never forgot the experience of seeing apparent enemies unite against them.

'Approximately fifty women were marooned between a march of young Asian men calling for a ban on *The Satanic Verses* and National Front supporters. Instead of tackling the National Front, the Asian men verbally and physically attacked Women Against Fundamentalism, which then had to rely on the police for protection whereas previously WAF members would have been marching alongside their Asian "brothers" against police and state racism!'

They were not all atheists, the women said. They just wanted to be modern British citizens, and to dispute the power of their fathers and brothers to force them into arranged marriages.

The Rushdie Affair became the Dreyfus Affair of our age because it revealed how, when faced the threat of violence, ordinary political categories collapse. Whatever your opinions, if you supported Rushdie, you supported the freedom to write, read and publish what you liked, even when (I would say especially when) books were being burned and death threats issued not in some far away and forgettable dictatorship but in your own land. You supported the rule of law, for Rushdie had committed no crime, and you placed the right of the individual to express him or herself above the rights of the collective. The enemies of Dreyfus said that they must keep an innocent man in prison to protect the collective honour of the French army and French state. The enemies of Rushdie said that the Ayatollah Khomeini's incitement to murder was understandable or excusable because it protected the collective honour of Muslims. No one who professed a belief in freedom of conscience and thought could hesitate for a moment before taking Rushdie's side.

Gita Sahgal and her sisters at Women Against Fundamentalism did not have the smallest doubt that Rushdie's struggle was their struggle, and that Rushdie's enemies were their enemies. 'At the heart of the fundamentalist agenda is control of women's minds and bodies, such as the imposition of restrictions on the right to abortion, on free and equal education and on the right of women to organise autonomously,' said the group's statement on Rushdie. 'We reject the idea the fundamentalists can speak for us. We will continue to doubt and dissent and will carry on the fight for our right to determine our own destinies, not limited by religion, culture or nationality … We are taking this opportunity to reaffirm our solidarity with Salman Rushdie.'

How hard was it to be on their side? Who in conscience would not choose to stand with them and against Jamaat-e-Islami, craven Indian politicians, apartheid South Africa, Islamist Iran, Wahhabist Saudi Arabia, the Tory intelligentsia, the Tory government, shabby Labour MPs playing Chicago politics, book-burners, life-deniers, witch-finders and murderers?

I can place public figures of my generation by where they stood on Rushdie. His friends believed in imaginative freedom and the right of the individual to argue with the world. Even if they did not agree with him, they knew that those who were trying to silence him would silence millions if they could. His enemies did then and have since put the collective before the individual. The conservatives among them talked about real-politik and keeping the natives happy. The leftists talked of the rights of 'the other' and cultural imperialism. Both would throw out freedom of thought, freedom of speech and the rights of women, if sectarian power or realpolitik demanded it.

Hundreds of thousands of people thought that the choice between defending Rushdie or joining his critics was no choice at all. They ensured that the censors could not stop *The Satanic Verses*, although the censors inflicted a terrible price. An unknown assailant murdered Hitoshi Igarashi, *The Satanic Verses*' Japanese translator, by stabbing him in the face. Ettore Capriolo, the Italian translator, was knifed in his apartment in Milan, but lived. William Nygaard, Rushdie's Norwegian publisher, was shot three times and left for dead at his home in an Oslo suburb. Nygaard was not a man who frightened easily. He recovered, and published the Bangladeshi writer Taslima Nasrin, who had described the massacres of Hindus in the 1971 genocide, and received the obligatory death threats. In Turkey, the satirist Aziz Nesin started a translation. On 2 July 1993 he attended an Alevi cultural festival in the central Anatolian city of Sivas. Alevis are a tolerant and egalitarian Shia sect, and suffer the consequences. A mob gathered around the hotel where the Alevis were staying, calling for Sharia law and death to infidels. Nesin and many guests escaped. The killers murdered thirty-seven others.

The victims did not appear to have suffered in vain. Rushdie lived, and *The Satanic Verses* remained in print and sold around the world. Battered but unbeaten, liberalism triumphed.

Or appeared to triumph.

For here is something strange. Between the fatwa and the present, religious killers have murdered just one Western artist – the Dutch director Theo van Gogh, assassinated in 2004 for making a film with the Somali feminist Ayaan Hirsi Ali. Yet in the same period Western culture changed, and not for the better. The change can fit into a sentence. No young artist of Rushdie's range and gifts would dare write a modern version of *The Satanic Verses* today, and if he or she did, no editor would dare publish it.

## RULES FOR CENSORS (2):

### *A Little Fear Goes a Long, Long Way*

Free societies are not free because their citizens are fighting for their freedom. They are free because previous generations of citizens *have* fought for their freedom. When put under dictatorial pressure, they must start old fights anew. Once the struggle begins, you can never guarantee in advance that the citizens of the United States, Holland or Britain will be braver than the citizens of Iran, Zimbabwe or Burma. National and political differences are no protection against the universal emotion of fear. Not the immediate fear that causes the eyeballs to dilate and the fight-or-flight response to kick in, but the niggling fear at the back of the mind that warns of the pressing need to avoid a fight in the first place.

Hitoshi Igarashi was the only person associated with *The Satanic Verses* to pay for the Ayatollah's blood lust with his life. Compared to the millions killed in wars and genocides in the years that followed the fatwa, the pain the enemies of the novel inflicted was small. But it was sufficient. The threats against Rushdie produced a fear that suffused Western culture and paralysed its best instincts. From then on, authoritarians seeking to restrict civil liberties or members of the political right led the opposition to militant Islamism. Liberals, who had the best arguments against theocracy, and who might have offered immigrants to Europe – particularly women immigrants to Europe – a better future, went absent without leave.

The society around them imitated the craven politicians, bishops and rabbis rather than the workers in the bookshops and the editors at Penguin. It displayed little or no willingness to defend the potential victims of terror. In one of his rare interviews, Peter Mayer, Penguin's chief executive, praised the bravery of everyone in the book trade who had defended his right to publish, but then told a bleak story about how strangers treated his family. He had received many death threats. Someone went to the trouble to cut themselves and send him a letter scrawled in blood. An anonymous telephone caller told Mayer that 'not only would they kill me but that they would take my daughter and smash her head against a concrete wall'. Far from rallying to defend an innocent girl and her innocent father, the parents of her classmates demanded that the school expel her. What would happen, they asked, if the Iranian assassins went to the school and got the wrong girl?

And Mayer thought, 'You think my daughter is the *right* girl?'

The same cowardice greeted him when he applied for a co-op apartment in New York. 'There were objections that the Iranians could send a hit squad and target the wrong apartment. As if I had done something wrong.'

The intimidation became too much for Penguin to bear. Rushdie's relationship with Mayer broke down as he came to think that his publisher was trying to avoid releasing a paperback edition of *The Satanic Verses*. 'Months of pressure began to tell on Mayer,' Rushdie remembered, 'eroding his will … He began to persuade himself, it seemed, that he had done all he needed to do.' The trouble was that any delay in publishing the paperback would cause the Islamists to redouble their efforts. The 'affair' would never go away as long as Rushdie's enemies thought they could claim the partial victory of stopping the paperback edition.

Articles carrying quotes from apparently senior sources at Penguin criticising Rushdie appeared in the press. When Rushdie went to call on Penguin, company lawyers attended their meetings. The common front of author and publisher broke down. A disillusioned Rushdie managed to create a consortium to publish the paperback, but after that last act of bravery, everything changed.

After Rushdie, the fear of a knife in the ribs or a bomb at the office meant that liberals who stuck by liberalism were in the wrong. They knew the consequences now. If someone killed them, they were guilty of provoking their own murder. In the eyes of most politicians and most of the journalists, broadcasters, academics and intellectuals whose livelihoods depended on the freedom to debate and criticise, the targets of religious violence had no one to blame but themselves. The intensity of the rage against Rushdie allowed them to turn John Stuart Mill on his head. Mill argued that censorship could be justified only if a writer or speaker caused a direct harm – by urging on a mob to commit a crime, was his example. Rushdie did not incite violence. His opponents did. The harm was all on their side. However, governments and cultural bureaucracies came to believe that when religious mobs showed that they were prepared to murder Rushdie, they provided the justification for the censorship they sought.

The attack on *The Satanic Verses* appalled liberals. The fight to defend it exhausted them. Knowing what they now knew, few wanted to put themselves through what Rushdie and Penguin had been through. Unlike the Western campaigns against apartheid, Franco, the Greek colonels and the Soviet Empire, a campaign for free speech would involve them running a slight risk of becoming the target of violence themselves. They soon found high-minded reasons to avoid it, and redefined their failure to take on militant religion as a virtuous act. Their preferred tactic was to extend arguments against racism to cover criticism of religion. Or rather, they extended them to cover arguments about minority religions in Western countries. It remained open season on Christianity for liberal writers and comedians, even though Islamist pogroms in Pakistan, Nigeria, Egypt and Iraq and communist oppression in China made Christianity the most persecuted of the major religions.

Writers taking on religious themes, journalists writing about Islamist extremism, or police officers, teachers and social workers investigating the abuse of women, knew that they now ran the risk of their opponents accusing them of a kind of racial prejudice. The charge of 'Islamophobia' would not always stick, but its targets understood that their employers would take it seriously and their contemporaries would regard them as tainted until they had cleared their names. The accusation was not always fatuous. As the millennium arrived, racists and nativist conservatives, who hated Muslims because they were immigrants or came from immigrant families, could develop the most unlikely interest in human rights. If liberalism gave them a new means of attack, they were prepared to feign an interest in it. The only principled response to their hypocrisy was to oppose racism and radical Islam in equal measure and for the same reasons. The best conservatives and liberals managed that, but most settled into the ruts described by a liberal Muslim think tank in 2011. 'Sections of the political left have not done enough to challenge Islamism, yet, encouragingly, they have challenged anti-Muslim extremism,' it said. 'Similarly, sections of the political right have been reluctant to challenge far-right extremism yet are willing to challenge Islamism.'

The fear the Ayatollah generated among liberals thus operated on several levels. Critics of religious obscurantism, most notably liberal Muslims and ex-Muslims, feared violent reprisals. Beyond the worries about direct threats lay the fear that religious groups, bureaucrats, left-wing politicians and newspapers would accuse critics of insensitivity or racism, and that racist groups or websites would confirm the accusation by repeating their critiques. The fear of the vilification and ostracism that would follow was often the most effective deterrent against speaking out. 'Society can and does execute its own mandates,' said John Stuart Mill. 'It practises a social tyranny more formidable than many kinds of political oppression, since, though not usually upheld by such extreme penalties, it leaves fewer means of escape, penetrating much more deeply into the details of life, and enslaving the soul itself.' He might have been writing of modern Europe.

The nature of intellectual life made retreat the likely option. Whatever radical postures they strike, writers and journalists in Western countries are not the equivalents of soldiers or police officers. Nor are they members of a revolutionary underground. They do not begin an artistic or journalistic career expecting to risk their lives. They do not work in well-protected police stations or military bases alongside colleagues who have access to firearms. They work in university campuses or offices, or, in the case of many authors, at home surrounded by their families. Rushdie's marriage broke down under the strain of the fatwa. Police moved the couple fifty-six times in the first few months, and his wife walked out. The desperate Rushdie tried everything to persuade his pursuers to let him live in peace. He apologised to Iran and converted to Islam. Nothing worked. His enemies just laughed at him and pressed on with the terror campaign. Should other writers spend years in hiding with no hope of escape? Did they want to see their relationships disintegrate, as Rushdie had done?

They could rely on the police for protection, but only up to a point. Ordinary criminals, including ordinary murderers, want to escape from the scenes of their crimes. Visible security measures deter them. The likelihood of arrest and prosecution makes them think twice. Suicide bombers, brainwashed to believe they are on their way to paradise to ravish an assortment of virgins, do not care about arrest and prosecution once they have detonated their bombs. They reason that the police cannot prosecute a corpse.

If they had discovered a general resolve to take on militant religion, then writers and editors might have found safety in numbers. Instead, they were united by their fear. An inversion of the usual processes of publishing began. In normal circumstances, publishers look for controversy the way boozers look for brawls. Nothing delights them more than an author or newspaper columnist who arouses anger. When Margaret Thatcher's government tried and failed to suppress the memoirs of Peter Wright, a retired MI5 officer, his paranoid book became an international bestseller. The British authorities' trial of *Lady Chatterley's Lover* for obscenity in 1960 turned the lawyers and expert witnesses on D.H. Lawrence's side into liberal heroes, and the publishers into happy men and women. Forty years on, admiring newspaper features and television drama documentaries still recalled how E.M. Forster, Richard Hoggart and Raymond Williams had revealed to the jury the artistic merit behind Lawrence's use of the words 'fuck' and 'cunt'. The prosecutor, the hapless Mervyn Griffith-Jones, earned his dismal place in the history books when he revealed how out of touch the fuddy-duddy establishment of the 1960s had become by asking the jury if this was the kind of book 'you would wish your wife or servants to read'.

Before Rushdie, publishers praised themselves for their business acumen in buying a book that offended the authorities. After Rushdie, the smart business move was for a publishing house to turn down books that might offend religious zealots. Publishers knew that their business rivals would not pick up the discarded title; they would be equally frightened, and no more inclined to run risks. A cost-benefit analysis lay behind their calculations. Authors can be touchy creatures: vain, grasping and needy. But say what you must about us, no author has ever murdered an editor for *not* printing a book, or bombed the home of a television commissioning editor for *not* broadcasting a drama.

Censorship is at its most effective when its victims pretend it does not exist. If intellectuals had stated that they were too scared to cover subjects of public concern, then at least they would have possessed the courage to admit that they were afraid. Western societies would then have been honest with themselves, and perhaps that honesty would have given birth to a new resolution. But the psychological costs of a frank confession were too high to contemplate. Honesty would have exposed contemporary culture as a culture of pretence.

The grand pose of intellectuals and artists in liberal democracies in the years after the fatwa was that they were the moral equivalents of the victims of repressive regimes. Loud-mouthed newspaper columnists struck heroic postures and claimed to be dissenting voices bravely 'speaking truth to power'. Their editors never had to worry that 'power' would respond by raiding their offices. Publicly funded BBC comedians and state-subsidised playwrights claimed to be the edgy breakers of taboos as they denounced the wars of the Bush/Blair era. Although they never said it, they knew that Bush and Blair would not retaliate by cutting grants or putting artists on trial for sedition – nor did governments fighting wars on two fronts think of imposing military censorship on civilians. Few admitted that what made liberal democracies liberal was that 'power' would not throw you in prison, whether you spoke the truth to it or not, and that taboos had been broken for so long that the most 'edgy' thing an artist could do was conform to them. If the transgressive had come clean, they would have had to accept that they lampooned the bigotry of Christianity and the wickedness of Western governments because they knew that Christians were not so bigoted and Western leaders were not so wicked that they would retaliate by trying to kill them, while the Islamists they ignored just might. Their fear caused them to adopt out of nervousness an ideology that Islamists adopted out of conviction. A partisan of Hizb ut-Tahrir, the Muslim Brotherhood, Jamaat or al Qaeda would not tolerate criticism of Muhammad, but had no difficulty in attacking the greed of Western corporations and the double standards of Western governments. As for denunciations of Christianity and Judaism from Western commentators, Islamists welcomed them, because they echoed their own denunciations of Zionists and Crusaders.

Journalists hoped no one would notice that we were living with a similar double standard. Newspapers ran accounts of Western soldiers torturing or mistreating prisoners in Iraq or Afghanistan. They could well have put troops' lives in danger as the Internet and satellite television sent images of abuse round the world. If anyone raised the matter with us, we replied that freedom of the press and the need to expose torture trumped all other considerations. It would have been a conclusive argument, had we not refused to publish articles and cartoons that might have put *our* lives in danger. As it was when Grayson Perry, a British artist who produced what Catholics would consider to be blasphemous images of the Virgin Mary, said what everyone knew to be true, his candour was so rare *The Times* treated it as news. 'The reason I have not gone all out attacking Islamism in my art is because I feel the real fear that someone will slit my throat,' he told the audience at a debate on art and politics.

Few others could bring themselves to say the same in public, or admit the truth to themselves in private. In the chilling phrase of Kenan Malik, they 'internalised the fatwa', and lived with a fear that dare not speak its name. They ignored the Indians, Pakistanis, Arabs, Africans and Turks who just wanted to get on with building a new life in the West, they forgot about the refugees who had fled to Europe to escape militant Islam, and took militant Islam to be the authentic voice of European Muslims.

You only had to look around to understand why they accepted that there might be something in the clash-of-civilisations hypothesis after all. The 9/11 attacks on New York and Washington were planned in Hamburg. The 7/7 attacks on the

London transport system were planned in Leeds and executed by men with broad Yorkshire accents. Most terrorist violence in Europe came from within. Meanwhile Britain exported terrorists to Pakistan, Israel, Iraq and Afghanistan, and Danish Muslims travelled the world to whip up trade boycotts against their own country.

Theirs were not typical cases. But those in charge of politics and culture were well aware that behind the terrorists were hundreds of thousands of people whose attitudes towards violence were at best ambivalent. In 2007 a survey of British Muslims found that, contrary to expectations, the sense of belonging to Britain was higher among the old, who were more likely to have been born abroad, than the young, who were more likely to have been born in Britain. A significant minority was turning to religious reaction. About one third of Muslims surveyed aged between sixteen and twenty-four wanted the introduction of Sharia law and supported the execution of apostates. Cheeringly, two thirds did not, but anxious cultural bureaucrats were more impressed by those who might do them harm than by those who would leave them alone, particularly when the forces of reaction appeared to have history on their side.

In his caustic *Reflections on the Revolution in Europe: Immigration, Islam and the West*, the American conservative writer Christopher Caldwell saw a continent that was declining in numbers and paralysed by political correctness. It had become too weak to face down the 'adversary culture' of militant Islam. He and others on the right held that post-Christian, post-imperial, post-Holocaust, post-modern, post-just-about-everything European countries lacked the patriotic pride and religious certainties of strong societies, and were wide open to attack from those who felt no comparable embarrassment about their beliefs. As I hope this book makes clear, I think that conservatives underestimate the power and appeal of liberalism. But the most striking feature of the twenty years after *The Satanic Verses* was that Western political and cultural grandees, who trumpeted their anti-Americanism, behaved as if American conservatives were right. They treated Muslims as a homogeneous bloc, and allowed the reactionaries to set the cultural agenda.

They might have looked to Salman Rushdie, to the feminists in Women Against Fundamentalism, to the Arab and Iranian dissidents and to liberals in immigrant communities struggling against the religious ultras. But a principled stand would have involved confronting their fears. However fantastic those fears were, they were not irrational. They could glance at the evening news and see Islamists slaughtering tens of thousands of civilians in Pakistan, Iraq, Nigeria and Afghanistan. They knew it could happen here, because in Rushdie's case it *had* happened here.

With religious censorship, as with censorship in all its forms, you should not just think about the rejected books, newspaper articles, TV scripts and plays, but remember the far larger class of works that authors begin then decide to abandon. The words that were never written, the arguments that were never made during two decades when argument was needed. In 2010, the BBC asked the Egyptian-American feminist Mona Eltahawy why ever-larger numbers of European women were allowing men to tell them that they must hide behind veils. 'I think it has become more prevalent because the space has been left completely uncontested to the Muslim right wing, which does not respect anyone's rights whatsoever except for this one right to cover a woman's face,' she replied. 'No one has pushed back against the Muslim right wing. Integration has largely failed across Europe, even in the UK.'

You can find many reasons why writers, journalists and politicians failed to push back against the Muslim right wing, or even to admit that a Muslim right wing existed. I accept that they were not always cowardly, and that an honourable wariness about the possibility of aiding the white right wing motivated many. But beneath the plausible arguments lay a base and basic fear.

It pushed the majority of Western liberals into adhering in whole or in part to the post-Rushdie rules of self-censorship:

1 They would defer to Islamists and engage in no criticism of the life and teachings of Muhammad.
2 They would treat the Koran as the inerrant word of God, as they would the sacred texts of any other religion which threatened violence, and not suggest that sacred texts are man-made.
3 They would carry on exercising their freedom to criticise, often justifiably, Western religions and governments, which were not threatening to kill them, while appeasing or ignoring those that might.
4 They would never admit to being hypocrites, or accept that their double standards favoured extremists.
5 They would minimise political differences within Muslim communities and refuse to risk their necks for Muslim or ex-Muslim liberals and feminists.
6 They would say that the dictatorial policies of religious regimes and movements were the fault of Western provocation.
7 They would argue that religious violence had nothing to do with religion.

If these rules were all there were, it would have been bad enough. But rules imply limits, and there were no limits. After Grayson Perry said he did not satirise Islam because he feared having his throat slit, he added a shrewd observation. 'I'm interested in religion and I've made a lot of pieces about it,' he said. 'With other targets you've got a better idea of who they are, but Islamism is very amorphous. You don't know what the threshold is. Even what seems an innocuous image might trigger off a really violent reaction, so I just play safe all the time.'

# THREE

## *Manufacturing Offence*

*One nineteen p.m.*
*No one seems to be going in.*
*Instead a fat baldy's coming out.*
*Like he's looking for something in his pockets and*
*at one nineteen and fifty seconds*
*he goes back for those lousy gloves of his.*

WISŁAWA SZYMBORSKA,
'THE TERRORIST, HE WATCHES'

No one doubted that Maqbool Fida Husain was India's greatest modern artist. Western conceptual art became so formulaic, so lost in mannerism and self-reference, that he may have been the world's greatest living artist, although writers risked ridicule when they made such ostentatious claims. I would defy any critic, however, to deny that Husain's work embodied the struggles and glories of India.

For half the year, he lived in London. If you had passed him in Mayfair before he died in June 2011 at the venerable age of ninety-five, you would have found him hard to ignore. He strode out from his studio to Shepherd's Market in bare feet or socks – he did not wear shoes, whatever the weather. Often he carried an oversized paintbrush, just to make sure that the curious could guess his trade. Yet most people in Britain who thought of themselves as cultured found it easy to ignore his work, because no one showed it to them. In part, the ignorance was the result of the parochialism of British culture. But that was not the only reason for Husain's obscurity.

London's Serpentine Gallery included a selection of his paintings in a wider exhibition of contemporary Indian art in 2008. Strange though it once would have been to say it, the gallery's staff deserved praise for their courage as well as their good taste. In 2006, the Asia House cultural centre in Marylebone tried to give the British public the first major solo exhibition of Husain's work. Threats from protesters closed it within days. Even though the Indian High Commissioner opened the show, they denounced Husain as an enemy of the Indian nation. Husain offended all Hindus, they said, with his pornographic and blasphemous art. The possibility of violence terrified the exhibition organisers, and they backed away from a confrontation with censorious extremism.

In India, Husain's position was worse. Hindu militants attacked his home and galleries showing his work. For twelve years, the Indian legal system aided and abetted them. Without understanding how his enemies were exploiting him, the old man became a cog in a machine that manufactured offence. Sectarian politicians exploited him to keep their supporters in a useful state of religious fury, a splenetic condition that delivers many votes to unscrupulous operators at election time.

Born into a Muslim family in Maharashtra in 1915, Husain began his career as a self-taught artist under the Raj. His family moved to Bombay when he was in his teens, and he went door to door offering to sketch portraits. 'What I discovered was that everyone, regardless of their looks, wanted to have their cheeks rosy. I could not do all these rosy cheeks, so I decided to paint Bollywood cinema hoardings instead.'

He painted posters for nearly twenty years, scaling scaffolding and sleeping on the pavement. 'I loved it, that street life. All art in India is viewed as celebration. That is what I've tried to put into my work.'

Husain's friends tell me that he travelled round India, and when he ran out of money he exhibited his drawings on railway station platforms and invited passing passengers to pay what they wanted for them.

When Nehru announced Indian independence in 1947, Husain joined the Bombay Progressive Artists' Group. It had the cosmopolitan project to make a new art for a new country by combining Indian traditions with the Western avant-garde. Husain stayed true to the progressive promises of the 1940s all his life. German expressionism and the modern movement influenced him, and Western critics called him 'the Indian Picasso', but he never lost his ability to straddle high culture and popular culture, which is as good a definition of greatness in art as I can find. In his paintings, gorgeous Bollywood stars appear alongside gods and goddesses of the Hindu tradition. 'For me, India means a celebration of life. You cannot find that same quality anywhere in the world,' he told an interviewer in 2008. 'I never wanted to be clever, esoteric, abstract. I wanted to make simple statements. I wanted my canvases to have a story. I wanted my art to talk to people.'

All India's religious traditions moved him. His family were from the Sulaimani Bohra branch of Shia Islam, which had absorbed many Hindu beliefs. His mother died when he was young, and his father sent him away from home when he was a teenager. 'I used to have terrible nightmares when I was about fourteen or fifteen. This stopped when I was nineteen. I had a guru called Mohammad Ishaq – I studied the holy texts with him for two years. I also read and discussed the Gita and Upanishads and Puranas. This made me completely calm.'

All of which is a long way of making a short point: Husain was from the roots of India. He painted for longer than the Indian republic has existed, and tried to tie its present to its past through his work. Until he was close to eighty, the suggestion that he had no right to include himself as a part of the Indian cultural tradition because he was from a Muslim family would have struck him and all who admired him as inexplicable. As would the notion that there was anything offensive about his nudes.

You only have to visit the Lakshmana temple at Khajuraho to see the erotic strain in Indian culture. The presence of naked gods and goddesses tells visitors that they are far from the taboos of the Abrahamic religions. Hinduism bears partial responsibility for the many crimes of the caste system, but its admirers defend it by saying that because it has no prophet or pope, it has room for those who believe in thousands of gods or none. 'You can cover up your goddess in the finest silk and jewellery,' wrote a sympathetic observer. 'Or you can watch her naked. You can look at the beauty of her face and admire the divinity of her halo, a sari wrapped around her, and her face made up like a Bollywood queen. Or you can see her with ample breasts heaving, her luscious lips parted seductively carved, her thighs wrapped in supreme sexual ecstasy around an athletic god or even goddess – carved for eternity on the walls of a Hindu temple ... At least that's the theory, and it has been the practice in large parts of India for thousands of years.' The sculptors of the Tantric and Shaktic traditions openly celebrated eroticism. Others placed erotic carvings on the outer walls of temples – not to excite visitors, but as a reminder that they should leave their desires behind before they entered. More often, artists used nudity in religious painting and sculpture to symbolise purity. Their work carried no more sexual charge than the nudity of the sadhus who wade into the Ganges at Kumb Mela.

Husain's sketch of Saraswati, the goddess of learning, did not compare with temple carvings of goddesses wrapping their thighs around gods. You could not even call the drawing a fully realised nude. Saraswati sits cross-legged beside a lute, holding a lotus flower above her head. There is nothing erotic – let alone pornographic – about his stylised white-on-black sketch in which only the contours of the body are evident. Husain's goddess is pure to the point of being ethereal. He drew her in the mid-1970s. No one complained. In 1996, a Bombay art critic included the sketch in a book on Husain. A writer on a sectarian Hindu monthly picked up a copy, saw the line drawing of Saraswati, and decided to create a scandal out of nothing.

'M.F. Husain an Artist or a Butcher?' ran the headline above an article accusing the artist of insulting Hindus. The provocateur had picked the right time to start a culture war. By the 1990s, religious parties and sectarian militias had infested the supposedly secular Indian state. They wanted to – they *needed* to – inflame their supporters. If they could not find real offences, they were happy to manufacture them.

Shiv Sena, a thuggish bunch of rabble-rousers, dominated Husain's Bombay. They saw a copy of the article, and instructed the police to file charges. Three days later, Hindu activists stormed a gallery showing his work and trashed his paintings. Husain's enemies had thrown him into the self-pitying and vicious world of Hindu sectarianism, whose malignancies the West should treat as a warning.

Identity politics contains a trap. Of all the reasons to be wary of religious leaders asking the state to suspend freedom of speech to spare their tender feelings, not the smallest is that selective censorship leaves liberals with no argument against sectarians from the dominant denomination or ethnic group. The Indian version of identity politics has led to the majority – or demagogues claiming to represent the majority – *behaving as if it were a persecuted minority*. The various Hindu sectarian parties complained that the state gave special treatment to the descendants of India's former Muslim masters. Rajiv Gandhi's Congress government banned *The Satanic Verses* to please Muslim sentiment. It agreed to exempt Muslim men from paying the alimony to divorced wives the secular law demanded, while not allowing Hindu men to benefit from the cheap rate authorised by Sharia. Look, cried the Hindu sectarians, look at how the elite panders to the minority while penalising the majority.

The worst thing one could say about the Hindu nationalist charges was that they were true. By departing from equality before the law, Gandhi had left India with no argument against sectarianism, in whatever form it came. Hindu nationalists saw an opening, and poured through it. They told the mass of Indians that they remained the victims not just of their former Muslim conquerors, but of the former British conquerors too. The Raj's final imposition on India was to indoctrinate Nehru and his anglicised, British-educated contemporaries with alien democratic and secular ideas. Like militant Islamists and so many pseudo-leftist Western academics, Hindu nationalists damned human rights, including the right to free expression, as colonial impositions.

Bal Thackeray, Shiv Sena's leader, showed where the rejection of secularism led in one of his many declarations of admiration for that ultimate cultural relativist, Adolf Hitler. Thackeray announced that Hindus must 'shake off their stupor' and consider protecting their civilisation and culture. 'If telling it like it is makes one a Nazi, I say: Fine, better that than the spineless, deaf, dumb, numb and blind state exalted as Nehruvian secularism. I wouldn't even spit on it.' Thackeray and the many politicians like him said that Hindus were put upon and cozened. To end the injustice they must free themselves from their former Muslim and British oppressors and become a force the world must reckon with. Hence the destruction in December 1992 of the Ayodhya mosque, allegedly built by the conquering Mughals in the sixteenth century on the site of a Hindu temple, and the slaughter of thousands in the communal riots that followed. Hence the threats to the lives of historians who said that India had always been an amalgam of cultures, religions and ethnicities, and that some Hindu princes had been as keen on sacking Hindu temples as the Mughal invaders were. And hence the campaign to persecute Husain, who, as a supporter of Nehru's ideals and a Muslim to boot, was their perfect target.

As soon as Shiv Sena filed lawsuits against him, Husain had to cancel his planned attendance at a commemoration in the city of the achievements of the Progressive Artists' Group. If he had come, the police would have arrested him for 'disturbing communal harmony' – and there was a chance a religious mob might have killed him too. A group of young artists unfurled a banner at the party reading 'Husain, we miss you', but other guests were unimpressed when a Western collector insisted that they speak out on Husain's behalf. 'Why doesn't he understand?' said an artist's husband. 'This is like asking us to speak out in Berlin in 1936.'

As so often, the Hitler comparison was an exaggeration, although given Thackeray's pronouncements, you can see why the man reached for it. Fanatics threatened Husain and all associated with him with violence. They destroyed his paintings at every opportunity. When a TV network asked its viewers whether Husain should receive India's highest honour, religious yobs stormed the studios. In 1998, militants attacked Husain's Bombay home and wrecked it. Thackeray justified them and identified with them. 'If Husain can step into Hindustan, what is wrong if we enter his house?' he said as he redefined secular, multi-cultural India into mono-cultural 'Hindustan', and made Husain an enemy alien in his own city.

The logic of retaliatory sectarianism dictated that when Islamists offered a reward to anyone who would kill Danish cartoonists who had offended them, Hindu nationalist politicians offered a reward to 'patriots' who would chop off Husain's hands.

A dirty mind is a perpetual feast, and once they started looking for reasons to be offended, sectarians found them everywhere. Husain painted a nude woman whose body curved around a map of India. His persecutors denounced it as pornographic, and claimed he was insulting Bharatmata (Mother India). In truth, Husain had painted a severe work because it was his contribution to a charitable campaign to raise money for the victims of the civil war in Kashmir, and the cause demanded restraint. As might have been expected, the fact that the aid was going to Muslim Kashmiris made his opponents angrier still.

When they had finished with what he had painted, Husain's enemies questioned him about the subjects he had never painted. Why did he not paint Muhammad? Why did he paint nudes of Indian goddesses, but not of the Prophet's favourite wife Aisha? On the Web, they contrasted his abstract nudes of gods and goddesses with his fully clothed portraits of his wife and daughter, and of the Prophet Muhammad's daughter Fatima. 'Husain depicts the deity or person he hates as naked. He shows Prophet's Mother, his own mother, daughter, all the Muslim personalities fully clothed, but at the same time Hindus and Hindu deities along with Hitler are shown naked. This proves his hatred for the Hindus.'

India's lawyers and politicians helped at every stage of the campaign of harassment. India and America are the world's greatest democracies. But whereas America's founding fathers wisely protected free speech with the First Amendment, India's founders took their lead from the British colonialists. They believed that censorship could promote national unity, as many European politicians and bureaucrats believe today. Article 19 of the constitution grants Indians free speech – but adds opt-outs to allow censors to intervene in every important area of debate – the 'sovereignty and integrity of India, the security of the State, friendly relations with foreign States, public order, decency or morality, or in relation to contempt of court, defamation or incitement'. Article 295 of the criminal code penalises 'deliberate and malicious acts, intended to outrage religious feelings or any class by insulting its religion or religious beliefs'. For good measure, Article 153 mandates the punishment of those who promote 'enmity between different groups on grounds of religion, race, place of birth, residence, language, etc., [by] doing acts prejudicial to maintenance of harmony'.

The courts and the police, who never seemed to be to hand when criminals attacked art galleries, besieged Husain for more than a decade. Censorship was not promoting harmony, let alone the interests of justice, but allowing sectarians to pick grievances out of thin air. It took until 2008 for the Delhi High Court to throw out all of the hundreds of criminal charges against Husain, and warn, 'In India, a new puritanism is being carried out ... and a host of ignorant people are vandalising art and pushing us towards the pre-renaissance era.'

By then Husain had had his fill. In 2010, at the age of ninety-four, and after years of exile, he renounced his Indian citizenship. Speaking with sadness but not bitterness, he said, 'I have not intended to denigrate or hurt the beliefs of anyone through my art. I only give expression to the instincts from my soul. India is my motherland and I can never hate the country. But the political leadership, artists and intellectuals kept silent when Sangh Parivar [Hindu nationalist] forces attacked me. How can I live there in such a situation?'

India must carry the shame of being the first country to ban *The Satanic Verses*, the work of its greatest novelist, and of following up that miserable achievement by driving its greatest artist into exile.

Why pick on Husain for sketches no one found disturbing when he first released them? Read his accusers, and they cannot justify their charges of blasphemy or obscenity. How can they, when Husain's paintings are not remotely pornographic, but part of a deliberate attempt by the artist and his contemporaries to continue Indian traditions? Husain's real offences were to be born into a Muslim family almost a hundred years ago, and to defend the secular dream of Nehru. That was it. His enemies wanted to feed their supporters a diet of indignation, and needed to supply them with new targets for their rage. The identity of the target was irrelevant. If they had not gone after Husain, they would have gone after someone else.

In his study of the crisis in Indian secularism, Salil Tripathi emphasises how unIndian Indian nationalism has become. 'Whenever Hindu nationalists attack an art gallery, or tear down posters they consider obscene, or demand bans on books they don't want others to read, or vandalise a research institute, or destroy the home of an editor, or threaten an academic, or run a campaign against a historian they disagree with, or force film studios to change scripts, or extract apologies from artists, or hurl eggs at scholars, or destroy mosques, or rape Muslim women, or kill Muslim men and children, they take India into a deeper abyss [and] push Hinduism into a darker age. They look and act like the Nazis and the Taliban ... [They] are untrue to the meaning of their faith and are disloyal to their nation's constitution. They shame a great nation and belittle how Rushdie saw India: "The dream we all agreed to dream".'

The self-satisfied might say how lucky we in Britain are that we do not suffer from India's censorship laws, and how proud we should be that we could offer Husain a sanctuary. Before we become too smug, we should go back to the forced closure of the Husain exhibition in London in 2006. The reaction to the attack on intellectual freedom in the heart of a city that boasted of being a great cultural capital was instructive. There was no reaction. The artists and intellectuals who are usually so keen to write round-robin letters to the press denouncing this policy or that injustice stayed silent. Journalists and politicians bit their tongues too, as they tacitly accepted the tyrannical proposition that if a writer or artist failed to show 'respect', then he or she must suffer the consequences. The denial by fanatics of the right of the public to see the work of a major artist did not warrant one paragraph in even the news-in-brief columns of any of the daily papers.

I must enter one further caveat. For all the bad faith behind their concocted accusations, the religious thugs had one good question: Why couldn't Husain paint Muhammad, or come to that, his favourite wife Aisha?

## 'God is love'

Sherry Jones gave every appearance of being a warm-hearted American. She covered Montana and Idaho for a business news service, until in 2002 she decided like so many reporters before her to try to break into fiction. She learned Arabic. She read academic studies of the history of early Islam. Then, like no other reporter before her, she sat down to write a novel about the life of Aisha bint Abu Bakr, whose father, according to popular accounts, betrothed her to Muhammad when she was six, and gave her away to be his wife when she was nine.

The wars of 9/11 moved Jones to seek reconciliation between peoples. 'We in the West know so little about Islam that we tend to demonise it,' she told an interviewer. Muhammad was 'fairly egalitarian in his attitudes to women', and got a 'bad rap' from feminists. The sooner Muslims, Christians, Jews, atheists and Buddhists realised that 'we are all human beings with needs, desires and fears … the closer we will be to achieving Paradise right here on Earth. Because Paradise means living continually in the presence of God, and, as the Bible says, God is love.'

Jones's novel, *The Jewel of Medina*, continues in this vein – at some length. The opening lines set the tone for the rest of the book: 'Join me on a journey to another time and place, to a harsh, exotic world of saffron and sword fights, of desert nomads living in camel-hair tents, of caravans laden with Persian carpets and frankincense, of flowing colourful robes and kohl-darkened eyes and perfumed arms filigreed with henna.'

As the above suggests, Ms Jones was writing a historical romance for the women's market. The New York office of Random House was impressed, and paid her an advance of $100,000 in a two-novel deal.

I defy any reader to guess how a religious, racial or other interest group could find grounds for offence in her work. As with the paintings of M.F. Husain, it is impossible for those who do not know what happened next to understand why even the most twisted censor would want to hurl Jones's book on the fire.

*The Jewel of Medina* is an anti-*Satanic Verses*. It replaces scepticism with reverence, and satire with solemnity. Jones's Aisha is a feisty girl, as all modern heroines must be. Muhammad is wise and good. Jones does not suggest for a moment that his teachings are inferior to Christianity or Judaism. For those who do not like to see their prophets or gods cast in a bad light, Jones puts the best possible gloss on an event that shocks modern sensibilities: an old man taking sexual possession of a young girl. Jones avoids the obstacle by pretending it isn't there. In the novel, they are married when Aisha is nine. Muhammad kisses the child and says goodbye. She reaches the age of fourteen. To her intense frustration, her marriage is still unconsummated. 'Each day flowered with hope – would Muhammad visit me today? – then dropped its petals like tears. The weeks dragged by like a funeral procession.' The waiting lasts for years, and the marriage is not consummated until after she reaches puberty.

This comforting view of Aisha's life is popular with apologists for religion, most notably Karen Armstrong, a former nun who now soothes modern readers by assuring them that there is little or nothing to worry about in Catholicism or any other creed she comes across. Her biographies of Muhammad and her history of Islam guided Jones as she worked on the plot of *The Jewel of*

*Medina*, and Jones seems to have been impressed by Armstrong's bold assertion that the emancipation of women was a cause dear to the Prophet's heart. To make it, Armstrong had to explain away the hadiths and verses in the Koran that support the beating and sexual exploitation of women, and the power the holy book gives husbands to divorce unwanted wives. On the question of men marrying little girls, Armstrong's Muhammad, like Sherry Jones's Muhammad, does the decent thing. He waits until Aisha reaches puberty before making love to her. As Armstrong explains:

> Finally about a month after she had arrived in Mecca, it was decided that it was time for the wedding of Muhammad with Aisha. She was still only nine years old, so there was no wedding feast and the ceremonial was kept to a minimum ... Abū Bakr had bought some fine red-striped cloth from Bahrain and this had been made into a wedding dress for her. Then they took her to her little apartment beside the mosque. There Muhammad was waiting for her, and he laughed and smiled while they decked her with jewellery and ornaments and combed her long hair. Eventually a bowl of milk was brought in and Muhammad and Aisha both drank from it. The marriage made little difference to Aisha's life. Tabari says that she was so young that she stayed at her parents' home and the marriage was consummated there later when she had reached puberty. Aisha went on playing with her girlfriends and her dolls.

Tabari, the ninth-century Koranic scholar, is not in fact such a comforting source. In his collection of stories about the Prophet, he quotes Aisha as saying, 'the Messenger of God consummated his marriage with me in my house when I was nine years old'. In other traditions he cites, he puts her age at ten. The hadith collections of Bukhari, which Sunni Muslims consider to be the most authoritative, also say that Muhammad consummated the marriage when Aisha was nine. For most of the history of Islam, there was nothing controversial about her age at the time of the wedding. Because it confirmed her virginity, it reinforced Aisha's status among the Prophet's wives, and gave her wishes added force in the power struggles within Islam after Muhammad's death.

Perhaps Jones, Armstrong and all those like them who avert their eyes from inconvenient evidence do so because they worry about Western racists, who use Muhammad's marriage to Aisha to taunt ethnic minorities. But it is as important to worry about religious extremists who use the arguments for male supremacy, homophobia and the exploitation of women and children in holy books to justify oppression – and to notice that there is not a great deal of difference between the ideologies of the religious and the racial extremists.

In *Does God Hate Women?*, their scholarly study of the links between religion and misogyny, Ophelia Benson and Jeremy Stangroom criticise Armstrong by making the essential point that when sacred texts are taken to be divine instructions, you cannot allow nervousness to inhibit criticism.

In Iran after the 1979 revolution, the Islamists reduced the minimum age of marriage for girls to nine. In 2000, under pressure from women's rights activists, the Iranian parliament voted to raise it to fifteen. However, the Council of Guardians, an anti-democratic oversight body dominated by traditional clerics, vetoed the reform, saying that the new ruling was contrary to Islamic law. (They had the example of Ayatollah Khomeini on their side. He had availed himself of the law's blessings and married a ten-year-old girl.) The case of Yemen is equally instructive. In 1998, the Yemeni parliament revised a law that had set the minimum age of marriage at fifteen. The new ruling allowed girls to be married much earlier, so long as they did not move in with their husbands until they had reached sexual maturity. Conservative clerics take this to mean that the consummation of a marriage can take place at the age of nine. Human-rights activists have fought to reverse this ruling, but to date they have been unsuccessful, because Islamic clerics can point to Muhammad's marriage to Aisha to justify their views.

'Although it would be a massive oversimplification to claim that Islam is the cause of these patterns,' Benson and Stangroom conclude, 'it is nevertheless the case that Islamic beliefs are sometimes a factor in child marriage.' As the Iranian reformers found, religion makes the task of stopping girls becoming the possessions of older men – sometimes far older men – harder. The men can always say that religious authority is on their side. Unless religious authority is challenged, they will win.

There are three possible challenges. The first, and to my mind the simplest, is to give up on religion. To reject communism, you do not need to know why Marx's beliefs in the inevitability of proletarian revolution were wrong, you just need to look at the vast crimes the communists committed, and resolve to have nothing to do with the ideology behind them. Similarly, to reject religion you do not need to understand the scientific and philosophical arguments about the extreme unlikelihood of God's existence, or go through the archaeological and literary studies which tell us that the early years of Judaism, Christianity and Islam were strikingly different from the accounts presented to believers. Knowledge of the vast crimes committed in the name of religion is once again sufficient.

Religious reformers must try subtler strategies. They cannot abandon their faiths, therefore they take, say, the problematic lines in Leviticus, St Paul's epistles and the Koran that license the persecution of homosexuals and try to reinterpret them.

Leviticus says:

*Thou shalt not lie with mankind, as with womankind: it is abomination.*

The prohibition appears to leave no escape hatches, but liberal Jews and Christians must find a way out so they can continue to practise their religions without sacrificing their tolerant instincts. American Christian homosexuals made a dogged effort when they formed a group with the splendid title of the National Gay Pentecostal Alliance. (Sadly, they later changed its name.) They did their own translation of Leviticus, and came up with a new version of the prohibition:

> *And a man who will lie down with a male in beds of a woman, both of them have made an abomination; dying they will die. Their blood is on them.*

They updated the language into contemporary English to produce:

> *If two men engage in homosexual sex while on a woman's bed, both have committed an abomination. They are to be put to death; their blood will be on their own heads.*

It did not sound much of an improvement. But the gay Pentecostalists were undaunted. 'Rather than forbidding male homosexuality', they decided, Leviticus simply restricts where lovemaking may occur. According to their reading, if a bisexual man takes a gay lover into the bedroom he shares with his wife, he is committing an abomination in the eyes of the Lord. But if he sneaks him into the spare bedroom, then everything will be fine with God, although not, I imagine, with his wife.

An ingenious American rabbi by the name of Arthur Waskow decided that Leviticus could have meant:

> *Do not sleep with a man as it were with a woman.*

Once more, there seemed to be no substantial change to the rules of engagement. But the rabbi decided that Leviticus was saying that men must make love like men, not women. If two men have sex, neither should be the passive, womanly partner, he explained. They must come out of the closet and revel in their masculine sexuality when they get down to business. As the authors of Leviticus issued prohibitions against everything from bestiality to sacrificing donkeys, it is improbable that they wanted men to be out, loud and proud when they made love. But you can see why a liberal rabbi wanted to twist the Torah's words.

These arguments are casuistic, because if a conservative theologian could prove that Leviticus or St Paul had an unswerving opposition to homosexuality, liberal believers would not shrug and accept defeat, but would try to reconcile religion and liberalism by another tortuous method. However, the liberals' bad faith is not complete. They may be trying to get round inhumane prohibitions of homosexual love with arguments that are close to being ridiculous, but they never pretend that the inhumane verses do not exist. If they did, their conservative opponents would rout them. They would simply point to the relevant passages in the Torah or the New Testament and win the argument.

Muslim feminist reformers try a third and braver tactic when they confront Koranic justifications for sexism or the endorsement of child marriage. They tell believers 'to reject literal reads of the Koran and recognise that these verses were communicated during specific moments of war, and they aren't edicts for all time. We, as Muslims, must reject the notion that we read these words literally.' The reformers want to persuade the faithful that not every verse is true. Again, they do not wish away the difficulties of the enterprise by talking as if there is no conflict between modernity and tradition.

The task of pretending that a fundamental schism between liberalism and religious authoritarianism does not exist has fallen to the generation of post-Rushdie apologists. They do not say that believers should ignore the hadiths that describe Muhammad's consummation of a marriage to a nine-year-old girl. Nor do they reinterpret them, or argue that the hadiths do not constitute reliable evidence as their collectors did not find them and write them down until long after Muhammad's death. (Bukhari lived two hundred years after the Prophet died.) Instead, they write as if the uncomfortable passages are not there.

Sherry Jones strikes me as less culpable than others who self-censor to avoid offence. *The Jewel of Medina* is a novel. She is not offering readers a factual account, but telling a story. She ignores unpleasant evidence because she is a warm woman, with a heart throbbing to the passionate rhythms of sentimental fiction, and a soul brimming over with love for humankind.

Why would anyone want to hurt her for that?

## The Rise of the Religious Informer

Random House was delighted with *The Jewel of Medina*. It set a publication date for August 2008, and told Sherry Jones it would send her on a nationwide tour.

Days later, it pulled the book. Random House explained that 'credible and unrelated sources' had given it 'cautionary advice not only that the publication of this book might be offensive to some in the Muslim community, but also that it could incite acts of violence by a small, radical segment'. For 'the safety of the author, employees of Random House, booksellers and anyone else who would be involved in the distribution and sale of the novel', it had to abandon its planned publication of *The Jewel of Medina*.

Jones was devastated. She could not understand how anyone in the Muslim community could have found her book offensive. *The Jewel of Medina* was her first novel. Random House had told her it would be a bestseller. Her chance to become a novelist, her hopes of a big break, had been snatched from her. There is no record of her reaction when she found that one of the 'credible sources' who had damned the book was not a Jamaat activist in the Indian subcontinent or an ayatollah in Tehran, but a Western academic.

One of the creepy consequences of living in an age of religious extremism is that readers start thinking like police spies. 'She can't expect to get away with that,' we mutter as we put down the book and wait for the inevitable protests. 'She must know she's asking for trouble.'

Usually, demands for censorship and retribution come from members of the confessional group that has been insulted, or can simulate an offended manner, but not always. In an atmosphere of cultural tension, the small-minded discover that they cannot allow debates to be won on their merits. They must take it upon themselves to play the informer and point the finger at offenders.

Of all people, academics ought to have a professional interest in unconstrained intellectual freedom. If an American president were to demand the dismissal of leftish professors on US campuses for criticising American foreign policy, his targets would cry 'McCarthyism'. Liberal opinion would rally behind them and defend their right to speak their minds. Yet academics who depend on freedom of thought are among the first to deny its benefits to others. The twisted legacy of the 1968 generation carries much of the blame. The original attempts of the baby-boomer 'New Left' to promote equality were honourable, and conservatives who sneered at political correctness revealed nothing more than their own brutishness. Those who spoke up for black, Hispanic, female and gay students were asking for fair treatment. They wanted universities to ensure that no man or woman was refused the education they deserved to receive.

Treating people as equals means treating them as adults who can handle robust argument, not as children who need to be told fairy stories and tucked up in bed. But as the culture wars raged, fairy stories were what the universities delivered. Topics and arguments were ruled off-limits; real and imagined heresies denounced with phlegm-spitting vehemence; and comforting histories promulgated on how black Egypt was responsible for the philosophies of ancient Athens, or how Amazonian tribes were noble savages living in a state of prelapsarian harmony until wicked whitey came along.

Islamism came into universities whose academics had the good liberal motive that they should not discriminate against students because of their race or religion, but whose intellectual defences had been weakened by the hysterical attitudes the culture wars fostered. By the end of the first decade of the twenty-first century, academia had acquired a further bias. In general, academics hated George W. Bush and Tony Blair's wars in Afghanistan and Iraq, and worried about illiberal restrictions on human rights that the post-9/11 anti-terrorism legislation imposed. Many academics went on to find justifications for terror. An interventionist foreign policy and an authoritarian criminal justice policy were 'recruiting sergeants' for terrorism, they said. When they met students and preachers who promoted hate-filled ideologies, they could not argue against them with the vigour with which they argued against the hatreds of the white far right, because they thought Islamist hatred was justified in part.

Fear caught their tongues, too: the fear of accusations of 'racism', 'neo-conservatism', 'Islamophobia' or 'orientalism'; the fear of having to admit that their vague commitments to anti-imperialist solidarity were feeding reactionary movements; and the fear of violence. At City University, London, an investigation by liberal Muslims found students who preached, 'When they say to us the Islamic state teaches to cut off the hand of the thief, yes it does! And it also teaches us to stone the adulterer ... When they tell us that the Islamic state tells us and teaches us to kill the apostate, yes it does! Because this is what Allah and his messenger have taught us, and this is the religion of Allah and it is Allah who legislates and only Allah has the right to legislate.' Lesbian, gay and Jewish students reported feeling intimidated, while journalists on the independent student newspaper received threats after they covered the story.

They were not alone in that. 'A couple of years ago, UCL allowed the Islamic Society to put on a show of Islamic art,' recalled Professor John Sutherland of University College, London, in 2010. 'A friend of mine, an eminent scientist, strolled in to take a look. Was he a believer, asked an obviously Muslim student. No, replied my friend, he didn't believe in any god, as it happened. "Then," the young man confidently informed him, "we shall have to execute you." He wasn't joking; he was predicting. He wasn't going to draw a scimitar that minute and lop off the godless one's head, but he implied that at some future point such things would happen.' Sutherland was dragging up his memories of this old confrontation because on Christmas Day 2009 a graduate of University College, Umar Farouk Abdulmutallab, tried to detonate plastic explosives hidden in his underwear and murder the 289 passengers and crew on a Northwest Airlines flight from Amsterdam to Detroit.

Abdulmutallab had come to Britain from a good home – his father had been chairman of the First Bank of Nigeria. He was radicalised in the Dostoyevskian world of London extremism where the white far left meets the Islamist far right. Lonely and sexually frustrated – 'The hair of a woman can easily arouse a man. The Prophet advised young men to fast if they can't get married but it has not been helping me,' he wrote on a Web forum for young Muslims – he drifted towards his university's Islamic society.

He found himself in a religious atmosphere saturated with conspiracy theory. Speakers at the UCL Islamic Society had advocated anti-Semitic hatred. Jews are 'all the same', said one.

'They've monopolised everything: the Holocaust, God, money, interest, usury, the world economy, the media, political institutions ... they monopolised tyranny and oppression as well.'

A TV crew caught another on camera saying that homosexuals should be thrown off cliffs and that the testimony of a woman was worth half that of a man. A common theme was that although Westerners were murderous, tyrannical, corrupt and licentious, they were also perilously seductive. 'Today, the culture of Coke and the Big Mac, the culture of the Americans, the culture of the Europeans, these cultures are dominant and they are all-pervasive,' a third guest was on record as saying. 'We stand in awe of their culture and we are imitating them in everything. This culture, this evil influence, this imitation of the kuffar.'

After Abdulmutallab became president of the UCL Islamic Society in 2005, he organised martial-arts training and an 'anti-terror week', which featured a video of clips of violence, accompanied by a hypnotic soundtrack. The film-maker included footage of British left-wing politicians saying that the West believed that Palestinian blood was cheaper than Israeli blood, and of a former prisoner of war alleging that the Americans tortured him at Guantánamo Bay.

'When we sat down, they played a video that opened with shots of the twin towers after they'd been hit, then moved on to images of mujahedeen fighting, firing rockets in Afghanistan,' one member of the audience said. 'It was quite tense in the theatre, because I think lots of people were shocked by how extreme it was. It seemed to me like it was brainwashing, like they were trying to indoctrinate people.'

When the FBI arrested Abdulmutallab, journalists wanted to know why the university had not done more to fight extremism. The response of the university authorities was an education in itself. They denounced the 'quite disturbing level of Islamophobia' the case had aroused. Their inquiry decided that Abdulmutallab's radicalisation had happened after he left university, despite the evidence to the contrary. At a meeting at UCL to discuss the controversy, I watched academics and student leaders abuse the university's critics. They were the real racists and bigots, not the guests of the Islamic Society. They were the ones who needed 'de-radicalising', not the religious reactionaries.

It is less surprising than it ought to be that academics were on the side of repression when censors came for a harmless novel by a well-meaning writer.

Among those who received advance copies of *The Jewel of Medina* was Denise Spellberg, an associate professor of Islamic history at the University of Texas in Austin. Jones had read Spellberg's *Politics, Gender, and the Islamic Past: The Legacy of 'A'isha Bint Abi Bakr* while researching her novel, and the publishers might have hoped that Spellberg would supply a puff quote.

If they did, they were disappointed. Spellberg phoned Shahed Amanullah, a lecturer at her university, and the editor of altmus-lim.com, a popular site for American Muslims. 'She was upset,' Amanullah told the *Wall Street Journal*. She asked him to 'warn Muslims' that a novel that 'made fun of Muslims and their history' was on its way. Spellberg confirmed to the paper that she hated the book. It was a 'very ugly, stupid piece of work', she said and quoted a scene which takes place on the night when Muhammad consummates his marriage with Aisha. Spellberg said that Jones was guilty of a 'deliberate misinterpretation of history', and of producing soft porn. She did not seem to grasp that novelists are not historians, and in any case, if *The Jewel of Medina* was misinterpreting history, it was misinterpreting it in Muhammad's favour.

Amanullah dashed off an email to his graduate students: 'Just got a frantic call from a professor who got an advance copy of the forthcoming novel, *Jewel of Medina* – she said she found it incredibly offensive.'

The next day, a blogger posted Amanullah's email on a website for Shia Muslims, Hussaini Youth, under the headline 'Upcoming Book, *Jewel of Medina*: A New Attempt to Slander the Prophet of Islam'. His readers rallied to the new cause. 'In the garb of Freedom of Speech enemies of Islam are attacking Islam,' said one poster. 'You have the freedom of throwing the stones in the sky. But you can be prosecuted if it injures or kills someone.'

The publishers soon heard the commotion. A manager at Random House told her colleagues, 'There is a very real possibility of major danger for the building and staff and widespread violence. Denise says it is a declaration of war ... explosive stuff ... a national security issue ... thinks the book should be withdrawn ASAP.'

In a letter she later wrote to the *Wall Street Journal*, Spellberg said that she was not alone in wanting to see the book stopped. 'I never had this power [to cancel publication], nor did I single-handedly stop the book's publication. Random House made its final decision based on the advice of other scholars, conveniently not named in the article, and based ultimately on its determination of corporate interests. I felt it my duty to warn the press of the novel's potential to provoke anger among some Muslims.'

The good, old cause of freedom of speech was upheld not by editors in New York, still less by academics in American universities determined to defend their country's Bill of Rights, but by American Muslims. Asra Q. Nomani wrote the *Wall Street Journal*'s story about the incident, and concluded her piece with a personal note: 'This saga upsets me as a Muslim – and as a writer who believes that fiction can bring Islamic history to life in a uniquely captivating and humanizing way. For all those who believe the life of the Prophet Muhammad can't include stories of lust, anger and doubt, we need only read the Quran (18:110) where, it's said, God instructed Muhammad to tell others: "I am only a mortal like you."'

Shahed Amanullah, Denise Spellberg's colleague, met Sherry Jones and liked her. 'Unlike so many other times in our recent history where we are struggling against people who are really out to vilify us, I sensed from the beginning that you were doing this out of appreciation or respect,' he told her, and then found the words that ought to have been in the mouths of American professors and publishers. 'The best response to free speech ought to be more speech in return. Anyone should have the right to publish whatever he or she wants about Islam or Muslims – even if their views are offensive – without fear of censorship or retribution. In an ideal world, both parties would open their minds enough to understand the other point of view.'

Even the protests on the Shia website were not as menacing as they appeared. Its readers' action plan consisted of a letter-writing campaign.

Rival publishers realised that Random House had not just failed to defend free speech, but worse – much, much worse – had failed to think about the bottom line. Beaufort Books decided the fears of a violent attack were twaddle, and snapped up *The Jewel of Medina*. Sherry Jones had her bestseller, and foreign houses bought the overseas rights. Jones and everyone associated with her book seemed safe.

In her eerie poem 'The Terrorist, He Watches', the Polish poet Wisława Szymborska describes a terrorist looking at a bar in the minutes before his bomb will explode. Some people escape danger just in time, although they do not know it. Others walk into the bar and to their deaths. It is the terrorist's detachment that gives the poem its power. Everyone in and around the bar is in his killing zone. Whether they live or die is down to luck. The terrorist sees a bald man leave, then turn back to collect his gloves. He will die. Another man gets on a scooter and rides off. He will live. The terrorist does not mind who his targets are, as long as he has targets.

The publishers who bought *The Jewel of Medina* did not realise that they were now in the zone. It did not matter that Jones had avoided the issue of sex with children in an admiring account of Muhammad's life, and that American Muslims had praised her work. However briefly, her name had been associated with an 'insult to Islam'. Whether someone would respond by targeting her or her publishers was now down to chance.

Ali Beheshti was an admirer of Omar Bakri Muhammad, a Syrian-born militant living in London, and founder of the British extremist group al-Muhajiroun. 'We don't make a distinction between civilians and non-civilians, innocents and non-innocents,' Bakri said as he explained the group's ideology, 'only between Muslims and unbelievers.' Beheshti was not a sleeper, hiding from the police until the moment came to strike. He made no effort to play the undercover agent. He embraced radical Islam and thrust himself in front of the police. He gained international notoriety in 2006 when he took his twenty-month-old daughter on a demonstration outside the Danish embassy against cartoons of the Prophet Muhammad which had appeared in the Danish newspaper *Jyllands-Posten*. He made her wear a hat carrying the slogan 'I ♥ Al Qaeda'. Around her, furious men chanted 'Bomb, bomb the UK' and 'Europe, you will pay with your blood.'

Beheshti had the motive. The opportunity was there for the taking. The owner of the Gibson Square publishing house, which bought the British rights to *The Jewel of Medina*, ran his business from his home, and his promotional literature carried its address. Beheshti found the means on the night of 27 September 2008, when he and two accomplices put a barrel of diesel into the boot of a Honda Accord. The police had bugged the car, and heard Beheshti ask his co-conspirator, 'You wanna be the emir [leader], yeah?'

'That would be you.'

'You know what we gotta do, anyway, innit?' Beheshti added.

They poured the diesel through the letterbox in the publisher's front door and set it on fire. They failed to kill anyone, and the police picked them up. Iraqis or Pakistanis looking at the terrorist slaughters that were taking place in their countries would have thought the failed firebombing a lame effort. But in the Western democracies the attack on Gibson Square reinforced the message that capricious violence might strike anyone, anywhere. All it needed was for someone to denounce an author, and for that denunciation to spread on the Net. In the 1980s, mullahs in Tehran and clerical reactionaries in Pakistan ignited violence. By the 2000s, anyone could deliberately or inadvertently set off a panic – a blogger, a reviewer, an academic or indeed a reporter.

The muscling in of my trade of journalism into the business of manufacturing offence was an ominous development, because journalists are skilled at making news out of nothing. We come across a fact we suspect will outrage a pressure group/political party/guardian of the nation's morals. We call the pressure group/political party/guardian of the nation's morals and ask, 'Are you outraged?' 'Yes we are,' the pressure group/political party/guardian of the nation's morals replies, allowing us to generate the headline 'Pressure Group/Political Party/Guardian of the Nation's Morals Outraged by ...'

In 2009, Ophelia Benson and Jeremy Stangroom published *Does God Hate Women?*, which criticised the soothing story about Aisha's life that Karen Armstrong, Sherry Jones and others promoted, and presented evidence that contradicted it. The *Sunday Times* greeted the book's arrival with the headline 'Fears of Muslim Anger Over Religious Book'. The report explained that it 'could cause a backlash among Muslims because it criticises the Prophet Muhammad for taking a nine-year-old girl as his third wife'.

The word to concentrate on in that sentence is '*could*'.

Religious militants were not in fact preparing a 'backlash', because they did not know of the book's existence. The journalist who wrote the piece phoned Anjem Choudary, a self-styled Sharia judge from al-Muhajiroun, the group Ali Beheshti was associated with when he had targeted Sherry Jones's British publishers. The obliging 'judge' told the *Sunday Times* that as well as targeting Sherry Jones's book, Islamists could also target the critics of Sherry Jones's version of history. 'Talk of Aisha as a child when she married is not true,' he said. 'At nine, she reached her menses and in those days a girl was considered to be mature when that happened. No one will swallow talk about child brides. It would lead to a huge backlash, as we saw with *The Jewel of Medina*.'

The journalist phoned the publisher of *Does God Hate Women?*, and told him he was being 'brave'. The poor man had not appreciated that he was being brave, and called on the services of an 'ecumenical adviser', a religious censor modern Europe thought it had seen the last of. The ecumenical adviser said that although he did not like the book, the authors had substantiated their claims, and that in his opinion the publisher should allow the public to read their work.

Because of an inoffensive sketch he drew in the 1970s, Hindu fanatics drive an Indian artist from his country in the 1990s. Because an academic from Texas denounces an American romantic novelist, terrorists firebomb a publisher's home in north London. Because two intellectuals write a study of feminism and religion, and a journalist invites extremists to find offence, an editor calls in a religious adviser to rule if he can publish a book in a country that was once proud to number John Milton, John Stuart Mill and George Orwell among its greatest writers.

## RULES FOR CENSORS (3):

# *Go Postal!*

Imagine a dictatorship. Let us call it Authoritania. It could be a gulf sheikhdom, an African nationalist kleptocracy, a relic of pan-Arabism, a post-Soviet republic or a communist 'people's democracy'.

Our imaginary dictator has learned from the twentieth century that cooperating with crony capitalists is more profitable than spouting slogans about proletarian revolution. He pushes most of his subject country's earnings through a sovereign wealth fund, and forms alliances with oligarchs in the private sector. Public and private enterprises – the distinction between the two is fine – provide jobs that bring maximum reward for minimal effort to the dictator's supporters, relatives and mistresses. In return, he harries free trade unions and allows both state and private companies to operate without restraint. Corruption and exploitation follow. The state's medical service publishes no official records of industrial injuries, or of the high rates of depression, for fear of what they may reveal about the state's luckless subjects. Doctors play down the Aids epidemic, because they know that honest reporting would show how many desperate women have become prostitutes. The secret police arrest opposition leaders and deny them access to the state-controlled television channels. The state's prosecutors harass the few opposition newspapers and radio stations. Although Authoritania's constitution declares its commitment to freedom of speech and of the press, its 'Law of Social Responsibility' allows the courts to impose hefty fines on journalists and editors found guilty of 'offending' or 'denigrating' the authorities. The official 'Press Law' goes further, and imposes prison terms on writers who criticise the president or incite actions that 'undermine state security'. The police arrest journalists who cover 'illegal' strikes – legal strikes are impossible – or protests by the owners of small businesses, who face continuous demands for bribes from bureaucrats. With considerable initiative, prosecutors charge reporters with organising the demonstrations they had gone to observe.

Authoritania seems sewn up. But it remains a dictatorial, not a totalitarian state. Opposition parties can stand in elections, although the bureaucracy ensures that they can never win. Writers and journalists face intimidating restrictions, but because the government casts the restrictions as laws, dissidents can work round them and subvert the apparently rigorous censorship. The bureaucracy is not a monolith, but contains competing interests and rival factions. Many in authority are happy to see mild criticism of the leader, and give journalists the leeway to target their enemies in the state apparatus.

Like Andrzej Wajda in post-Stalinist Poland, or the writers and directors of the Iranian new wave, the country's film-makers produce haunting tales of fear and disillusionment, which are far better than the offerings of Hollywood. Their films are not explicitly political, but the audience finds the political message just below the surface. Theatres produce surrealist and absurdist dramas to avoid the laws banning direct criticism of the regime. Their favourite play, however, is a traditional story. They keep staging an apparently innocuous folk tale about an official who stands up to a tyrannical king. Everyone knows why it interests them so.

The small opposition press uses similar tactics. It does not tackle the fraud of the kleptomaniac state head-on, for a direct assault would be too dangerous. It focuses on small cases of corruption instead, and uses them to hint at the sickness of the wider society.

To the president's fury, his power and pomp mean nothing to visiting foreign journalists and human-rights groups. In their eyes, it is the marginal artists, writers and trade unionists who speak for his country, rather than his ministers in their air-conditioned offices and bulletproof cars.

He summons the chief of the secret police.

'How can I silence these shits?'

'Go postal!'

'What?'

'It's a phrase from neo-con America, Excellency. A man with a gun, often a postal worker for reasons no one understands, walks into an office or school where he thinks he was once humiliated and kills people at random.'

'You mean I should kill the leaders of the opposition?'

'I will happily do so, Excellency, if you command it. But that's not the idea. You need to pick on slights and humiliations that are so small they seem not to be humiliations at all, and punish them with unreasonable ferocity. Random violence creates the necessary conditions for order. A leader of the opposition expects us to arrest him from time to time, but a writer making a veiled criticism of your rule, or a man who grumbles about you in a shop queue, does not. By randomly attacking a few people who speak sedition, we tell many people that the only safe option is to avoid all talk about politics. The aim is to create a state where everyone knows it is best to say nothing, and the bastards shut up.'

A story from Mao's China illustrates the hopelessness engendered by a truly random terror. Mao imitated Stalin by purging the Communist Party of anyone who might defy or threaten him. He prepared the ground by turning society upside down, so that it would be in no position to resist. Mao changed the balance of power between the old and the young by telling schoolchildren that they could torture and murder their teachers for filling their minds with 'bourgeois ideology'. However bestially they behaved, the police would not intervene. The students killed their first recorded victim on 5 August 1966, when pupils at a Peking girls' school seized their headmistress. The girls kicked and trampled the fifty-year-old mother of four, and poured boiling water over her. They ordered her to carry heavy bricks back and forth, and thrashed her with leather belts with brass buckles until she collapsed and died. If the teacher had seen her life flash by her in her dying moments, she would have realised that nothing she might have done could have spared her. She had obeyed the communists, spouted their dogmas, taught Mao's own daughters ... but Mao still killed her. There had never been a smart move to make, no moment when she might have chosen a safer course, and escaped her execution.

Most modern dictators are not like communist totalitarians. They do not kill loyalists as well as enemies. When they slip towards terror, they use disproportionate violence against minor critics instead. Just as the relatives of the victims of a mass murderer who goes berserk in a school because he felt its teachers humiliated him can find reasons for the deaths, so the victims of dictatorial violence can understand the reasons for their suffering. It is just that the 'offence' is out of all proportion to the retribution visited on the offenders.

Robert Mugabe was not the equivalent of Saddam Hussein or the organisers of the genocide in Darfur. After taking power in 1980, he presided over one act of mass terror, when he sent the 5th Brigade of the Zimbabwean Army to Matabeleland and the Zimbabwean Midlands to murder three thousand of his opponents. After that atrocity, he practised cruelty at a lower level. He wrecked the economy by seizing white-owned farms and handing them over to cronies, and failed to tackle the Aids epidemic.

But although parliament was neutered, the judiciary subverted and the country reduced to beggary, Mugabe allowed some opposition – at the time of writing there are opposition politicians in his government. Wilf Mbanga, the editor of the *Zimbabwean*, told me that outsiders would be surprised at how much journalists and artists can get away with – when the security services relax.

In 1999, Oliver 'Tuku' Mtukudzi's song 'Wasakara' was the hit of the year. The chorus ran:

> Admit, hey, admit
> Admit you have gotten old
> Admit you are worn out.

As Mtukudzi sang, helpful members of the concert crew beamed a spotlight onto a portrait of the wizened Mugabe. When the police questioned him, Mtukudzi told them that his lyrics came from observing his family and acquaintances, and criticism of the geriatric despot could not have been further from his mind.

Such small acts of resistance are typical of stable times in dictatorships. In Burma, an official in the national bank protested against the arrest by the military junta of Aung San Suu Kyi, whose National League for Democracy had been the legitimate winner of a free general election in 1990, by enhancing rather than debasing the national currency. His superiors had asked him to design a new one-kyat note. It had to include a picture of Aung San Suu Kyi's father General Aung San, who in 1945 had led Burma to independence. The designer used light strokes to soften the jawline as he gently transformed the face of the father into that of the daughter. Around the portrait he drew four circles of eight petals to mark the date of Burma's democratic uprising on 8 August 1988 – 8/8/88. For months the portrait of 'the lady', as Aung San Suu Kyi was known, was admired by the citizenry, until the generals realised their mistake, withdrew the 'democracy note' from circulation, and made possessing it a criminal offence.

Like the Burmese generals, Mugabe did not tolerate veiled criticism for long. He retained power because he mixed periods of relative quiet with outbreaks of capricious repression. The courts sent an unemployed man to prison for asking two boys with Mugabe's face emblazoned on their T-shirts, 'Why would you want to wear a wrinkly old man on your clothes?' The police arrested a human-rights campaigner who exposed the brutal conditions in an army-controlled diamond mine. 'That kind of behaviour, if proved, is treacherous and abominable, particularly in these times of national economic strife,' the judge said as he denied him bail. Such inflated rhetoric is characteristic of dictatorships on the rampage. To justify censorship their lackeys magnify the offence, as the judge did when he turned a criticism of the working conditions of miners into an act of economic treason.

Neither the campaigner for workers' rights nor the man talking to the boys in the Mugabe T-shirts was a direct threat to the regime. But as Wilf Mbanga said, 'Every now and again he wants to send a message to all and sundry. He wants to keep journalists and activists on their toes, so we don't know what we can get away with from one day to the next.'

The prudent Mr Mbanga edits the *Zimbabwean* from a seaside town in southern England.

# A Cartoon Crisis

Modern religious violence, even in its most barbaric forms, is not comparable to the absolute terror of communist totalitarianism. In Afghanistan, Pakistan and Iraq, men can stay alive if they do not cross the Taliban or al Qaeda (women, obviously, face additional dangers). Like the Nazis, Islamists do not slaughter their own supporters. In the democracies, the fear spread by religious violence is closer to the fear of excessive punishments for inconsequential slights that modern dictatorships generate.

To put the same thought another way, we are living through a Mugabification of religious argument.

Even conscious acts of anti-clericalism, an essential part of any campaign to cut down over-mighty religions, bring a response as disproportionate as the assault on Sherry Jones's unconscious 'insult'.

The Danish cartoon crisis of 2005 – and it tells you everything about the overwrought state of democratic opinion that policy-makers and pundits could talk about a 'cartoon crisis' with a straight face – was almost as phoney as any manufactured act of outrage. The religious censorship it engendered met the criteria of dictators engaged in random retaliation:

- A modest critique produced an excessive reaction.
- Legitimate criticism of terrorist murder and the oppression of women was turned into something it was not, in this instance a prejudiced hatred of all Muslims.
- The threat of violent punishment hung in the air.
- Critics learned that the safe course was to say nothing, because they did not know where fanatics would draw their lines.

Intellectuals discuss freedom of speech in the abstract. But it always arises as a political issue in response to changes in society. The Danish press did not commission cartoons of Muhammad for a laugh, but because they could see new forces at work in their country. A group of Muslim fundamentalists had attacked a lecturer at Copenhagen University because he had quoted from the Koran to non-Muslims. Sunni traditionalists had threatened Sufi Muslims for staging a concert, because they claimed that music was unIslamic. The most disturbing story came in press reports about how a writer called Kåre Bluitgen could not find an artist prepared to illustrate a guide to

Muhammad and the Koran for schoolchildren. The artists he approached muttered about the murder of Theo van Gogh, and the assaults on the lecturer at Copenhagen University. They maintained that Islam proscribed representations of Muhammad, although that was not true, as the portraits of Muhammad from the golden age of medieval Islam demonstrate. More probably, the wavering Danish illustrators reasoned that certain sects in modern Islam denounce images of Muhammad as idolatry, and that those sects were, as it happens, the sects most likely to kill them.

Flemming Rose, the editor of *Jyllands-Posten*, a Danish daily with a circulation of about 150,000, invited cartoonists to treat Islam as they treated other religions, and show that demands for censorship were incompatible with contemporary democracy and freedom of speech. 'One must be ready to put up with insults, mockery and ridicule,' Rose said in an article accompanying the cartoons. Reject that idea and 'we are on our way to a slippery slope where no one can tell how the self-censorship will end'. Despite his defiant words, his blasphemy fell short of being a full-frontal satirical assault on religious conviction. The twelve cartoons that were to provoke such fury were a tame collection.

Among them was an image of Muhammad with a bomb in his turban. The drawing suggested that extremists had used Islam as an excuse for terrorism, a view that was hard to argue with. It caused the most offence, because it could also be interpreted as suggesting that all Muslims supported terrorism, an argument which was not true, although the protesters against the newspaper undermined their case when they resorted to violence. The tender-minded found three other drawings offensive. An ambiguous portrait of Muhammad may or may not have been insulting. The artist drew him with a glowing object above his head. Readers could interpret it as a halo, a pair of devil's horns or Viking's horns, or the Islamic crescent. You had to work hard to find the 'devil' insult, although, as always, that did not stop those determined to be offended from putting in the effort. Next was a cartoon which showed a Muhammad in heaven, greeting suicide bombers with the words, 'Stop, stop, we've run out of virgins!' Of all the cartoons, it came closest to making a joke that was actually funny. Complainants also decried a picture of an aggressive Muhammad, in which the artist had blocked out his eyes with a black line to prevent his identification. The line paralleled the eyeholes in the hijabs of two women with frightened expressions behind him, the rest of whose bodies were draped in black robes.

Several cartoonists mocked Flemming Rose, Kåre Bluitgen and themselves rather than Muhammad. In one drawing, a cartoonist sweats with fear as he draws a straight portrait of Muhammad. A self-fulfilling prophecy, since the artists duly received death threats. In another, a figure (presumably Muhammad) attempts to calm down two furious armed followers with the words, 'Relax, it's just a drawing by a cartoonist from the south-west of Denmark.' One artist showed Bluitgen wearing a turban and holding up a stickman portrait of Muhammad. An orange bearing the slogan 'PR Stunt' is perched on the turban's top. The orange baffled foreigners, but local readers got the point that Bluitgen was seeking to up his profile and make money out of the controversy, because in Danish the phrase 'to have an orange drop into your turban' means to receive undeserved good fortune. Another artist had an everyman character saying that he is unable to pick out Muhammad from an identity parade of religious figures. Among them is Kåre Bluitgen, who is holding up a sign which says 'Kåre's public relations, call and get an offer'.

Nor did the cartoonists miss the argument that in Saudi Arabia, Pakistan and Iran, Islam was the religion of clerics with real power to ruin the lives of others, but in Denmark it was the religion of immigrants on the margin of society. In one drawing, by Lars Refn, a schoolboy captioned as 'Mohammed' from 'Valby

School class 7A' – which identified him as coming from a poor immigrant area of Copenhagen – taunts the editors at *Jyllands-Posten*. The boy has written a slogan in Farsi on a blackboard, which reads '*Jyllands-Posten* journalists are a bunch of reactionary provocateurs'. Little good did Refn's decision to attack the newspaper and defend immigrants do him: he was the first of the cartoonists to receive death threats. Apparently there are people who will kill you for drawing pictures of boys called 'Mohammed'. The remaining cartoons were unremarkable. One was an abstract drawing of a group of women whose heads are formed from traditional Arabic symbols of a star and a crescent, along with a poem criticising the Prophet for 'keeping women under yoke'. Then there was a picture of Muhammad with a star and crescent forming one eye and the outline of his face. And finally, a reverent picture of the Prophet leading a donkey through the desert, entirely suitable for use in a children's book.

If writers and artists were required under pain of death to be careful about how they mocked the papacy's ban on contraception, they would not be able to make an effective critique of how religious dogma facilitates the spread of the Aids epidemic. Satire generalises. It speaks with a clear voice or no voice at all. Satirists cannot argue with caveats, particularly when the caveat the religious insist on is that satirists remove religion from criticisms of religious violence and religious oppression.

I will not pretend that the publication of the cartoons was met with equanimity. Jamaat-e-Islami, inevitably, urged the Pakistani government to issue a reward for anyone who killed the cartoonists, and many Danish Muslims were offended. About 3,500 people attended a protest in Copenhagen, and the police moved two cartoonists to safe houses. Imams and ambassadors from Muslim countries demanded meetings with the Danish prime minister, Anders Fogh Rasmussen. He replied that a meeting was pointless, because 'free speech goes far and the Danish government has no influence over what the press writes'.

Quite properly for a democratic leader, he said that what the press printed was not the business of his government, or of foreign dictatorships for that matter. The police found no grounds for prosecution because, as the prime minister had said, Denmark was a free country.

For all the initial demonstrations, the fact remained that Rose published the cartoons on 30 September 2005, but the violence did not begin in earnest until January 2006. In the interval, newspapers in many countries, including the Egyptian weekly *El Fagr*, printed the cartoons, without raising significant protests.

Much of the credit for turning a mild satire into a crisis must go to three reactionary imams, to whom Denmark had offered asylum. French television gave viewers a glimpse of their ideology when it caught one of them, Ahmed Akkari, on camera implicitly threatening a liberal Muslim leader, Naser Khader, a member of the Danish parliament. According to the footage, Akkari said: 'If Khader becomes minister of integration, shouldn't someone dispatch two guys to blow up him and his ministry?' He later said he was 'jesting'. For a man who wanted to ban cartoons, he had a broad sense of humour. The imams had a political as well as a religious interest in whipping up a crisis that might place them at the head of Danish Islam. A survey in March 2006 found that Khader was Danish Muslims' most popular spokesman, followed by a left-wing Pakistani doctor who shared Khader's beliefs in secularism and sexual equality. Akkari and his friends trailed well behind their liberal rivals.

In December 2005 – two months after the paper published the cartoons – the three imams went to an Arab League meeting in Hosni Mubarak's Egypt. The league issued a statement condemning freedom of speech being used as a pretext to defame religion. A separate delegation briefed Bashar Assad's Ba'athist dictatorship in Syria. The imams carried with them a forty-three-page dossier which contained all twelve of the *Jyllands-Posten* cartoons. Helpfully, someone had added three other images, supposedly of Muhammad – one of a man wearing a plastic pig mask, one of a praying man being sodomised by a dog, and one of a devilish Muhammad – all of which were considerably more offensive than anything the paper had published. The imams claimed that they had been included for context, to 'give an insight into how hateful the atmosphere in Denmark is towards Muslims'. But where did these pictures originate? In two cases, no one knows if they were anything more than the sort of scrawl which is regularly found on toilet walls. Bloggers quickly identified the 'pig' picture as an Associated Press photograph taken in August 2005 at an agricultural fair in Trie-sur-Baïse, in the French Pyrenees, which had nothing to do with Muhammad. Instead of showing the Prophet, it showed Jacques Barrot, a French farmer, who was competing in the village's annual 'pig-squealing competition', complete with plastic snout and pig's ears. Along with other locals, he was dressing up and demonstrating his pig-imitating skills as part of an annual promotion of the region's excellent pork dishes. Barrot didn't even win.

After the briefing by the imams came a direct call at the beginning of February 2006 from Yusuf al-Qaradawi, the spiritual leader of the Muslim Brotherhood, for 'an international day of anger for God and his prophet'. Danes and anyone associated with them became a target.

As the crisis grew, *Jyllands-Posten* received more than a hundred credible threats. Syria, Kuwait, Saudi Arabia and Libya withdrew their ambassadors from Denmark. In Gaza, gunmen stormed the EU offices demanding that Europe apologise. In Libya, the police shot fifteen people dead who were protesting against reports that an Italian minister had worn a T-shirt with the cartoons on it. In all 139 people were to die, as police fired into crowds in Nigeria and Afghanistan as well as Libya. The owners of *France Soir* fired the paper's editor for running the cartoons as a gesture of solidarity with his Danish colleagues, and then rehired him. In Damascus, demonstrators attacked the

Danish embassy and the Norwegian embassy. Iranian militants attacked the Danish embassy in Tehran and firebombed it. Demonstrators in Lahore attacked branches of the American-owned Pizza Hut, Kentucky Fried Chicken and Holiday Inn chains, while Muslim customers boycotted Lego, Bang & Olufsen and Arla Foods, which at least had the merit of being Danish-owned. Osama bin Laden blamed Jews and Crusaders for the cartoons, and said no apology could stop the rage.

As late as January 2010, a Somali armed with an axe and a knife broke into the home of Kurt Westergaard, who had drawn the picture of Muhammad with a bomb in his turban. Westergaard dived into a panic room and pressed the alarm, as the Somali tried to batter the door down. The police shot the intruder in the leg, but a spokesman for the Somali al-Shabaab terror group implied that there would be plenty more where he came from: 'We appreciate the incident in which a Muslim Somali boy attacked the devil who abused our prophet Muhammad and we call upon all Muslims around the world to target the people like him.'

As striking as the violence was the reaction of liberals. Across the world, demonstrators were attacking the embassies and nationals of a small social democratic country in northern Europe and boycotting its goods because of twelve cartoons. Its prime minister had held true to the values of anti-fascism and anti-communism and refused to abandon freedom of speech within the law, despite the pressure on him to go along with repression. The assault on Denmark was political, and not only because radical imams were seeking to supplant their liberal rivals and make themselves the 'authentic' voice of Danish Islam. The countries that demanded that Denmark apologise had political agendas of their own. George W. Bush's plan to extend democracy to the Middle East appalled the Egyptian dictatorship. By manufacturing a scandal about Danish cartoons, Mubarak hoped he could show the naïve Americans that 'Western' freedoms were not for Egyptians, and it was better to leave them under the control of the elite, a fiction he succeeded in maintaining until his subject people contradicted him in Tahrir Square in 2011. The Iranian and Syrian dictatorships used the crisis to bolster their regimes by whipping up hatred against the Western enemy, the better to distract attention from their grim rule.

From the behaviour of the majority of Western liberals, you would never have guessed that dictatorial regimes and ideologies were attacking fundamental principles for self-interested reasons. In 1989, a large section of liberal opinion rallied to Salman Rushdie, regardless of whether it thought *The Satanic Verses* was a good book or not. By 2006, many liberals had abandoned the basic tenet of a free society that the intention of a speaker or writer is irrelevant to his or her right to enjoy freedom of speech and publication. If Flemming Rose had commissioned cartoons mocking America and the Bush administration had protested, liberals would have clasped him to their pounding chests, because his intention would have been *good*. But because he had allowed cartoonists to criticise Islam, albeit mildly, his intention was *bad*, and therefore the enemies of liberalism could take their revenge on him, his cartoonists and his country.

Bill Clinton and European rabbis said the drawings reminded them of the anti-Semitic cartoons of fascist Europe – an odd comparison, because the leaders of Syria, Iran and the Muslim Brotherhood were anti-Semites. Jack Straw, the then British Home Secretary, praised the British press for not running the cartoons, while the Council of Europe criticised the Danish government for invoking the apparently irrelevant concept of 'freedom of the press' when it refused to take action against the 'insulting' cartoons.

The reaction of the Yale University Press encapsulated Western deference. Without waiting to receive a threat, it censored pre-emptively, and refused to carry pictures of the cartoons in a supposedly serious academic book about the

controversy. The book's author treated arguments about freedom of speech and women's rights as if they were ancient
notions that need not detain the modern reader, and could not
have been 'fairer' to their opponents. Nevertheless, Yale said it
would have had 'blood on its hands' if it had shown readers the
cartoons its author was analysing. Murders would not be the
responsibility of the murderers, but of the publishers, because
'republication of the cartoons by the Yale University Press ran a
serious risk of instigating violence'.

Until the twentieth century, Western writers were frightened
of criticising Christianity. Britain took until 2008 to abolish its
blasphemy law, although it had fallen into disuse long before
then. America's constitutional protection of free speech and
press freedom meant that blasphemy had never been an offence
in the United States, but social pressures and the potential of
Christian groups to stage protests and boycotts made it a de
facto crime. That power to censor has gone. Trey Parker and
Matt Stone, the creators of *South Park*, acknowledged its passing
at the time of the cartoon crisis: 'It really is open season on Jesus.
We can do whatever we want to Jesus, and we have. We've had
him say bad words. We've had him shoot a gun. We've had him
kill people. We can do whatever we want.'

Islam was another matter. *South Park*'s network Comedy
Central would not allow the show to run a simple image of
Muhammad during the affair, but at least it was honest about its
reasons. Other US networks that banned images of Muhammad
said they were censoring because they were liberals who wanted
to display their respect and tolerance. 'No you're not,' Stone said.
'You're afraid of getting blown up. That's what you're afraid of.
Comedy Central copped to that, you know: "We're afraid of
getting blown up."'

In autumn 2011, the French satirical magazine *Charlie Hebdo*
responded to the depressing success of an Islamist party in
Tunisia's first election after the Arab Spring. As its target was a

religious group, it satirised religious beliefs – what was it meant to do? The cover featured a cartoon of Muhammad with a bubble coming from his mouth saying, 'One hundred lashes if you don't die laughing.' An arsonist bombed *Charlie Hebdo*'s office. French politicians defended freedom of speech, but the guardians of liberal orthodoxy could not match their fortitude. *Time* deprecated the 'notoriously impertinent paper' and others who 'openly beg for the very violent responses from extremists their authors claim to proudly defy'. By then the notion that religious criminals did not have moral responsibility for their crimes was everywhere. Muslims were an undifferentiated block, naturally prone to violence, rather than a vast denominational group with reactionary and liberal strands.

As the old Christian punishments withered, Islamists pushed the West into accepting a new blasphemy law. It was not a law debated by congresses or parliaments. No legitimate authority spelt out its limits in a statute book. No judge protected defendants' rights to a fair trial. No jury said that it must find the accused guilty beyond reasonable doubt before conviction. The accused could break the law without knowing it, and be condemned without appeal. It was sufficient that someone, somewhere, deemed that the defendant had failed to show proper respect, and had the means to threaten retribution.

When I spoke to Flemming Rose he made a direct link between the modern acceptance that an 'insult' to a religion justified punishment, and the ideologies of the twentieth-century dictatorships. Rose had worked as a foreign correspondent in the old Soviet Union, and had learned to despise 'the trick of labelling any critique as an anti-Soviet insult to the state. You can catch anyone that way: Andrei Sakharov, Vladimir Bukovsky, Alexander Solzhenitsyn, Natan Sharansky, Boris Pasternak … the regime accused them all of anti-Soviet propaganda, and many in the West went along with that.'

His comparison was not as far-fetched as it seemed.

FOUR

# The Racism of the Anti-Racists

*It is time to extend our solidarity to all the rebels of the Islamic world, non-believers, atheist libertines, dissenters, sentinels of liberty, as we supported Eastern European dissidents in former times. Europe should encourage these diverse voices and give them financial, moral and political support. Today there is no cause more sacred, more serious, or more pressing for the harmony of future generations. Yet our continent kneels before God's madmen, muzzling and libelling free-thinkers with suicidal heedlessness.*

PASCAL BRUCKNER, 2007

Affectation had no place in Ayaan Hirsi Ali's writing. She did not play the coy dissident and smuggle coded messages past the censors, or imitate the magical realists by wrapping a critique inside a spinning narrative. She wrote plainly, in a precise voice of restrained outrage, and behaved as if she were a free woman with no reason to fear those who would silence her permanently – although she had reasons aplenty.

You needed to spend just five minutes in her company, or read a few pages of her work, to realise that indignation about the oppression of women drove her forward. The baby-boomer cliché that 'The personal is political' ignored the reality that in most of the world, and for most of history, the personal could not be political for women, because the power of religious and cultural authority prevented a political response to personal oppression. For a moment when Hirsi Ali was young, that power seemed to be breaking. Her father was a Somali socialist involved in revolutionary politics. But revolution in Somalia, like revolutions everywhere, turned to dictatorship. The local strongman threw her father in jail. The family fled into exile, and found a haven in Kenya, where Hirsi Ali learned that, revolution or no revolution, her sex determined her fate. When she and her sisters went to pray in a mosque, her father explained to the confused girl that she must stand behind him and the rest of the men. At school, she saw her friends dreaming of marrying a husband they loved, but then being forced to marry old men by their parents. Her grandmother arranged for what euphemists call 'female circumcision' – that is, for an amateur surgeon to cut away a girl's clitoris and her outer and inner labia, and scrape the vaginal walls. Hirsi Ali learned the hard way that she 'was a Somali woman and therefore my sexuality belonged to the owner of my family: my father or my uncles. It was obvious that I absolutely had to be a virgin on marriage, because to do otherwise would damage the honour of my family and whole clan – uncles, brothers, male cousins – forever and irretrievably. The place between my legs was sewn up to prevent it. It would be broken only by my husband.'

The retreat of poor-world radicals from the dying creed of socialism and into religious and tribal fanaticisms was well underway in Kenya by the time Hirsi Ali was a teenager. In Europe and America as well as Africa and the Middle East, the Muslim Brotherhood was the vehicle for religious reaction. Although conceived in Egypt as a totalitarian movement, which would impose a theocratic caliphate on the whole of humanity, the Brothers were not always agents of dictatorial revolution. In the West, they sought to 'engage' with liberal establishments to ensure that their sectarian version of Islam received state funds, and that they were allowed to define who was and was not an authentic Muslim among immigrant populations. Elsewhere, they could be plotting to seize control of Arab states or lying low. The Brotherhood followed the tactics of twentieth-century Marxists-Leninists. It could adopt an entryist strategy of infiltrating existing power structures or try insurrection depending on circumstances.

The Brotherhood's willingness to play along with Western governments should not disguise its extremism. It was the world's largest anti-Semitic organisation. Yusuf al-Qaradawi, the Egyptian scholar the Brotherhood most admired, declared that throughout history, God had imposed upon the Jews avengers who would punish them for their corruption. 'The last punishment was carried out by Hitler. By means of all the things he did to them – even though they exaggerated this issue – he managed to put them in their place. This was divine punishment for them. Allah willing, the next time will be at the hand of the believers.' His combination of partial Holocaust denial – 'even though they exaggerated it' – with genocidal fantasy – divine punishment awaits the Jews – marked him as a religious counterpart of Europe's neo-Nazis, whose fantasies allowed them to pretend that Auschwitz wasn't a death camp while dreaming of the death of the Jews.

The young Hirsi Ali was briefly attracted to the Brotherhood, but it was no place for an independent-minded woman. Qaradawi permitted husbands to beat disobedient wives, and allowed genital mutilation – 'Whoever finds it serving the interest of his daughters should do it, and I personally support this under the current circumstances in the modern world' – while the Brotherhood recommended a lifetime of submission. She got enough of that at home, and drifted away.

More useful to her was an altogether less holy tradition. At her Kenyan school, she read the novels of Charlotte Brontë, Jane Austen and Daphne du Maurier. Outside class, she and her friends swapped trashy paperback romances. Not a particularly radical education, you might think. But romance contains an idea more subversive than half the political philosophies devised by men. Hirsi Ali's heroines fell in love and defied their families to marry the husbands of their choice. In East Africa, and in much of the world, this was then, and remains now, a thrillingly revolutionary idea.

Her father arranged for her to marry a distant cousin from Canada she had never met. En route to Canada, she turned romance into rebellion. The plane touched down in Germany. Instead of flying on to Canada, she took a train from Dusseldorf to Holland and claimed asylum. Realising that in refugee law the personal was not political, and that no country would grant her asylum so that she could escape an arranged marriage, she claimed to be a victim of political persecution in Somalia. Once she had secured asylum, her intelligence and determination ensured that she could build a new life. She helped fellow refugees find work, went to university, became a Dutch and therefore a European citizen, and began to publish her thoughts on her new homeland.

I can think of no better antidote to Western ennui than the writings of poor-world liberals. Hirsi Ali came to Europe, and was liberated and inspired. The notion that the world could be explained without reference to the 'fairy tales' of monotheism enchanted her. Secularism, stability, peace, prosperity and rights for women were wonders. 'The very shape of Holland seemed like a challenge to Allah,' she said at one point. 'Reclaiming land from the sea, controlling flooding with canals – it was like defying God.' At university in Holland, she embraced the liberal tradition of free speech and religious tolerance, and studied, Locke, Mill, Russell, Popper and Baruch Spinoza, whom Amsterdam Jews excommunicated for his free-thinking in the 1650s, and whose works Catholic and Protestant divines banned for their blasphemy. Given her sufferings and her intellectual self-confidence, it was always likely that she would abandon her religion.

9/11 shook her faith, and she found a ready supply of Western moralists willing to denounce her as a 'new atheist'. Their label was self-evidently foolish – the 'new atheists' of the twenty-first century were not so different from the old atheists of the twentieth (they still did not believe in God, to mention the most prominent continuity). The newness of the 'new atheists' lay solely in their determination after 9/11 to state their beliefs without embarrassment. The dangers of religious extremism were clear, even to those who had not wanted to see. The new atheists thought that the best argument against Islamist terror, or Christian fundamentalism, or Hindu or Jewish nationalism, was to say bluntly that there is no God, and we should grow up. Fear of religious violence also drove the backlash against atheism from those who felt that appeasement of psychopathic believers was the safest policy; that if we were nice to them, perhaps they would calm down. Prim mainstream commentators decried the insensitivity and downright rudeness with which the new atheists treated the religious. The complaints boiled down to a simple and piteous cry: 'Why can't you stop upsetting them?'

You cannot, if like Ayaan Hirsi Ali you are confronting clerical oppression. In 1792, Mary Wollstonecraft's *Vindication of the Rights of Woman* stood alongside the pamphlets of the French revolutionaries as a founding feminist text. Wollstonecraft was alert to the danger that religion could suffocate her belief that 'It is vain to expect virtue from women till they are in some degree independent of men.' Although a radical dissenter from the English non-conformist tradition rather than an atheist, she took on the myths Judaism and Christianity had thrust on humanity: that God made Eve from Adam's rib to be his help-mate, and that Eve damned women by taking the apple from the tree of knowledge.

Suppose, Wollstonecraft wondered in the liberated intellectual climate after the French Revolution, that the conservative clerics of the 1790s were right, and God had formed women from Adam's rib to please men. The conclusion that 'she ought to sacrifice every other consideration to render herself agreeable to him: and let this brutal desire of self-preservation be the grand spring of all her actions' would be just, and women must submit to being stretched on the 'iron bed of fate'. But Wollstonecraft thought that dependence made an 'ignoble base' for human society – unworthy of a supreme being. So she begged leave to doubt whether God had created woman to please man. 'Though the cry of irreligion, or even atheism, be raised against me, I will simply declare, that were an angel from heaven to tell me that Moses's beautiful, poetical cosmogony, and the account of the fall of man, were literally true, I could not believe what my reason told me was derogatory to the character of the Supreme Being.'

In the later 1790s, as the reaction against the French Revolution swept Britain, anti-Jacobin writers denounced women's emancipation as the doctrine of 'hyenas in petticoats'. They seized on the miseries of Wollstonecraft's private life, and held them up as a terrible example to other women of the dangers of rebelling against God and nature. After her death in childbirth, her husband, the silly radical philosopher William Godwin, supplied her critics with the ammunition they needed. He stripped 'his dead wife naked' in the words of Robert Southey, by publishing frank accounts of her love affairs, illegitimate child and suicide attempt. Conservatives could not have been more grateful. Challenge traditional society and you will end up like her, they said – deprived of feminine charm, cursed with bastard children, betrayed, dejected and suicidal. But Wollstonecraft won a posthumous victory. Not even Tories and bishops can bring themselves to read the anti-Jacobin attacks on her now, while her work survives to enthuse succeeding generations. The triumph of her ideas did not happen by some benign process of osmosis. The opponents of the subjugation of women had to fight for their ideas, and endure abuse and hatred.

Ayaan Hirsi Ali reacted to life in Holland with a feminist revulsion Wollstonecraft would have recognised. Freedom was everywhere except in the lives of refugee women, who were still tied to the 'iron beds' fate had prescribed for them. As an interpreter, she visited Somali wives whose husbands beat them. Alongside the bruises and broken bones, she found Vitamin D deficiency. Dutch social workers thought it was the result of a poor diet caused by poverty. Hirsi Ali had to explain that the women were sick because their husbands would not let them leave their homes and walk in sunlit streets. The women did not complain, because they believed that in 'accepting systematic merciless abuse, they were serving Allah and earning a place in heaven'.

Hirsi Ali protested against the white society which tolerated such abuses as much as she did against the abuse itself. She came to believe that guilt crippled Europe: guilt about imperialism, guilt about Nazism, guilt about the Holocaust; guilt about the past but never about the present. Like many others, Hirsi Ali noticed that in the name of anti-racism European liberals were following a racist policy. When mass immigration began, they resolved to emphasise what divided rather than what united people, and to show their compassion by respecting the culture of 'the other'. Compassion sounds a fine virtue, which ordinarily leads the compassionate to help those less fortunate than themselves. In Europe, it produced indolence and indifference: a squishy liberal version of apartheid in which the authorities downplayed the genital mutilation of girls on kitchen tables and the murder of women who refused to accept arranged marriages because the women on the receiving end of the abuse were not white.

The appeal of respectable reasons for doing nothing should not be underestimated. Nor should the readiness of Ayaan Hirsi Ali to confront the double standard.

The first thing that strikes you when you meet her is her extraordinary calm. She is chatty and funny, but when the conversation turns to politics, stillness envelops her, as if her life had brought her to one unshakeable conclusion: the oppression of women by whatever authority must be fought. Blasphemous though her simple idea may be to some, she reasoned that Holland was a land where sex and drugs were openly on sale, and where comedians could fire at Christianity at will. Surely there would be no repercussions if she asserted the obvious? She campaigned against male violence, and renounced Islam on national television. By 2000, she was active in politics, an achievement worth mentioning for a black immigrant who arrived in Holland unable to speak Dutch in 1992. She marched under the banner of the Labour Party, before the left's hypocrisies pushed her into joining the centre-right liberals. I would be being unfair if I suggested that the whole of the Dutch left was too frightened to support her. Hirsi Ali's memoirs record the camaraderie of individual social democratic politicians. She joined the centre-right because as a collective the European left remained stuck in the identity politics of the 1968 generation. They were interested in group rights – the rights of blocs of immigrants not to be penalised for their colour or creed – rather than rights of individuals not to be persecuted by their own 'community'.

If the historians of the future have one ounce of morality, they will damn the European left for its inability to oppose racism and support individual liberty simultaneously. Hirsi Ali was not prepared to wait for posterity's judgement, and forced the Dutch police to recognise the extent of 'honour' killings of women in her country. After she renounced her religion and criticised the abuse of women, she learned that the descendants of the clerics who had banned Spinoza's books remained at large in Amsterdam. The police sent bodyguards to protect her. Her fellow MPs wondered if they needed to 'protect her from herself', a true example of white condescension towards 'the other' which she rejected with disdain.

She linked up with Theo van Gogh, a distant relative of the painter. Friends and critics alike described him as a provocateur: a typical loud-mouthed showman, who was always trying to get himself noticed by épatering the bourgeoisie. *Submission*, the ten-minute film he directed in 2004 from Hirsi Ali's script, belied much that critics said about him, and much of what he said about himself. It is a formal, sombre work, in which the camera flits over the faces and bodies of young women. The first woman describes how she fell in love, and was whipped in accordance with the Koranic injunction that 'The woman and the man guilty of adultery or fornication, flog each of them with a hundred stripes; let no compassion move you in their case, in a matter prescribed by God, if ye believe in God and the Last Day; and let a party of the believers witness their punishment.' A second describes how her family compels her to marry a man who repels her. She pretends to be 'unclean', but when she can pretend no longer he forces himself on her. She submits because the Koran tells men, 'When they have purified themselves, ye may approach them in any manner, time or place ordained for you by God.' A third is raped by her uncle. 'When I told my mother, she said she would take it up with my father. My father ordered her – and me – not to question his brother's honour.' Now she is pregnant, and knows her father will kill her for losing her virginity. She wants to kill herself, but cannot. The film ends with her saying, 'I know that in the hereafter the one who commits suicide shall never count on Your mercy. Allah, giver and taker of life. You admonish all who believe to turn towards You in order to attain bliss. I have done nothing my whole life but turn to You. And now that I pray for salvation, under my veil, You remain silent as the grave I long for. I wonder how much longer I am able to submit!'

If van Gogh had produced a film on the religious oppression of puritan women in seventeenth-century Holland, or Orthodox Jewish women in nineteenth-century Poland, the jury at Cannes might have applauded. But he and Hirsi Ali wanted to challenge contemporary injustice, not to excavate the past.

He laughed when the first death threats arrived. 'No one kills the village idiot,' he told Hirsi Ali.

On the morning of 2 November 2004, Mohammed Bouyeri, a second-generation Moroccan immigrant who had joined the local jihadist sect the Hofstad Network, approached van Gogh on an Amsterdam street with a handgun. Van Gogh's last words were, 'Can't we talk about this?'

There was to be no conversation.

Bouyeri shot van Gogh eight times in the chest, slit his throat and stuck a letter to Hirsi Ali onto his warm corpse with a butcher's knife.

In the millions of words that have been written about Hirsi Ali, few commentators discuss what Bouyeri, or the ideologue who drafted the letter for him, said. The contents were too embarrassing, for they placed Europeans under an anti-fascist obligation to stir themselves. Hirsi Ali was going to be next, Bouyeri said. Because she had argued for women's rights, she, like Salman Rushdie before her, had become the tool of 'Jewish masters': 'It is a fact, that Dutch politics is dominated by many Jews who are a product of the Talmud schools; that includes your political party-members.' Hirsi Ali was not Jewish – how could she be? – so the Hofstad group decided that because she had renounced religion she was 'an infidel fundamentalist' manipulated by the Elders of Zion. She did not 'believe that a Supreme Being controls the entire universe'. She did not 'believe that your heart, with which you cast away truth, has to ask permission from the Supreme Being for every beat'.

You can find the same reasoning among all varieties of religious rightists. The American evangelical Jerry Falwell said the 9/11 attacks on New York and Washington were God's punishment on 'the pagans, and the abortionists, and the feminists, and the gays and the lesbians who are actively trying to make that an alternative lifestyle, the ACLU, People for the American Way, all of them who have tried to secularize America'. Like Bouyeri, Falwell saw a vengeful God enforcing his punishments on decadent secularists.

In Amsterdam, the city of Spinoza and Anne Frank, anti-Semites had murdered a director for making a feminist film, and forced a black liberal into hiding. Hirsi Ali had good reasons to criticise European liberals, but she might have expected that they would have stood with her as she faced down murderous enemies. She was to learn a hard lesson. The response to van Gogh's murder could not have been more different from the response to the attempts to assassinate Salman Rushdie. Instead of defending the victims of armed reaction, liberal opinion turned on them.

## The New Anti-Jacobins

Liberal immigrants to Europe are caught on a fork. Native conservatives in their new country are against them because they are immigrants. Religious conservatives in their 'community' are against them because they are liberals. They ought to be able to turn to white liberals for support, but liberalism in Europe has turned septic. In the name of tolerance it is happy to abandon its friends and excuse its enemies.

The Dutch media went to work on Ayaan Hirsi Ali after van Gogh's murder. A television crew travelled to East Africa and revealed that she had not fled from the war in Somalia, as she had said on her asylum application, but from a comfortable home in Kenya. The story was true, but it was not a revelation:

she had told the leaders of her party long before that she was fleeing an arranged marriage. The journalists then alleged that she was not fleeing an arranged marriage. Of course I was, Hirsi Ali replied. My father had said that I must marry a distant cousin – and 'My father is not a man who takes no for an answer.'

Once, attacks on bogus asylum seekers and illegal immigrants were confined to the right-wing press. But those who attacked Ayaan Hirsi Ali used the language of the left. One Dutch commentator explained that the Dutch public did not support her because the 'neo-conservative wave that swept Holland in recent years is running out of steam and turning in on itself'. Let me remind you that Hirsi Ali and van Gogh had made a film that criticised rape, wife-beating and the flogging of 'immoral women'. The response of elements in the Dutch left was to assert that opposition to the oppression of women made a feminist a neo-conservative. Ordinary Dutch society behaved no better. Just as the neighbours of Penguin's Peter Mayer did not want him or his children near them, so Hirsi Ali's neighbours wanted to remove her from the safe flat where the Dutch police had hidden her. Appeal court judges accepted a suit from families living in the apartment block. In a ruling beyond satire, the court said that the decision of the Dutch police to put her in a place of safety was a breach of her new neighbours' human rights. Because Hirsi Ali defended the rights of immigrants, she was a threat to the human rights of the natives. Her presence endangered their security, the court said, and lowered the value of their properties – an unforgivable offence in the eyes of the European bourgeoisie. Of the fourteen apartment-owners in the complex, only three were prepared to offer her their solidarity.

Rita Verdonk, a leading figure in Hirsi Ali's Liberal Party, moved against her next. Verdonk was a populist, who gave the Dutch electorate a tough line on immigration. True to form, she said that because Hirsi Ali had lied in her asylum application, the state must strip her of her Dutch citizenship. Her attack on

Hirsi Ali split her party, and Verdonk had to back down. But it remained an eye-opening event. After the courts ejected an atheist feminist from her place of safety, Dutch politicians threatened to make her a stateless woman again. If they had succeeded, the Dutch authorities would have been under no obligation to protect her. They could call off her police escort and leave Hirsi Ali in a free-fire zone. Such was the price elements in the Dutch establishment wished Hirsi Ali to pay for upholding the ideals they professed to hold themselves.

Nor were the majority of the wider liberal intelligentsia prepared to offer support to a woman hitmen wanted to assassinate because she had protested against patriarchy. Their assaults on Hirsi Ali were ominous in the extreme, for they revealed the retreat from universal values.

Even before her neighbours demanded that the courts eject Hirsi Ali from her secure apartment, anyone could see that large numbers of European liberals did not want to defend their principles, if defending them put their lives and property at risk. The Dutch journalist's accusation that standing up for human rights made you a 'neo-con' was widely held by his contemporaries. They could not maintain a belief in universal human rights and criticise George W. Bush at the same time. The accusation became a self-fulfilling prophecy in Hirsi Ali's case. Rejected by Dutch leftists and the Dutch Liberal Party, she eventually found a home at the neo-conservative American Enterprise Institute in Washington, DC. She became what her enemies said she was because when her natural allies abandoned her, their opponents were the only people who would take her in.

Identity politics played their part too. The proposition that 'Europeans believe defending Muslim women from mutilation and abuse constitutes a racist attack on Muslims' is an oxymoron that is so morally and logically contemptible it demolishes itself. Few of Ayaan Hirsi Ali's enemies could admit to holding such a detestable notion, although many behaved as if they did.

Liberal intellectuals did not force their readers to be honest with themselves. Instead the Anglo-Dutch journalist Ian Buruma and the Oxford academic Timothy Garton Ash stepped forward to provide a 'liberal' critique of Hirsi Ali. The unthinking consensus in which they operated was best revealed by their failure to explain why they felt it necessary to add to her troubles. Nothing in their writing betrayed the smallest awareness that others would find it strange that men who called themselves liberals should turn on a woman clerical censors were persecuting because of her commitment to the equality of the sexes. When the fashion in Manhattan, London and Paris is to slide away from universal principles, those leading the slither can never admit that modern liberalism contains contradictions and dark motives that require an explanation. Self-awareness and self-criticism would puncture the assumption of moral superiority, which is liberal culture's greatest strength.

In Buruma's book *Murder in Amsterdam* and in a series of articles for the *New York Review of Books* and the *New York Times*, Buruma and Garton Ash acknowledged Hirsi Ali's bravery with a passing nod, and then men who had no fear in their own lives passed judgement on a marked woman who could not step outside without bodyguards.

Her call for the emancipation of women marked her as an extremist, they decided. Van Gogh's assassin had denounced her as an 'infidel fundamentalist'; Garton Ash and Buruma adapted the insult, and denounced her as an 'Enlightenment fundamentalist'. As if those who believed in the subjugation of women, the Jewish-conspiracy theory of history and the murder of homosexuals, adulterers and apostates were the moral equivalents of those who did not. As if there was nothing to choose between the two. As if the principled liberal response to the conflict between them was to dedicate time and energy to condemning Enlightenment 'fundamentalism' while ignoring the Enlightenment's enemies.

Buruma decided that Hirsi Ali was not a victim but a victim-iser, an elitist with contempt for ordinary women. The way she waved her hand at a guest arguing with her during a debate at a refuge for battered women unsettled him. It was a 'gentle gesture of disdain', he decided, an 'almost aristocratic dismissal of a noisome inferior'. Her attitude towards the Dutch was no better. The ingrate immigrant regarded the inhabitants of her new homeland as being in a pit of 'moral decadence'. She said she supported Enlightenment values, but Buruma maintained she had no right to compare herself to Voltaire. He was a brave man who fought the mighty Catholic Church of the eighteenth century. She was, he implied, a bully who was picking on weak Muslims, 'a minority that was already feeling vulnerable'. By renouncing Islam, he concluded, she had made herself a woman of no importance. She had cut herself off from European Muslims. Her voice had no legitimacy among the women she sought to address, so she was an irrelevance as well as an elitist and a bully. It apparently never occurred to him that Mary Wollstonecraft and her successors in the nineteenth century had to take on established Christianity. Although devout women at the time would not have liked their repudiation of Genesis, their lives and the lives of their daughters could not have been improved until divinely sanctioned oppression had been challenged.

Garton Ash and Buruma dwelt on Hirsi Ali's brief interest in the Muslim Brotherhood when she was young. She had walked away, as we saw, but they decided that the change in her politics was more superficial than real. She was a Muslim fundamental-ist then, and an 'Enlightenment fundamentalist' now. Politic Europeans should have nothing to do with her. Garton Ash concluded by turning Hirsi Ali's good looks against her. 'It is no disrespect to Ms Ali,' he said with the condescension Oxford dons habitually mistake for wit, 'to suggest that if she had been short, squat and squinting, her story and views might not have been so closely attended to.'

The West still had intellectuals prepared to defend the honour of liberalism, and Garton Ash and Buruma's attacks on Hirsi Ali, and the willingness of the liberal *New York Times* and *New York Review of Books* to run them, provoked rousing counterblasts in North America and Europe. The New York intellectual Paul Berman filled half of an issue of the *New Republic* with a dissection of how the affair exposed the 'reactionary turn' twenty-first-century liberal thought had taken. In a ringing conclusion, he declared:

A sustained attack in the intellectual world on a persecuted liberal dissident from Africa, a campaign in the press that has managed to push the question of women's rights systematically to the side, a campaign that has veered more than once into personal cruelty, a soft vendetta but a visible one, presided over by the normally cautious and sincerely liberal editors of one distinguished and admired journal after another, applauded and faithfully imitated by a variety of other writers and journalists, such that, in some circles, the sustained attack has come to be accepted as a conventional wisdom – no, this could not have happened in the past.

In Paris, Pascal Bruckner, heir to the best traditions of the French Enlightenment, said that as well as living in fear, Ayaan Hirsi Ali has had 'to endure the ridicule of the high-minded'. In the eyes of the 'genteel professors' she had 'committed an unpardonable offence: she has taken democratic principles seriously'. For that they called her a 'fundamentalist', and could not see that 'the difference between her and Muhammad Bouyeri is that she never advocated murder to further her ideas'.

For all the brilliance of the polemics in the pamphlet war over Hirsi Ali, no fair observer could doubt that Buruma and Garton Ash represented the dominant tendency in liberal opinion in the West. In Britain, the Archbishop of Canterbury and the Lord

Chief Justice supported the use of Sharia law in divorces and other family disputes – the Lord Chief Justice in a Jamaat-e-Islami-influenced mosque, appropriately. The women priests of the Church of England, so keen to have their equal right to be bishops asserted, and women lawyers at the Bar, who complained so vociferously about the law's glass ceiling, did not accuse the archbishop and the judge of sexism. They left the fight to a group of ex-Muslim women, who pointed out that Sharia law already existed informally in Britain, and 'women are often pressured by their families into going to these courts and adhering to unfair decisions. If they refuse to go they faced threats and intimidation, or at best being ostracised.' Too many liberals ignored the protest, and showed they were prepared to endorse one law for women with white skins and another for women with brown skins.

With equal insincerity, the nominally left-of-centre and perennially two-faced Labour Party instructed the Foreign Office to appease Islamist sentiment at home and abroad. It embraced the Muslim Brotherhood and Jamaat-e-Islami, and declared that they were 'reformist groups' with a 'moderate' and 'progressive' ideology. Britain's 'progressives', nitpickingly politically correct in all other matters, stayed silent as they did it.

Ayaan Hirsi Ali was not the only dissident they left behind.

## The Scaremongers and the Scared

In 2009, I was standing with a group of young men and women whose courage made me want to hug them. They called themselves British Muslims for Secular Democracy, and they had come together to defend freedom of speech and demand the separation of Church and state. We were demonstrating in central London against Islam4UK, a front organisation for radical Islamists, whose fellow travellers were more than willing to turn violent, as the publishers of The Jewel of Medina had learned. 'Laugh at those who Insult Islam', read one of my companions' placards. 'Liberal democracy will rule the world', read another. 'Secularism is coming to Britain,' their organisers said. 'We are all free to worship or not to worship according to our own conscience.'

Well, I thought, I've waited a long time to see this. Behind us on the steps of Eros at Piccadilly Circus was a separate protest organised by beery football fans, draped in Union flags. Its members explained that they were from a new organisation called the English Defence League. They had had enough of Islamists wrecking the solemn ceremonies to mark the return of the bodies of British troops from Iraq and Afghanistan. They would fight back, they told me, but not as racists. I had been waiting a while for that, too. Liberal-left politicians could not deplore prejudice and then welcome Islamists into Whitehall without expecting a backlash. The Archbishop of Canterbury and the Lord Chief Justice could not call for Sharia law, and think that no one would notice. There was bound to be a reaction, and it was good to see that it appeared to be of an earthy and democratic kind. Or as the wife of an EDL member said to me, 'I'm not walking three paces behind any fucking man.'

My illusions lasted less than an hour. I walked into a nearby bar with a young woman who was as British as anyone else in London that day. 'You're not welcome here,' EDL members spat at a Muslim so integrated that she would walk into a pub with a casual acquaintance. 'Fuck off back to Pakistan.' I learned then that the English Defence League was not against Islamists, but against all Muslims. As I expected, the League soon became home to those far-rightists who hated Muslims more than they hated Jews.

A few weeks later, I addressed a meeting of students, and praised the secular Muslims for defending liberal values. A leftist in the audience was having none of it. He denounced British Muslims for Secular Democracy as the English Defence League's allies and collaborators, citing as evidence the 'joint demonstration' at Piccadilly Circus. I told him there had been no joint demonstration, and I had seen with my own eyes the white racists abuse the secular Muslims. I was there, he was not; but it did not matter what I said. He and his comrades had already spread the required smear round the Net. To their minds, liberal Muslims were Uncle Toms. Authentic Muslims could only be bearded men with a Koran in one hand and a Kalashnikov in the other.

By that time, it was hard to know whether left or right was more culpable of inciting violence. With a neat symmetry, campaigners against white neo-fascism wrote to the right-wing *Daily Star* in 2010 to complain that the paper exaggerated 'the importance of tiny Muslim extremist groups', and risked creating 'a dangerous backlash among non-Muslims which in turn will feed groups such as the EDL and the British National Party'. Within weeks, liberal Muslims at the Quilliam Foundation complained to the leftish executives of Channel 4 that they took speakers from Islamist groups and supporters of the Iranian theocratic regime to 'represent mainstream Muslim opinion', and reinforced 'negative stereotypes of Islam to non-Muslims' by doing so. Right-wing newspapers pretended extremists were immigrants' authentic representatives because they wanted to whip up the fear of the other. The liberal media gave platforms to reactionary and paranoid men because they wanted to revel in the exoticism of the other. The motives were different, but the effect was the same.

In Holland, the Islamophobic Party for Freedom overtook the Christian Democrats to become the largest conservative force in the country. The French National Front enjoyed a resurgence of support, while the Sarkozy government banned women from wearing the burqa – a direct assault on freedom of choice and freedom of religion. American conservatives believed that Muslim immigration was turning Europe into 'Eurabia', as the example mentioned earlier from Christopher Caldwell's writing shows. Immigrants, the theory ran, had huge families and an uncompromising religion. Godless, pacifist Europeans, their will sapped by secularism and relativism, their numbers diminished by their hedonistic determination to have sex without having babies, lacked the moral certainty to fight militant Islam and the birth rate to outbreed it. They were losing the battle of ideas and the battle in the maternity wards. Muslims would make up 30, 40 or 50 per cent of the population of Europe by 2050, according to which alarmist forecast you read. It would become an anti-American, anti-Semitic, anti-Western continent, too frightened of its new inhabitants to stand up for democratic values.

These figures were nonsense. Even when they were not outright inventions, they included the assumption that current immigrant birth rates would remain high, when statistics suggested they were falling. The premise behind conservatives' fears was equally dubious. European Muslims did not form a cohesive bloc capable of collective action in favour of the causes of Islamist militants. The best reason for rejecting the paranoia of the right, however, was that it did not look at the victims of violence.

Extremists of all persuasions committed atrocities. Islamists murdered 191 civilians in Madrid in March 2004 and fifty-two in London in July 2005. The neo-fascist Anders Breivik murdered seventy-seven in Norway in July 2011. Both the religious far right and the white far right were convinced that they were fighting diabolic conspiracies. The London bomber Mohammad Sidique Khan justified random murder by invoking a Western plot to destroy Islam. 'Your democratically elected governments continuously perpetuate atrocities against my people all over the world,' he said in a videotape released after he killed himself and murdered six others on the London Underground's Circle Line. 'And your support of them makes you directly responsible, just as I am directly responsible for protecting and avenging my Muslim brothers and sisters.' Breivik cut and pasted a manifesto from anti-Muslim blogs, and justified his massacre by saying that leftish multi-cultural elites were plotting to destroy Europe's old nations and create 'Eurabia' by flooding the continent with immigrants. His charge was not that European establishments were naïve or cowardly in their treatment of religious extremism – which they were on many occasions – but that a quasi-Marxist hatred of traditional Christian culture pushed them into collaboration with an alien enemy.

Although the two sides seemed to be diametrically opposed, when they went for specific targets, rather than bombing random collections of civilians, they showed that what united them was more important than what divided them. Breivik's victims were not militant Islamists: most of them were young members of the Norwegian Labour Party. To his mind they were 'traitors' to their race and culture. Similarly, those Islamists marked for suffering were not far-rightists who dreamed of an all-white Europe, or conservatives who bewailed the decline of the Christian West. The leaders of most European far-right parties could operate without fearing a bullet in the head. It never occurred to Tea Party Republicans, who wittered about a demographic explosion producing a jihadist Europe, that jihadis might retaliate by gunning them down. With the exception of Geert Wilders of the Dutch Party of Freedom, who was the target of threats and one assassination attempt, the scare-mongers knew no fear.

Unlike panic-stricken conservatives, Islamists did not regard European Muslims as a bloc which was theirs to command. They understood that there was no unified Islam, that most immigrants were just trying to make a living, and many were experimenting with new ideas and freedoms. The first aim of religious violence is to stop experiment by the faithful and to enforce taboos. Naturally, the first targets of Islamists in Europe were liberal Muslims and ex-Muslims, who like Salman Rushdie were 'traitors' to their religion. Potential victims ought to have been able to count on the steady support of a European mainstream that opposed Islamism and neo-fascism in equal measure, and recognised that both drew on a common totalitarian impulse. But as the example of Ayaan Hirsi Ali showed, principled anti-fascism was hard to find.

Liberal societies treated the Islamist wave with a disastrous mixture of authoritarianism and appeasement. On the one hand, they passed anti-terrorist laws that conflicted with basic liberties, banned burqas and imposed new immigration controls, which were controls on Muslim immigration when you stripped away all the humbug around them. On the other, they complemented their anti-terror strategy with a policy of 'engaging' with Islamists of the Muslim Brotherhood variety, who were extreme but not violent. They hoped that by co-opting religious zealots, they could reduce the pool of potential terrorists. If we concede ground and don't challenge them too rigorously, they thought, perhaps they won't turn malevolent. The consequence of their double standards was that they had to attack Hirsi Ali and those like her who were not afraid to point out their hypocrisy or ignore the suffering of immigrant women 'engagement with Islamists' brought.

Naser Khader, the Danish Muslim politician whose defence of free speech during the cartoon crisis provoked one radical imam to discuss the possibility of him being blown up – as a 'jest', you will remember – viewed the manoeuvres of mainstream opinion with abhorrence. 'They take a minority in a minority to represent everyone,' he told me. 'When the minority in the minority demands the right to oppress the majority within the minority, they give it to them.' Khader has had to live with threats from extremists of all kinds. The intimidation from white racists bothered him less than the threats from Islamists from the religious far right. The police ought to know the identities of activists in local white extremist movements, he reasoned, and be able to monitor them. But radical Islam had a global network – a Comintern of the faithful – that stretched far beyond the jurisdiction of the Danish state. Just before I spoke to Khader, he had suggested in a television debate that schools should spare Muslim children the Ramadan fast because teachers had told him that hungry pupils were tired and listless during lessons. Someone in Denmark heard him, and passed details of his offence to the Middle East. A threatening message ordering him to mend his ways or suffer the consequences arrived from Jordan. Maybe nothing would come of it, maybe it would, but the Danish police could not investigate a threat from extremists living almost two thousand miles away.

Maryam Namazie, who fled with her family to Britain to avoid the persecutions of the Iranian theocracy, responded to the Archbishop of Canterbury and the Lord Chief Justice by organising campaigns against Sharia. 'To safeguard the rights and freedoms of all those living in Britain, there must be one secular law for all and no religious courts,' she said. As with Hirsi Ali and Khader, religious extremists threatened her as soon as she spoke out. She received a message warning, 'You are going to be decapitated.' If the American government or the British state had menaced her, she would have been a heroine. The press and the broadcasters would have defended and succoured her, and given encouragement to all who wanted to defy authority. As it was, she remained a virtually unknown figure.

On occasion, liberal society stirred itself. The self-taught Moroccan-Dutch artist Rachid Ben Ali responded to the murder of Theo van Gogh by producing pictures of 'hate imams' spewing bombs and excrement. As if to prove his point, death threats followed. Ali, like so many others, confessed to being frightened, but said that he remained determined to use his art to show that people of Muslim origins can be 'absolutely free in their thinking'. His gallery stood by him, and paid for his security guards.

Such moments of solidarity were rare. Ali's fellow artist Sooreh Hera was not so fortunate after she tried to confront religious hypocrisy. 'They condemn homosexuality, but in countries like Iran or Saudi Arabia it is common for married men to maintain relations with other men,' she said as she explained her project. 'Works of art can be provocative. It is not an artist's job just to paint flowers. Art should shine a light on social issues.' She photographed gay Iranian exiles wearing masks of Muhammad and Ali, the Prophet's son-in-law, sitting half-naked in modern bedrooms. The director of her Dutch gallery loved her protests against the execution of gays by the Iranian regime – Such a transgressive critique of hegemonic power structures! So edgy! So fizzing with contemporary relevance! – until he realised that 'Certain people in our society may perceive them as offensive,' and removed them from the show. Hera went into hiding, after receiving charming emails along the lines of 'We're going to burn you naked or put a bullet in your mouth.' Like Khader, she was well aware of the international reach of her enemies, and feared that agents of the Iranian state might target her. The Dutch government and the left-wing press refused to support her. 'Freedom of expression has become an illusion in Europe,' she said. 'We think we have freedom of expression, but in fact we live under a sort of hidden censorship.'

Because it was fighting a religious culture war and targeting newspapers, artists and novelists who offended it, radical Islam posed the greatest threat to freedom of speech of the anti-liberal movements. There is no guarantee that others will not imitate its tactics. In the summer of 2011, a British literary festival cancelled an event featuring an Islamist speaker after the English Defence League threatened to disrupt the meeting. Maybe I should not make too much of an isolated event, but the white extreme right could not have failed to have noticed that the habit of agreeing to the demands of menacing men had become ingrained in cultural bureaucrats. Religious radicals could dictate who spoke and wrote, so why shouldn't they do the same?

If the fears of feminists, artists, politicians and writers seem remote from ordinary life, consider the case of Deepika Thathaal, who like many girls did not dream of growing up to be a painter or a novelist, but a pop star. She started as a child singer in her native Norway. By seventeen, she was doing what teenage girls do, rebelling against authority, dressing in skimpy outfits and listening to the music of her day. Her second album, released in 1996, was a sensation in Norway. She mixed the influences of Asian music, Massive Attack and Portishead, and looked stunning as she did it. She thought she was on a smooth path to success, until the intimidation began.

Her parents had to change their phone number because of the hate calls. Five men burst into her school calling her 'a slut, a whore, a prostitute'. The confused teenager could not see why they were upset. 'I had the first brown face to appear on the front of the showbiz magazines. They ought to have been pleased.' She was attacked on the street and on stage during a concert in Oslo. She moved to London, where she decided to relaunch her career as Deeyah, 'the Muslim Madonna'. With a naïvety that could make you weep, she thought Britain would be a safer and better country than Norway because she had visited it as a child, and been impressed to see Asian women in Western clothes. Performers like her would be freer here, she reasoned, because immigrants had had longer to integrate.

'I first realised that something was wrong when my new manager told me that there was no competition. No other Muslim woman was doing what I was doing. He thought it was great, but I wondered, "Why am I the only one?"'

She soon found out. In 2006, she released a single, 'What Will it Be'. 'We don't take it lightly when you threatenin' women/How you have so much hate and faith in religion?' she sang on the video as she danced in a bikini top. To pile offence on offence, she supported women's refuges and campaigns against 'honour killings'.

British religious reactionaries forced her to hire bodyguards. Middle-aged men spat at her in the street and phoned her to say they would cut her to pieces not just because of her clothes, she told me, but because the sight of a woman making any kind of music was anathema to them. Callers demanded that Asian music channels ban her videos, and the channels' abject managers agreed. A spokesman for the Islamist organisations the Labour government, the Archbishop of Canterbury and the Lord Chief Justice were appeasing condemned her by saying women should not draw unnecessary attention to themselves.

'It was just the same in Britain as it was in Norway,' Deeyah said. She moved to an American city where no one knew her to find peace of mind and the time to pull herself together.

Deeyah talks as if liberal Europe had betrayed her, a common feeling among dissidents. Naser Khader, whose defence of gay rights and freedom of speech would once have marked him as a leftist, has given up on the liberal left and has joined the Danish conservative party. Gita Sahgal, who organised the pro-Rushdie demonstrations in Parliament Square in 1989, went on to work for Amnesty International. She and the organisation seemed natural allies. Sahgal was a feminist. Amnesty International was the world's pre-eminent liberal campaign group. She resigned in 2009 because she could no longer tolerate Amnesty allying with Islamists. Liberal-leftists in Europe and North America assume that good people will always recognise the inherent goodness of the liberal left and join it. I would not count on that happening with the coming generation of dissenters from Muslim backgrounds. The most radical voices – to use 'radical' in its true sense for once – have good reason to turn away. The first principle of liberalism, a principle that predates the Enlightenment, was freedom of conscience. No man should have the power to force others to accept his religion. Europe had hundreds of politicians, activists, intellectuals, writers, artists and exiles who found that freedom denied to them as they tried to criticise religious beliefs. Beyond Salman Rushdie and Ayaan Hirsi Ali were many others whose cases rarely made the papers. They had come to Europe because they wanted freedom of speech and freedom of conscience. When they tried to exercise those rights, they were threatened, attacked or forced to go into hiding. Mainstream society, which could cry so piteously for the persecuted in far-off lands, did not even know their names, let alone find the courage to defend their liberties.

## *Say that it is Bigoted to Oppose Bigotry*

Attempting to define 'chutzpah', and finding that 'gall, brazen nerve, effrontery, incredible guts, presumption plus arrogance' did not quite capture the awe the word carried with it, the Yiddish linguist Leo Rosten tried again. Chutzpah, he said, is 'that quality enshrined in a man who, having killed his mother and father, throws himself on the mercy of the court because he is an orphan'.

The skill of the practised chutzpahean lies in his ability to manipulate his listeners' guilt. He knows that no one wishes to be accused of picking on the vulnerable, and so will make you forget that the self-made orphan is a murderer, and the self-anointed victim an oppressor.

From Salman Rushdie on, Islamists have supplemented the threat of violence with appeals to the sometimes irritating but often well-justified arguments for fair treatment made by the politically correct. They have claimed that they are the victims of racism or religious phobia, and said that democratic countries must punish or ostracise those who affront their prejudices or question their faith. It is a breath-catching demand, because blasphemy is a victimless crime. What has the blasphemer injured? Is it religious ideas? If so, must we protect ideas from criticism as we protect children from abusers? Are we to regard concepts as persons who can suffer physical harm and financial loss? Perhaps the tender feelings of believers are the victims. If so, is their faith so weak that mockery and doubt can threaten it? Or maybe the defendant stands accused of insulting whatever god or gods the faithful follow. If that is the case, are the delicate deities in question so thin-skinned that their 'self-esteem' can only recover if their followers perform human sacrifices and present them with the corpses of their critics?

In practice, the injured party on whose behalf the state brings its action or the terrorist kills his victim is the tribe or imagined community. Blasphemy is the means by which it enforces group identity by condemning internal critics as heretics and apostates, and silencing sceptical outsiders. The religious transfer legal rights from individuals, where they belong, to abstractions such as faith or God. The 'insults' and 'offences' they penalise are vague and subjective. Given the impossibility of defining what they mean with anything like the clarity we expect in law, let alone of demonstrating real physical or financial harm, the 'crime' of blasphemy gives censors, judges and poisonous nuisances enormous leeway. Reviewing the blasphemy laws not just of the Islamic world but also of Poland and Greece, the human-rights group Freedom House said in 2010 that blasphemy allowed extremists to cement a mobbish alliance between Church and state. 'No matter what the political environment, blasphemy laws lend the power of the state to particular religious authorities and effectively reinforce extreme views, since the most conservative or hard-line elements in a religious community are generally the quickest to take offence and the first to claim the mantle of orthodoxy. Virtually any act has the potential to draw an accusation and prosecution' – a sentiment that M.F. Husain and Sherry Jones would have agreed with.

Religious freedom – including freedom from religion – requires freedom of speech. Restrict freedom of speech, and Christians can persecute Muslims and Jews for denying that Jesus was the son of God. Muslims can persecute Jews and Christians for denying that Muhammad was God's messenger.

Jews can persecute Christians and Muslims for saying that Christian and Muslim doctrines superseded theirs. And every religion can persecute free-thinkers.

To cite the most striking example, the United Nations Human Rights Council demanded in 2009 that member states forbid the 'defamation of religion'. The council is a sick joke, which has included Russia, China, Saudi Arabia and many another dictatorship among its members. Its proclamations are a regular source of shame, but its attack on freedom of speech was its nadir. The UN did not say that states should forbid persecution on religious grounds – if it had, China and Saudi Arabia would have been in the dock – but that they should forbid criticism of religion. It gave no definition of the meaning of defamation, but Pakistan, the promoter of the motion, said it was against the 'negative stereotyping of religions [and] the frequent and wrong association of Islam with human-rights violations and terrorism'. Irony is always lost on the authoritarian mind, and the representative of Pakistan could not allow himself to remember that Islamists were reducing his country to a failed state by using religion to justify human-rights violations and terrorism.

Clearly floundering as he tried to find a moral justification for censorship, he went on to say that the motion must be passed, because laws against the defamation of religion were needed to protect religious minorities from 'discrimination and acts of violence'. The insincerity behind the worthy sentiment was plain to see. As Pakistan talked of the need to end discrimination, its judiciary and Islamist terrorists persecuted Christians, and Shia, Ahmadi and other 'heretical' versions of Islam.

The most notorious case was that of Asia Bibi, a Christian mother of five. The police arrested her after she argued with Muslim women who refused to drink water she had carried, saying that she was impure. A mob surrounded the police station in her village in the Sheikhupura district of the Punjab. Its leaders told the authorities that she had insulted Muhammad.

For this blasphemy, the court sentenced her to death. Not much respect shown for her minority rights, then. Nor for the rights of Salmaan Taseer, the governor of the Punjab, who denounced the death sentence as the work of a 'black law'. He and his wife visited Asia Bibi in prison, and promised that she would receive a presidential pardon. Taseer's fellow politicians, from the president downwards, could not emulate his bravery. Fearing a religious backlash, they abandoned him. (One went so far as to say that not only would he not soften or repeal the blasphemy law, he would personally kill anyone who blasphemed.) Their cowardice left religious talk-show hosts free to run a hate campaign against Taseer. A police constable, charged by the state to protect him, then pumped twenty-six bullets into his body, while other members of his bodyguard stood by and let him do it.

Once you concede ground to religious extremists, their demands grow more impertinent. The supporters of Taseer's killer did not claim that the governor had blasphemed by asserting that the Koran was the work of men, not God, or that he had insulted the Prophet Muhammad. He was murdered for criticising the workings of a lethal blasphemy law, and urging judicial restraint. He had not blasphemed against God, only blasphemed against blasphemy law, but for that small 'offence' he had to die.

Pakistan's use of the language of victimhood to sweeten repression was not a one-off. In 1990, the foreign ministers of the Organisation of the Islamic Conference launched the Cairo Declaration on Human Rights in Islam. It established Sharia as 'the only source of reference' for the protection of human rights in Islamic countries, thus giving it supremacy over the principles of the United Nations Declaration of Human Rights. Both documents claim to protect freedom, but the former is a sickly and deceitful alternative to the latter. On 10 December 1948 the United Nations responded to the gas chambers and saturation bombings of the Second World War and the crimes of Stalin and

Hitler by stating that 'disregard and contempt for human rights have resulted in barbarous acts which have outraged the conscience of mankind'. Article 1 of the Declaration consists of the straightforward statement that 'All human beings are born free and equal in dignity and rights. They are endowed with reason and conscience and should act towards one another in a spirit of brotherhood.' Article 1 of the Cairo Declaration of 1990 is a more shifty piece of prose: 'All human beings form one family whose members are united by submission to God and descent from Adam,' it asserts, as it at once distances itself from universal brotherhood by limiting membership of the human family to those who believe in God and submit to Him. If the Cairo Declaration had upheld human rights, the appeal to religion would have mattered less. Instead, the drafters offered human rights with one hand and then snatched them away with the other. Article 2 says: 'Life is a God-given gift and … it is prohibited to take away life except for a Sharia prescribed reason.' The Declaration says that safety from bodily harm is a guaranteed right, and 'it is prohibited to breach it without a Sharia prescribed reason'. Murder and torture are prohibited, except when Sharia says they are not. The Declaration asserts the right to free speech, and then removes it from those who 'violate sanctities and the dignity of Prophets, undermine moral and ethical values or disintegrate, corrupt or harm society or weaken its faith'. Its authors produced a human-rights declaration that from the point of view of free speech offers no protection against terrorists killing cartoonists, or courts passing death sentences for blasphemy, or ayatollahs ordering the murder of novelists for apostasy.

The Islamic states' hypocrisy shows that in our time opposing religious censorship means concentrating on authoritarian Islam. You can find many examples of appalling Jewish and Christian attitudes towards women and gays. Orthodox Judaism is a misogynistic creed, and Christian Africa is one of the most dangerous places in the world for homosexuals. In the past, Judaism and Christianity threatened freedom of speech as a matter of course. But their censorious power in the rich world has largely been contained by secularism – which is not to say that extremist Jews and Christians do not want to see it rise again. Israel has a blasphemy law. America does not, but it has a legal campaign group called the Alliance Defense Fund that employs Christian lawyers to force schools and libraries to censor when it can. As I have argued, the West underestimates the threat Hindu nationalism poses to Indian writers, academics and artists. When all the exceptions have been made, however, Islamic states and paramilitaries are in a league of their own when it comes to religious censorship.

Given the ethnic spread of the faith, their targets will usually have brown skins; yet a large section of white Western liberal opinion does not recognise that it is truly racist to refrain from condemning the clerics who seek to oppress them. Half-educated academics and gutless politicians maintain that, on the contrary, it is racist to argue that human rights are universal. They instruct us that formerly colonised peoples should have different human rights, even if these turn out on close examination not to be human rights at all. The chutzpah of the authoritarian regimes and movements which maintain that it is bigoted to criticise religious bigotry is dazzling. More dazzling still is the eagerness of fercockt Western putzes to go along with them.

# HOW TO FIGHT BACK:

## *John Milton and the Absurdity of Identity Politics*

The English unleashed the contemporary idea of freedom of speech in the 1640s. Ever since, the English establishment has being trying to rein it in. John Milton's *Areopagitica* – his title paid homage to the free-speaking assembly of ancient Athens – was the first critique of religious censorship to push ideas about freedom of conscience into the modern age. His words ring down the centuries, providing arguments and inspiration to all who must take on secular and religious tyranny.

Milton supposed that the Parliamentarians he supported in the war against Charles I were fighting to end the power of the state to tell men what they must believe and how they must worship. When the king ruled without Parliament from 1629 to 1640, his determination to impose religious orthodoxy, in the form of a Catholicised Anglicanism, on England helped convince Milton – and his fellow rebels – of the necessity of revolution against a monarch who appeared to be aiming for absolute power. Charles's Court of Star Chamber had lopped off the ears and sliced the cheeks of Protestant dissidents, and branded their faces with 'SL' – seditious libeller – for contradicting the king's theology, and questioning the authority of the king's bishops. (Such was Star Chamber's reputation for extracting confessions through torture that even now in England you hear people denounce kangaroo courts and arbitrary verdicts as 'Star Chamber justice'.) A 1637 Star Chamber decree made it a crime to print 'any seditious, scismaticall, or offensive Bookes or Pamphlets'. A publisher must obtain state approval, in the form of a licence, before he could sell a book. Charles, like his predecessors, insisted on pre-publication censorship – the most effective censorship there is – and mutilated those who refused to submit to the screening process.

When the costs of war with the Presbyterian Scots forced Charles I to recall Parliament in 1640 and England began its slide towards revolution, one of the first acts of the new House of Commons was to abolish the state licensing of book publishers, along with the Court of Star Chamber. For the first time in their history, the English enjoyed the freedom to publish and read what they wanted.

Milton revelled in the new liberty. He dived into the controversies about religion and politics, and briefly was more famous for his polemics than his poetry. As with so many revolutionaries since, he soon found it hard to tell the difference between the new boss and the old. The Presbyterian faction in the Westminster Parliament, strengthened by its alliance with the Scots, wanted to replace the uniformity Charles I had imposed through his bishops with a uniformity of its own. It reintroduced licensing in 1643. All printers had to register with the state and submit to pre-publication censorship. Parliament's officer had the power to seize and destroy books and arrest offensive writers and publishers.

Milton watched the vanquishing of his hopes for religious liberty with increasing alarm. His bitter quip, 'New presbyter is but old priest writ large,' anticipated Orwell's concluding scene in *Animal Farm*, in which the creatures looked 'from pig to man, and from man to pig, and from pig to man again; but already it was impossible to say which was which'.

Milton had personal as well as intellectual reasons for opposing the return of censorship. Orthodox Protestants had demanded that a pamphlet on divorce he had written in 1643 should be burned for contradicting Christ's teachings in the gospels and St Paul's in his epistles. For recommending that men and women should be free to separate if their characters were incompatible, the poet became 'Milton the divorcer', a dangerous thinker who threatened the family and promoted lasciviousness.

Milton wrote *Areopagitica* in 1644, when the outcome of the war between Parliament and the king was still uncertain. It takes apart the reasoning of those who would censor authors' works with the fury of a great writer directing all his intelligence against the mean-minded. As a mark of his intent, Milton refused to send his pamphlet to the licensers, but published it freely and at some risk to his safety. He argued as if his life depended on it, because what was at stake for Milton was the principle that was to inspire *Paradise Lost*. God had endowed man 'with the gift of reason to be his own chooser'. Censors denied the God-given right to find religious truth in the world. They wanted to impose a 'yoke of outward conformity' and push England back into a 'gross conforming stupidity'. It told Milton much about the contempt with which religious leaders held their flocks that they appeared to believe that 'the whiffe of every new pamphlet should stagger them out of their catechism'. What were they frightened of? If a writer was leading the faithful astray, why could they not challenge his arguments? Christ preached in public 'wherewith to justify himself [and] writing is more public than preaching; and more easy to refutation'.

The most stirring lines in the *Areopagitica*, which still have the power to bring a tear to English eyes, show Milton arguing for England to become a free-thinking country. 'Lords and Commons of England,' he said to Parliament, 'consider what nation it is whereof ye are, and whereof ye are the governors: a nation not slow and dull, but of a quick, ingenious, and piercing spirit, acute to invent, subtle and sinewy to discourse, not beneath the reach of any point the highest that human capacity can soar to.' The English should not allow clerics and politicians to infantilise them. Only by engaging in the battle of ideas, including the battle with false, foolish and blasphemous ideas, could they discover religious truth. When Milton said that he could not praise a 'fugitive and cloistered virtue, unexercised and unbreathed, that never sallies out and sees her adversary', he meant that religious truth could not be imposed from above by a king, priest, minister, rabbi, guru, ayatollah, 'community leader', judge or bureaucrat. The individual had to find it for himself in the heat of argument. The sentence all readers remember – 'Give me the liberty to know, to utter, and to argue freely according to conscience, above all liberties' – is an assertion that authority is no guarantee of truth, if authority is not tested.

Milton's advantage over modern writers and academics is that he had experienced censorship. He knew the humiliation of having to take work to a censor, and had a justifiable contempt for the type of man who would choose bowdlerising as a career. He wondered who would want to tell others what they could and could not write, and found that his question answered itself. No writer with any talent or respect for liberty would consider accepting the job. Censoring was 'tedious and unpleasing journey-work'. Only the 'ignorant, imperious, and remiss, or basely pecuniary' would wish to take money for blacking out the thoughts of others.

'*Milton! Thou shouldst be living at this hour,*' cried William Wordsworth in his sonnet to liberty of 1802.

> England hath need of thee: she is a fen
> Of stagnant waters: altar, sword, and pen …

Then as now, the temptation to see Milton as a modern man, whose words are weapons we can use to defend our freedoms, is overwhelming.

But the author of *Paradise Lost*, one of the greatest poems Christianity inspired, was not a forerunner of the Enlightenment, but a writer formed by the wars of religion. He could not bring himself to offer toleration to persecuted Catholics, and wrote a hack propaganda work for Oliver Cromwell before the general sailed off to massacre the Irish. Papists were so wicked to Milton's mind that they must be silenced. His pamphlet on divorce, that infuriated the clerics of seventeenth-century London, did not anticipate Mary Wollstonecraft and the first feminists. As his biographer Anna Beer says, Milton had no interest in the horrendous abuse of women by men that the seventeenth century tolerated. In *Paradise Lost*, he created one of the most loathsome images in English literature when he imagined 'Sin', a female figure who guards Hell's gates. Her own son has raped her, and she gives birth to fiendish dogs,

> hourly born, with sorrow infinite
> To me; for, when they list, into the womb
> That bred them they return, and howl, and gnaw
> My bowels, their repast; then, bursting forth
> Afresh, with conscious terrors vex me round,
> That rest or intermission none I find.

I think it is fair to say that John Milton was not wholly at ease with women's sexuality. I am certain that he could no more contemplate the emancipation of women than could his contemporaries. Milton did not support divorce because he wanted to free battered wives from private hells, but because he thought marriage was a restriction on the dominant male's right to live as he wished. He wanted to 'make it easier for men to divorce their wives' so that men could be 'masters of themselves again'. Later, in the 1650s, he reneged on the principles of *Areopagitica*, and censored on behalf of Parliament. His work survives despite, not because of, the man.

To put that thought more kindly, Milton was a creature of his time, as we all are. His relevance lies not just in his arguments for freedom. The reaction against him illustrated how supporters of the status quo justify suppression. Monarchs believed that their subjects must share their religion. Charles I had no difficulty in justifying the censorship of Milton's contemporaries, because he thought – rightly, as events were to show – that his power depended on his ability to suppress religious dissent. Seventeenth-century Presbyterians thought that they possessed the revealed truth, and had every right to use force to stop the 'lies' of blasphemers leading the faithful to perdition. Once again, their reasons for suppression strike us as dictatorial, but struck them as self-evident.

Today's supporters of religious censorship claim that they are different. They say they are not advocating censorship because they believe we must bow down before Church and state, but because we must respect different cultures and say nothing that might offend them.

If those who said, from the Ayatollah Khomeini's fatwa onwards, that we must censor and self-censor in the name of 'respect' could be transported to the London of the 1640s, how would they make their case?

I said that Milton was a creature of his time, and they might reply that Milton was offending the culture of his time and inviting punishment. But how would they define culture? Milton's views on divorce and freedom of speech undoubtedly conflicted with the views of the majority of his compatriots. But not even Milton's opponents would have said he was an enemy of English culture. He was one of the most English Englishmen who ever lived, whose patriotism is obvious to all who read him. In any case, what could a charge of offending

English culture have meant in the 1640s? Cultures are not unified or sealed in aspic; they change because men and women, propelled by circumstances and their own intelligence, fight to change them. Then as now, the English had many attitudes in common, but there was no such thing as a unified English culture, as the English of the 1640s proved by fighting a civil war to determine how the politics and culture of their country should change.

Our time travellers would fare no better if they substituted religious cultures for national cultures. It would take some nerve to accuse Milton of being a 'Christianophobe', and not only because of *Paradise Lost*. With Catholics fighting Protestants across Europe, a unified Christianity did not exist in the seventeenth century, any more than a unified Christianity, Hinduism, Judaism or Islam exists now. Could you say then that Milton was a heretical Protestant? His opponents claimed that he was, but the charge lacked force when Protestantism was itself divided into warring factions. The Presbyterians wanted to impose their views. A smaller group of independent Protestants, who believed in freedom of conscience, opposed them. Milton supported the independents, but the ranks of his comrades contained further divisions.

The faster you strip cultures down, the more you find contrariness and disputation, rather than a solid core, until eventually you reach the individual, a mammal shaped by evolution, material needs, cognitive biases and historical circumstances no doubt, but still a creature with a better right to state his opinions than kings and clerics have to silence them.

The faster you strip down the respectful arguments for religious censorship, the more you see the nation, tribe or community splintering, until you are left with one group of individuals with coercive power behind them demanding the right to censor another group of individuals because they disagree with them.

The one escape left from *reductio ad absurdum* for those who say we must censor to protect the majority within a religious group or any other community from the psychic harm that comes from hearing a strongly held view challenged, is for the 'liberal' proponents of censorship to admit that they support censorship on utilitarian grounds. They must believe that the harm to the tender feelings and brittle minds of believers caused by the publication of an argument, satire or exposé outweighs the benefit to the individual author of exercising his or her rights and of readers exercising theirs. They must take the possibility of violent reprisals as an honourable reason to ban a book rather than the best of reasons for defending it. To this way of thinking, even if the ayatollahs issuing death threats have not read the novel, and if the exposé of the subjugation of women is correct in all factual respects, liberals must join the religious in demanding suppression. They must hold that if the majority of a nation or community agrees on one issue – that divorce is immoral, in Milton's case; that mockery of the Prophet is blasphemous, in Rushdie's – it has the right to demand silence. (Even if the 'community' or nation is in other respects proving its lack of 'social cohesion' by fighting civil wars, as Protestants were in the 1640s.) They must mount the barricades against new thoughts that might torment and enrage the faithful, and say that no one can be the first to clamber over them, as Milton was the first Englishman to begin the argument for freedom of speech, or Mary Wollstonecraft was the first woman to argue for women's rights, or Salman Rushdie was the first novelist to subject the myths of the creation of Islam to ironic enquiry, or Ayaan Hirsi Ali was the first politician from the poor world to warn Europeans of the dangers of tolerating religious abuse.

In short, they must favour mob rule, the policy of demagogues, which liberals once earned what distinction they possessed by opposing.

# PART TWO

# *Money*

*If any opinion is compelled to silence, that opinion may, for aught we can certainly know, be true. To deny this is to assume our own infallibility.*

JOHN STUART MILL, 1869

# FIVE

# The Cult of the Supreme Manager

*Stardom isn't a profession; it's an accident.*

LAUREN BACALL

In 2003, I was trying to find a way of dramatising the widening gap between the broad mass of society and the emerging plutocracy. I hit on the idea of comparing the money the British public raised on Red Nose Day with the wealth of the super-rich. Foreign readers may need me to explain that after much consciousness-raising in the preceding weeks, the BBC devotes a day in March to exhorting the populace to donate to charities dedicated to the relief of poverty at home and abroad. As in every other year, the mandatory 'fun' in 2003 took the form of comedians filling the screens and cajoling viewers to help the cause. Tens of thousands of adults pestered their friends to sponsor their stunts – dressing up as a chicken, sitting in a bath filled with cold baked beans, going to work on a unicycle or some other rib-tickling wheeze. Twelve thousand telecom workers gave up their spare time to man phone lines, while a million or so schoolchildren wore red clown noses and extorted money from their parents. The relentless cheeriness ground down all but the most miserly. The organisers estimated that about five million people gave money, if only so the chickens and children would leave them in peace. The appeal raised £35,174,798 in total.

*That sum*, I cried in a voice that hit the soprano C of righteous indignation, *those hard-won proceeds* of Britain's largest exercise in communal altruism, counted for nothing when set against the rewards of the mighty. Red Nose Day's takings were dwarfed by the £157.7 million pocketed in 2002 by one man: Sir Philip Green, a retail tycoon the British Labour Party knighted even though he vested ownership of chain stores in the name of his wife, a resident of Monaco, so the family could avoid the taxes Labour imposed on the common people it once claimed to represent. The income of one tycoon made the charitable efforts of a large slice of the British public seem pathetic.

How risible my comparison seems now. The incomes of plutocrats have flown far beyond the levels of the early years of the century.

Statistics and anecdote dramatise how much wealth and potential power is now in the hands of a global elite. Between 2002 and 2007, 65 per cent of all income growth in the United States went to the top 1 per cent of the population. The financial crisis interrupted their enrichment, but after American and British governments, by which I mean American and British taxpayers, bailed out the financial system, the super-rich bounced back. The top twenty-five hedge-fund managers received on average more than $1 billion each in 2009, and overtook the records set in the bubble year 2007. In 2012 Emmanuel Saez, of the University of California, published a statistic that could change the way you thought about the world. After the great crash of 1929, those who had most to lose, lost the most. But when America bounced back after the great crash of 2007–08, the top 1 per cent captured 93 per cent of the income gains made in 2010. The top 1 per cent fared better in President Barack Obama's recession than they did in the recession of President George W. Bush from 2000 to 2002, Saez noted. To put it another way, the financial crisis was merely a slight setback in the forward march of the aristocracy of wealth.

The super-rich were the beneficiaries of a longer trend that began with the break-up of the post-war social democratic consensus in the 1970s. The pre-tax income of the richest 1 per cent of American earners increased from about 8 per cent of the total in 1974 to more than 18 per cent in 2007. The richest 0.01 per cent (the fifteen thousand richest families in the US) saw their share of pre-tax income rise from 1 per cent in 1974 to 6 per cent in 2007.

In 1997, the year Labour came to power promising to govern for 'the many, not the few', the collective wealth of the richest thousand people in Britain stood at £98.99 billion. By the time the tribunes of the masses were preparing to leave office in 2009, it stood at £335.5 billion. In the former Soviet Union, sharp operators moved in to plunder the assets of the defunct communist state by buying them cheaply or for nothing at all. In 1989, there were no Russian billionaires. By 2003, the country had more dollar billionaires in proportion to gross domestic product than any other major economy – thirty-six in all, fourteen more than in Japan, a markedly less corrupt, miserable and unhealthy society. Russia's wealthiest man was then Mikhail Khodorkovsky, with $15.2 billion. Vladimir Putin had Khodorkovsky jailed for crossing the autocracy, but those oligarchs who stayed out of opposition politics and found ways to – how shall we say? – make the burdens of office easier for the ruling clique to endure, saw their wealth grow and their numbers swell. Despite the crash of 2008, Forbes counted sixty-two Russian billionaires in 2009. In China, the number of billionaires ballooned to 128 in 2009, from seventy-nine in 2008. Only the United States, with four hundred, had more. It is the same in India, Brazil and Mexico ... everywhere in the world you look, the ranks of the super-rich are growing.

In 2005 Ajay Kapur, global strategist at Citigroup, and his colleagues described societies where a minority controls the majority of the wealth, and where economic growth becomes dependent on the fortunes of that same wealthy minority. The strategists said that it made sense to forget about national divisions and divide the world between the men and women at the top and the rest.

> There is no such animal as 'the US consumer' or 'the UK consumer', or indeed the 'Russian consumer'. There are rich consumers, few in number, but disproportionate in the gigantic slice of income and consumption they take. There are the rest, the 'non-rich', the multitudinous many, but only accounting for surprisingly small bites of the national pie.

Beneath the obscenely wealthy are the filthy rich. J.P. Morgan, the austere American financier, is reputed to have said that his executives should not earn more than twenty times the wages of workers at the bottom of his firms. How quaint his puritan limits seem a hundred years on. In 2009, the chief executive of the pharmaceutical company Reckitt Benckiser received £37 million – 1,374 times the pay of the average (not the lowest-paid) worker beneath him. The salaries of just two of the chief executives of the companies in the FTSE-100 passed Morgan's test. In the United States, the ratio of CEO pay to average worker pay rose from 42:1 in 1960 to as high as 531:1 in 2000 during the dotcom bubble, and fell back to 263 times more than the average worker in 2009.

Wealth always has its intellectuals, eager to find high-minded justifications for acquisitiveness. They have filled many books and many pages in the business press with their efforts to explain why fears of a plutocracy are groundless. I will not deny that they have a case. The collapse of Marxism was one of the most beneficial revolutions in history. In China alone, the end of Mao's terror and the replacement of his command economy with a limited market economy lifted hundreds of millions out of poverty. Globalisation, its defenders argued, inevitably created billionaires, because the global market and new technologies have allowed superstar brands, and with them superstar entrepreneurs, to emerge. Companies needed the best talent to handle disruptive technologies, because the difference between an average and a great manager was the difference between success and bankruptcy. If an Apple laptop delights, if Facebook puts its users in touch with the world, why should the citizen care about the incomes of the companies' founders? Lives for an increasing proportion of humanity are more comfortable, longer and healthier than they have ever been. In the rich world, the majority of what we used to call the working class is no longer engaged in hard manual labour, and mechanisation has removed the need for a peasantry to toil in the fields. Class hatred of the rich is therefore muted when set against the passions of the socialist era. Even the modern resentment of the bankers is a conservative emotion, comparable to the resentment of trade unionists who demanded state subsidies in the 1970s. Taxpayers loathe bankers not for being capitalists but for being failed capitalists, who picked the public's pockets. If they had been successes, the public would not despise them. Why worry?

The crash of 2008 showed a reason for not viewing the established order with complacency that is beyond the scope of this book. Financiers make up the bulk of the super-rich – a study of wealth in America in 2004 found that for every one company executive earning over $100 million there were nine Wall Street tycoons. When their speculative gambles pay off, they privatise the profits; when they fail, they nationalise the losses. America and Britain have a parasitic version of financial capitalism that exploits the taxpayer to cover the failings of wealthy and dangerous citizens. Andrew Haldane of the Bank of England estimated that between 2007 and 2009 the average annual subsidy for the top five UK banks was £50 billion – roughly equal to UK banks' annual profits prior to the crisis. With the understatement the

British mandarin deploys when he thinks the world has taken leave of its senses, he added, 'These are not small sums.'

For the purposes of this book, there is a further harm. I can think of few more important subjects for democratic citizens than the influence of the rich over politics, the damage business can do to the atmosphere and the environment, and the risks high finance brings to economic stability. Yet extreme wealth is creating societies in which it is harder to hold economic power to account. Writers in the Anglosphere concentrate on the failings and corruptions of our own elites – who, to give them their due, provide us with an abundance of material – and fail to see the wider corruption. In the rich world, the crash of 2008 hit democratic countries and public limited companies hardest. However useless they proved to be, they remained institutions whose structures allowed accountability, albeit imperfect. Citizens who questioned their behaviour did not run a personal risk. The new concentrations of wealth are not in democratic Europe or North America. Oligarchies with no traditions of freedom of speech or democratic government now hold much of the world's wealth, and those who try to hold them to account run considerable risks. In China, Russia and the Middle East, sovereign wealth funds or oligarchs who have paid off the local elites own the biggest banks and oil companies. Government-run energy companies in Saudi Arabia, Iran, Venezuela, Russia, China, India and Brazil control 80 per cent of the world's oil and gas supplies. India and Brazil are the only real democracies on that list, and the populations of both have to live with astonishing levels of inequality and corruption. It is not hysterical leftism to see a link between the two. In democratic India and America, and maybe soon in Britain and Europe too, corrupting the political system is the natural strategy for oligarchs to follow. It is a statement of the obvious to say that as inequality increases, 'the rich are likely to both have greater motivation and opportunities to engage in bribery and fraud to preserve and advance their own interests while the poor are more vulnerable to extortion'. But after making it, the American economists Jong-sung You and Sanjeev Khagram went on to demonstrate that while countries with authoritarian regimes are likely to have greater levels of corruption, the effect of greater inequality on levels of corruption will be higher in democracies. In free societies, the wealthy cannot employ direct repression by hiring private armies. They have to act covertly. One only has to look at how Wall Street's contributions to American presidential campaigns have prevented effective bank reform to see You and Khagram's theory operating in practice.

Contrary to all who believed that liberalism's triumph in 1989 was permanent, oligarchic countries did not suffer from the Great Recession of 2008. China boomed, and overtook Japan to become the world's second largest economy. It began to boast that it had nothing to learn from the Western model, and that the West should learn from China, which in the worst of ways we may do. For believers in liberal economics and for social democrats, who wanted to regulate market economies to produce the funds for welfare, 2008 was an ominous year. Vince Cable, now Britain's Business Secretary, saw an alignment of state and private interests across the world that 'promises all the worst features of capitalist economies – unfettered greed, corruption and inequalities of wealth and power – without the benefits of competitive markets'. The crimes and excesses of the age that has passed notwithstanding, we may look back fondly on the liberal supremacy of 1989–2008, and see the merits of its naïve belief that the world was destined to witness a victory of the free market and free societies.

I am not pretending that there is a clear division. The oligarchic world and the Western world are not separate entities, as NATO and the Warsaw Pact were in the Cold War. They are interlaced. At the level of the plutocracy there is no 'us' and 'them', and most certainly no 'other'. Of the fifty-three billionaires resident in London and the south-east of England for all or part of the year in 2010, twenty-four were foreign-born. Banks in New York handle the money made by 'high net-worth individuals', from whichever corner of the globe they come. German social democrat politicians promote the interests of the Russian gas giant Gazprom while they are in office, and take jobs from it when they retire. Libel lawyers in London protect the reputation of Saudi petro-billionaires and post-Soviet oligarchs.

Beyond the intermingling of their finances and interests, the Western rich and the oligarchic rich share an ideological affinity that is worth worrying about too: they are unshakeable in their belief that they are entitled to their wealth, and have every moral right to resist attempts to reduce it. It never occurs to them that they are lucky; that if they are Western speculators, they are lucky to have lived during a time when the negligent governments of America and Britain failed to regulate finance and allowed them to take incredible risks at no personal cost; that if they are post-communist oligarchs, they were lucky to be in place when the Soviet Union collapsed, and to have the connections and muscle to take control of the old empire's raw materials. To outsiders their luck seems self-evident. Yet nowhere in the recorded utterances of the plutocracy does one find a glimmer of an understanding that time and chance played a part in their good fortune.

Chrystia Freeland, a business journalist who works for Reuters, provided an archive of attitudes when she published interviews with the super-rich. As one might expect, the 'new men' of Putin's Russia were the most brazenly self-aggrandising. While he was still the richest man in Russia, Mikhail Khodorkovsky told her, 'If a man is not an oligarch, something is not right with him. Everyone had the same starting conditions, everyone could have done it.' American financiers were more careful in their choice of words, but their self-justifications were no different. They could accept no blame for the financial crisis, even though the public had bailed out the banks and lent hundreds of billions of dollars nearly free of charge to the financial system. The real culprits were the plebs who had bought homes they could not afford, or small-time investors who had over-extended their property port-folios. After hearing much more in this vein, Freeland ended on a portentous note: 'The lesson of history is that, in the long run, super-elites have two ways to survive: by suppressing dissent or by sharing their wealth.'

There are several forms of suppression available. The use of expensive lawyers to punish critics in libel courts, most notably in Britain, but in France, Brazil and Singapore as well, is an under-explored form of censorship that allows the wealthiest people on the planet to intimidate their opponents. The control by the wealthy of parts of the media is a kind of censorship, if not in the age of the Internet a censorship that is as effective as it once was. The most obvious restriction on freedom of speech, and the one which can cause the most damage to the common good, is so ubiquitous and accepted we do not even call it censorship, or think of tearing off the gag that silences us.

## The Censor in a Suit

Every time you go into your workplace, you leave a democracy and enter a dictatorship. Nowhere else is freedom of speech for the citizens of free societies so curtailed. They can abuse their political leaders in print or on radio, television and the Web as outrageously as they wish, and the secret service will never come for them. They can say that their country's leader is a lunatic, their police force is composed of sadists and their judiciary is corrupt. Nothing happens, even on those occasions when their allegations are gibberish. The leniency of free societies is only proper. Freedom of speech includes the freedom to spout clap-trap, as regular surfers of the Web know. If employees criticise their employers in public, however, they will face a punishment as hard as a prison sentence, maybe harder: the loss of their career, their pension, and perhaps their means of making a livelihood.

Britain has a formal legal protection for whistleblowers, but as so often with laws about free speech, the theory is one thing and the practice another. Workers are allowed to make 'qualifying disclosures' and warn of criminal offences, failure by their firms to comply with legal obligations, miscarriages of justice, threats to an individual's health and safety, and threats to the environment. The list sounds impressive, but the law says that an employee must first take his or her concerns to their employer. Only then can they raise the alarm and claim compensation if the boss fires them.

'It's like telling a mouse to go see the cat,' one of London's best employment lawyers told me. If the employer thinks for a moment that the employee may go to the press or a Member of Parliament, he will suspend him or her and deny them access to the computer system. In theory again, the law is aware of the problem, and allows an exception to the rule. If employees reasonably believe that they will suffer a 'detriment', or the employer will destroy evidence, they can go public without notifying their bosses. In practice, any worker who took the law at its word because he 'reasonably believed' his employer would destroy evidence or silence him would find himself in a catch-22. When his compensation case came to court, he would have to say, 'I went to the press without consulting my employers because I thought my employers would fire me.' To which the employer would respond, 'No we wouldn't, and because you didn't come to us first, you have no evidence that will stand up in this court that we would have.'

As soon as a whistleblower brings unwelcome news to his or her superiors, the human-resources department of any major public or private bureaucracy knows what it must do next. It will instruct its lawyers to secure a gagging injunction from the courts. All employment contracts include confidentiality clauses stating that the employee cannot release information about the organisation and its clients under any circumstances. Many now contain an additional catch-all clause stating that the employee must take no action that could bring the organisation into disrepute. Britain is a country where a council can sack a dinner lady for bringing her 'school into disrepute' by telling parents that their daughter was being bullied in the playground. Workers here do not speak their minds if they suspect their employers may find out. Even medics, who have a professional duty to protect the interest of patients, are exposed. The Nursing and Midwifery Council struck off a nurse who revealed the neglect of elderly patients by taking a camera crew into her hospital. The *British Medical Journal* said that when a doctor raised concerns about unsafe heart surgery in his hospital, 'his career stalled' and he moved to Australia to find work. Medical whistle-blowers, whose concerns touch on vital questions of who lives and who dies, 'find themselves the subject of retaliatory complaints and disciplinary action'. In one case of alleged research fraud, whistleblowers were advised to 'keep quiet or their careers would suffer'. When they did not, the regulatory authorities investigated them first, rather than the abuses they had uncovered.

In theory again, the courts will not issue a gagging order if the defendant can prove that he was seeking to release information that the public ought to know about. In practice, judges rarely refuse to gag, because the odds are stacked against the employee. Imagine a woman who has gone to her boss, maybe nervously, maybe filled with trust in her superiors' good faith. Instead of listening to her concerns, the employer tells security to escort her from the building. Her swipe card no longer works. She has no access to the computer system. Her belongings are in bin bags in reception, and she cannot afford expensive legal representation. Her case is lost before it has begun.

Lawyers know of just a handful of instances where employees have received compensation because they followed the correct procedure: first raising their concerns with their managers, and going public only when the company failed to address them. By one of those serendipities that can make the most atheist of authors believe that a supernatural power orders the universe, among the few was Gita Sahgal, who organised the Asian feminists who protested in defence of Salman Rushdie in Parliament Square in 1989. After her employer, the human-rights group Amnesty International, required her to leave for complaining to the press about its alliances with Islamists, her lawyers secured compensation for her.

Few have chosen to follow her path, because the driving desire in the minds of the overwhelming majority of employees is not the intricacies of the legislation or the possibility of compensation, but keeping their jobs and avoiding the need to go to law that speaking their minds would bring. Every whistle-blower I have known has ended up on the dole. Their colleagues know without needing anyone to spell it out for them that self-censorship is necessary if they are to enjoy future wealth and security. Speaking out in the public interest guarantees financial loss and unemployment. The primary concern of employees, public and private, is to avoid a confrontation. They work in hierarchies organised like armies. The managing director or CEO is the general, and a princely salary bolsters his or her status and pride. Beneath him or her are the staff officers, whose first duty is to show mindless obedience; and beneath them are the grunts, who are expected to take orders without question and not to answer back. The radical British economist Chris Dillow describes the strangeness of today's hierarchical organisations well. As the collapse of communism approached in 1989, conservative and soft-left commentators 'told us, rightly, that no one had enough knowledge and rationality to manage an economy. But they also told us that managers had enough knowhow to manage a firm.' While they condemned the hierarchical centrally planned economy, they praised the hierarchical centrally planned corporation or state bureaucracy.

If we take one lesson from the economic crisis, it should be that excessive wealth rendered the managers of banks unfit to run complex organisations. They had the most persuasive of economic incentives not to investigate the dangers of collapse thoroughly, because prudent banking would have cut the size of their extraordinary bonuses.

We should not be surprised that the managerial system that was so successful in the nineteenth and twentieth centuries experienced such a breakdown. Modern economies do not depend on producing goods on assembly lines, but on creative thinking, and you cannot command and control creativity, or order it to appear on time like a replacement machine tool. In the most advanced areas of the economy, most notably computing and biotechnology, small, light firms overtake established corporations because they know that information is scattered across organisations, not confined in the offices of executives. They tap it by encouraging cooperation, not subservience. As the costs of storing and retrieving information have collapsed, sharing expertise ought to be easy. But the cooperative approach based on openness and trust undermines the status of managers, whose wealth depends on the ability to create the impression that they have knowledge that their subordinates cannot be trusted to share.

All of the above are strong arguments against the managerialism that blights free countries. But the strongest stares us in the face. If managers looked to the inspiration for the technologies they deploy, they would find it comes from a scientific method that has no connection to the cramped, fearful ideologies of the managerial economy. The scientific method insists that researchers must go where the evidence leads, whatever the consequences. Status, salary and position should offer no protection from criticism, because no idea or person is sacred. Richard Feynman said that the differences between true sciences and the pseudo-sciences – a category that includes the management-speak of the business schools – was that the former try to be honest, while the latter do not.

Richard Dawkins illustrated the scientific ideal of egalitarian openness with the affecting story of a young zoologist challenging an old professor in Dawkins' zoology department. The professor believed that the Golgi apparatus (a microscopic feature on the interior of cells) was an illusion. 'Every Monday afternoon it was the custom for the whole department to listen to a research talk by a visiting lecturer. One Monday, the visitor was an American cell biologist who presented completely compelling evidence that the Golgi apparatus was real. At the end of the lecture, the old man strode to the front of the hall, shook the American by the hand and said – with passion – "My dear fellow, I wish to thank you. I have been wrong these fifteen years." We clapped our hands red. No fundamentalist would ever say that. In practice, not all scientists would. But all scientists pay lip-service to the ideal, [and] the memory of the incident still brings a lump to my throat.'

The scientific method is opposed to secrecy, and has no respect for status. It says that all relevant information must be open to scrutiny. The ideal it preaches – not always successfully, I grant you – is that men and women must put their pride to one side and admit mistakes. It is the opposite of the hierarchical cultures of business and the state, where status determines access to information, and criticism is met with punishment.

Nearly all of us work in hierarchies. Nearly all of us bite our tongues when we should speak freely. Yet few of the classic or modern texts on freedom of speech discuss freedom of speech at work, even though, as the crash of 2008 showed, self-censorship in the workplace can be as great a threat to national security as foreign enemies are.

## On the Psychology of Financial Incompetence

'The bullying is all I remember about him,' said a former execu-
tive as he recalled how dictatorial folly had brought down the
Royal Bank of Scotland, and helped to almost bring down the
British economy with it. 'He was just another angry guy.'

I could add that he was also a deluded, petty and ruthless
man who terrified his subordinates, but the dismissive tone of
'just another angry guy' is better than a sackful of adjectives.
When tyrants fall, and the chief executive of the Royal Bank of
Scotland was a tyrant of the workplace, people shake themselves
as if snapping out of a dream, and wonder why they ever feared
the reduced and ridiculous figure before them.

'Fred the Shred', or to give him his full title, Sir Frederick
Anderson Goodwin, was born in 1958. His father was an electri-
cian in Paisley, a suburb of Glasgow, who sent him to the local
grammar school. Young Fred went on to Glasgow University, the
first Goodwin from the family to receive higher education. He
graduated, and began to work his way up the corporate ladder.
He was not a fool. In 1991, as a young accountant, he helped
wind up the Bank of Credit and Commerce International, which
had financed Saddam Hussein, the Medellín drug cartel and
many another gangster and terrorist. He impressed his superiors
by recovering money they thought had disappeared into crime
families' safe-deposit boxes for good.

Goodwin earned his nickname by shredding jobs after he
moved from accounting to become a manager at the Clydesdale
Bank. His determination to cut costs may not have impressed
his junior colleagues, but it won him many admiring glances
from institutional shareholders and directors. RBS made him its
deputy CEO in 1998, and he took overall control shortly after it
purchased the National Westminster Bank in 2000.

The takeover was a triumph for RBS, and you can understand
why success inflated Goodwin's pride. Despite the glories of

Scottish culture, there is a strong sense of inferiority among the Scottish elite. However well careerists do in Edinburgh, they cannot escape the feeling that the prizes worth having in politics, business, the arts and the media are won on the big stage down south; that if they do not make it in London, their achievements will feel trifling. The battle for NatWest overturned English superiority. Edinburgh beat London. The men from the New Town outsmarted the men from Chelsea. NatWest managers had precedent and money on their side, and few gave the Scots a chance. RBS was one third of the size of its English rival. The deal RBS was offering was seven times the size of the previous biggest hostile takeover in the UK, and no hostile takeover of a major European bank had been successful before. City analysts assumed it would fail, but their scepticism could not stop RBS, whose dynamism and aggression saw it through.

Goodwin's triumph was twofold. He believed that 'naysayers' ran the NatWest, cautious and to his mind lazy bankers, who turned down good lending opportunities and missed the seductive prospect of speculating in the derivatives market. Once in charge, he tore into the bank's costs, slashing staff and merging departments, and ordered its remaining bankers to go out and find business. Profits ballooned, and Goodwin could say to himself that not only had he fought the City in a takeover battle and won, he had also gone on to show that the supposed superstars of London finance had missed an opportunity for profit that had been staring them in the face.

In 2002, *Forbes* named him its businessman of the year – not bad for a boy from Paisley who had been working for an Edinburgh bank in a backwater of global capitalism. As his fame grew, all the psychological flaws of the egotistic authoritarian personality feasted on his mind. He had no time for collaborative decision-making, or respect for collective wisdom. He was the meritocratic master, the proven winner, who instinctively knew what was right. 'I always work on the five-second rule,' he told *Forbes*. 'How a job offer makes you feel in the first five seconds when you hear the idea, before you spend ages agonising, is what you should do.' He required his subordinates to obey without question. At 9.30 a.m. he held his 'prayer meetings', at which he would caustically review the performance of his lieutenants, and assert his power with exercises in public humiliation. 'Executives would hate going to meetings with him,' a senior manager told me. 'They would sit at the table, eyes down, chin on chest, thinking, "I hope he doesn't pick on me this time."' Goodwin was adept at using his control of targets to frighten those below him. 'People would work for months on plans for the next year, trying to get costs down and profits up. Then he would tear up what they had done in front of their faces and say that the plans were too timid. Costs must always go down; profits must always go up, even if the targets were impossible. So back we would go, and try again.' The culture of the quick buck and the fast deal demoralised the corporation. Anyone who raised doubts about the tiny amounts of capital backing lending, or the failure to invest in computer systems that could cope with the bank's trades, heard managers tell them in threatening voices that they were 'Business Prevention Officers'. Carry on getting in the way, and the hierarchy would mark them as fifth columnists whose naysaying was destroying the bank's viability and the chance for bonuses for everyone working in it.

Let one vignette stand for the whole man. RBS was about to move staff into an office on Bishopsgate in the City. Goodwin inspected it just before it opened, and noticed that the carpet colour was not quite right. The minor breach with corporate branding did not matter: Bishopsgate was a home for administrative workers, not a place for customers. The exception was Goodwin's suite, which filled the eleventh and twelfth floors, and had an express lift so he and his guests could reach his private hospitality lounge without encountering the riff-raff. Linking the eleventh and twelfth floors was a sweeping staircase, which Goodwin descended to greet important guests as if he were a star in his own movie (the 'Fred Astaires', his underlings called it). Goodwin had previously insisted that every RBS branch in the world must have matching fixtures and fittings, that every RBS executive must wear a white shirt with a tie sporting the RBS logo, and that every plate of biscuits for RBS executives must include digestives, but not pink wafers. One of his guests might notice that the carpet was slightly wrong, so Goodwin ordered it to be ripped up and replaced, at a cost of £100 per square yard. His employees were reminded that he was their capricious lord, whose lives were his to control.

As an amateur psychologist could have predicted, Goodwin believed he could find fortune in the future by sticking to the strategies that had turned him from a provincial banker into a global player. The result was a bank collapse that made the failure of Bank of Credit and Commerce International seem like a blip.

Goodwin's insistence on making deals had transformed the culture of his corporation. RBS was once a bank whose conservatism was a source of pride to Scots. Before Goodwin, it specialised in 'value' banking. It would try to spot the best asset-financing opportunities – by setting up the Tesco Bank, say, or developing Canary Wharf – and profit when the deals came good. The trouble with value banking in a bonus-hungry City was that even if a bank invested early in a good venture, it would take years for the profits to come through. Equally depressingly, it would have to set capital aside as a regulatory cost in case the deal turned sour. Dealing in derivatives and using securities as collateral was much more satisfying. Bankers at RBS and everywhere else could claim their deals created no regulatory costs, and their banks did not have to hold capital against default because AAA securities were free of credit risk. Hence they could increase paper profits – and boost the bonus pot. The deals depended on everyone forgetting that the securities in question were ultimately dependent on saps in American trailer parks who had fallen for introductory teaser rates on sub-prime mortgages they would never be able to repay to buy condos whose keys they would have to return. RBS said it had 'stress tested' its securities, but like the geniuses in so many other banks, its geniuses never worked out that the securities might be worth 50p, 5p or 0p in the £1, and that they did not have the regulatory capital set aside to absorb the bad debts. 'Don't get high on your supply,' say drug dealers. As elsewhere, bankers at RBS ignored the wise advice of their colleagues in the opium-derivative markets. They did not offload the risk by selling on securities to the greater fool, but treated them as their own capital and held on to them.

Goodwin continued with his takeover binge. The battle for NatWest had made him famous, and he carried on expanding into Asia and the US at a frenetic rate. At the top of the market, just when liquidity was vanishing, he won a takeover battle against Barclays and paid £48 billion for the Dutch bank ABN AMRO, which he thought would give him a 'global platform'. The crash revealed what RBS should have known: bad debts weighed ABN down. Far from being a global platform, it was a sprawling mess of a bank with fifty-seven IT structures in eighty countries that would take years for a properly run business to integrate or even understand.

Goodwin's career ended in a scene so perfect it might have been taken from fiction. On 7 October 2008, three weeks after the collapse of Lehman Brothers had frozen the global financial markets, he stood in front of a roomful of investors in the ball-room of the Landmark Hotel near London's Marylebone station. In a thirty-minute presentation, he described the company's broad portfolio of businesses, strong balance sheet and opportu-nities for growth in Asia. Despite the turmoil in the markets, RBS remained as solid and reliable as it had always been. As he talked, word reached the hotel that the market had fallen again. A fund manager put up his hand. 'In the time that you have been speaking, your share price has fallen 35 per cent. What is going on?'

Goodwin went pale, and mumbled an answer. He cancelled his remaining meetings and rushed back to RBS's offices. A few days later the state nationalised the bank, and pumped in £37 billion from the British taxpayer. Goodwin retired with a pension pot of £16.5 million, also from the British taxpayer.

## Keep Mum, it's not so Dumb

Insiders knew. The greatest crash in the financial markets since 1929 did not come without warning. In the wake of the catastrophic loss of the jobs and homes of millions of workers, whose employers had never paid them a bonus in their lives, the previously somnolent media belatedly paid tribute to those who had tried to raise the alarm. In 2005, Raghuram Rajan of the International Monetary Fund addressed a meeting of central bankers. In the audience were Alan Greenspan of the US Federal Reserve, and Larry Summers, who along with Greenspan had done Wall Street's dirty work for it by preventing a few honourable officials in the Clinton administration from regulating the new derivatives market. Rajan's speech was prescient. He warned that derivatives and credit default swaps were providing lucrative financial incentives to bankers to take risks in the mistaken belief that the deals would never unwind.

Also mentioned in dispatches was Nouriel Roubini of New York University, who warned in 2006 that changes in economic fundamentals – real income, migration, interest rates and demographics – could not account for the surge in US property prices. America was in the grip of a speculative bubble pumped up by hot money and extraordinarily risky lending that would end with a 'nasty fall', he said. Again, his prescience was faultless.

But singling out the few – shamefully few – financiers, business journalists and economists who emerged from the early

2000s with their reputations intact is to miss a wider point. Thousands of people in banking knew the deals they were closing were dangerous, and suspected that money and egomania had turned their masters' heads. They may not have been able to predict a global liquidity crisis, but they knew that in their firms a lust for self-enrichment had replaced the principles of prudent banking. Goldman Sachs persuaded its gullible customers to invest in sub-prime securities that the company's investment bankers privately dismissed as 'crap' and 'shitty deals'. They knew. In Iceland, where a tiny population sat on a heap of volcanic rock, three banks ran up loan books of $110 billion – 850 per cent of Iceland's GDP. The official inquiry into the Icelandic financial collapse, which left every Icelandic man, woman and child nominally liable for $330,000, said that insiders were withdrawing their funds days before the bubble banks went bust. I think it is fair to say that they knew too. At RBS, everyone except Fred Goodwin knew that they were paying over the odds for ABN AMRO. As early as 2005, City analysts diagnosed that their chief was suffering from 'megalomania'. His staff did not need outsiders to tell them that. They knew from experience that he was also a sociopath, who was capable of leading their bank to ruin.

Goodwin's sociopathic tendencies seem exceptional, but if Barclays rather than NatWest had won the battle for ABN AMRO, Barclays would have collapsed, and journalists would now be writing about the character flaws of its executives. One cannot reduce the failures of management to the failures of a few bad apples that somehow ended up at the top of the sack. Instead, you have to look at the structural weaknesses of managerialism that encourage delusion. A fundamental flaw of modern capitalism is that businesses promote bombastic people. As Cameron Anderson and Sébastien Brion of the University of California, Berkeley, showed experimentally, 'In conditions where there is any ambiguity in competence and performance (which is common in organisations), overconfident individuals will be perceived as more competent by others, and attain higher levels of status, compared to individuals with more accurate self-perceptions of competence.' They think even better of themselves when they are promoted – 'If my employers say I'm a top dog, I must be' – and their elevation gives them the hiring power to surround themselves with sycophants, or 'my team', as they describe them.

The question therefore ought not to be who knew, but why so few spoke out. The answer reveals why financial institutions pose greater potential dangers to society than any other private business. The strongest link between the inequalities of wealth at the top and the destruction of the living standards of those underneath lies in the incentives the hierarchical system gives its participants to self-censor.

All bubble markets carry perverse incentives. During the dotcom bubble of the 1990s, analysts and fund managers on Wall Street and in the City who warned that worthless companies had issued bubble stocks were not thanked by their employers for their honesty, or congratulated when the crash in the dotcom market vindicated their scepticism. By staying out of the bubble, they missed the chance to profit as the bull market roared ahead. The investors who made money suspended their disbelief, feigned ecstasy about the market's prospects, and sold on before the crash. It was not enough to be right. One had to be right at the right time. The bonus culture of the first decade of the twenty-first century institutionalised financial false consciousness. Everyone in the City I interviewed emphasised that you should not just look at the money made by the alleged stars of the dealing rooms and the CEOs. All employees in a position of power or knowledge within the organisation were caught up by the determination to run risks and to jack up their bonuses. 'An ordinary risk manager or accountant at a bank can make £100,000 basic and £100,000 bonus,' said one. 'There is no way he can get that kind of money anywhere else. He is going to be as keen as the CEO on authorising risky trades.'

Suppose, though, that junior employees or indeed senior bankers realise that their managers are making catastrophic mistakes. They still have no reason to speak out. In the good years they will have pocketed salaries and bonuses. The state will not confiscate their homes and empty their accounts if their bank collapses, but will allow them to hold on to their assets and their winnings. If they have not caused trouble, they should be able to find another job in another bank. If the state coerces the taxpayer into bailing out the failed institution, they can carry on in their old job as if nothing had happened – but now drawing their salaries and bonuses at public expense. Within three years of the taxpayer bailing out RBS, two hundred of its staff were receiving million-pound bonuses. The recession, unemployment, higher taxes, reduced public services fell hard on everyone except the originators of the banking crash.

Silence in a banker's private interest brings no penalty. Speaking out in the public interest, however, would mean that he would never work in banking again. Even if he could use whistleblowing legislation – and as we have seen, that is no easy matter – the compensation he would receive would usually be one year's wages – pin money in comparison to the wealth the bank or the taxpayer would give him if he bit his tongue. Perhaps the banker could go to the regulatory authorities privately. Even assuming that they were not slumbering, his employers would find ways to force him out if they found out what he had done. And executives in rival hierarchies would ensure that he would *never work in banking again*. Therein lies the ultimate sanction. Whistleblowing in banking, and many another trade, does not mean you lose just your job, but *all other possible jobs* in your field. No rival manager would want you on his 'team', because you might expose him as you exposed his predecessor. In banking, business and the public sector, challenge one hierarchy and you challenge them all. Speaking out within the firm is equally dangerous. 'A risk manager once told me that to raise an issue that undermined the bank's multi-billion-dollar profits would have been to "sign his own death warrant", said a Wall Street derivatives trader after the crash. 'This inability to challenge trading desks generating billions in phantom profits was endemic.'

If a whistleblower had gone to journalists privately, there is no guarantee that they would have listened to him, because the same forces that were boosting high finance were destroying good financial reporting. In the 1840s, *The Times* thundered against the railway mania which ruined so many Victorian investors. In the 1990s, the *Economist* heaped scorn on the boosters of dotcom stocks, and won many admirers for its forthright journalism. In the 2000s, not one of the media organisations that covered business – not the *Wall Street Journal*, Bloomberg News, the *New York Times*, the *Economist*, *Forbes*, the *Financial Times* or, I should add, the mainstream British press and the BBC – saw a crash coming, or campaigned for a change in regulatory policy. Individual journalists served their readers well, but to pretend that the writing of Allan Sloan of *Fortune* or Gillian Tett of the *Financial Times* represented the media is like pretending that the work of Rajan and Roubini represented the collective wisdom of economists and financial analysts.

A post-mortem examination by the *Columbia Review of Journalism* noticed an alarming deterioration in the ability of reporters to investigate the wealthy and hold them to account. In the early 2000s, the American press printed much it could be proud of. Journalists found stories worthy of Upton Sinclair or Émile Zola as they exposed how Lehman, Citigroup and other Wall Street banks were throwing money at poor Americans to generate securities from sub-prime debt. The most haunting was the tale of an illiterate quarry worker who was already $1,250 in debt because he had borrowed money to buy food.

Citigroup's sub-prime subsidiary bought the debt and convinced him to refinance ten times in four years until he owed $45,000, more than half of it in fees. Repayment took more than 70 per cent of his income.

Such was the rock on which Alan Greenspan and George W. Bush built their economic miracle. Here were the 'economic fundamentals' that underlay Gordon Brown's boast that there would be 'no return to boom and bust'.

As the market went manic, it left the press behind. Wholesale fraud and forgery were rampant. Wall Street's demand for mortgages became so frenzied that managers expected female wholesale buyers to trade sex with retail brokers for securities. Bank underwriters, who approved mortgage loans, demanded bribes from wholesalers before they would pretend that the deals were prudent. Yet the American press ignored the wave of white-collar crime, and offered its readers pap pieces in which reporters praised the dynamism of CEOs and gasped like porn actresses at the size of their bonuses. Every bubble market captures journalists as it captures regulators and investors. The longer a speculative mania goes on, the more normal it seems. Journalists who ignore the euphoria that grips their colleagues and warn that the collapse will be all the worse when it comes risk hearing their editors tell them that they are bores who are not worth publishing. 'Where's the crash you promised me? Where's my story? All I can see are happy people out there working hard and making money.'

The *Columbia Review of Journalism* found other reasons for the media's inability to anticipate the crash of 2008. The decision of the Bush administration to call off the regulators, copied by Gordon Brown in Britain, was the most prominent among them. Regulators had provided reporters with leads. Once they dried up, the stories dried up as well. To anyone who worked on a newspaper in the early 2000s, however, one reason the *Review* gave for the failure of journalism rang as true as a funeral bell:

'The financial press is ... a battered and buffeted institution that in the last decade saw its fortunes and status plummet as the institutions it covered ruled the earth and bent the government.'

The instant electronic communications that allowed speculators to deal globally were destroying newspapers' business models by taking readers and advertisers away to the free sites of the Internet. A whistleblower who risked the sack and went to an old media institution with a possible story could not be sure that it would have the resources to follow the lead. The British media faced the further fear of libel actions. Fred Goodwin threatened to sue the *Sunday Times* for saying that he had wanted his own private road built from Edinburgh airport to RBS's Scottish headquarters, and had tried to jump the waiting list for membership of an elite golf club. The legal action never came to anything – the golf club backed the newspaper, and confirmed that Goodwin's 'people' had passed on words to the effect of 'Do you know who I am?' But as the decade progressed, newspapers that could see money haemorrhaging from their balance sheets could not afford to accept the costs of taking on the plutocracy's lawyers.

Nor were the British and US governments interested in learning the truth from insiders. The nominally left-wing Tony Blair, Gordon Brown and Bill Clinton, as well as the confidently right-wing George W. Bush, were certain that the best regulation of finance was less regulation.

One of the few honourable men monitoring the crazed market that followed was Paul Moore, the risk manager of the Halifax, a bank whose history tracked the decline of British self-reliance. It had once been a mutual building society formed by respectable working- and lower-middle-class families in Victorian Yorkshire to pool their savings and allow them to buy homes. Margaret Thatcher – who, contrary to myth, was the enemy of the best Victorian values – allowed the building societies' managers to enrich themselves by converting the mutuals into banks. The Halifax merged with the Bank of Scotland (which was not the same institution as the Royal Bank of Scotland, but was just as spivvishly managed), and the new company spewed out mortgages.

As its risk manager, Moore was under a legal duty to ensure it behaved prudently. He found a hyperactive sales culture. Managers rewarded sales teams if they sold mortgages, and mocked and demeaned them if they failed to persuade punters to take the bait. Moore thought that there 'must have been a very high risk if you lend money to people who have no jobs, no provable income and no assets. If you lend that money to buy an asset, which is worth the same or even less than the amount of the loan, and secure that loan on the value of that asset purchased, and then assume that asset will always rise in value, you must be pretty close to delusional. You simply don't need to be an economic rocket scientist or mathematical financial-risk-management specialist to know this.' When he tried to make the case for responsible lending, one manager told him he could never hit his sales targets if he behaved ethically. Another leaned across a desk and said, 'I warn you, don't make a fucking enemy out of me.'

Moore was a Catholic gentleman, who was educated at Ampleforth and trained as a barrister. He saw no conflict between business and morality. He went to the board and warned that its demand for sales growth at any price was putting the company at risk. The board received him warmly. A month later, the chief executive, James Crosby, called him to his office.

'I'm doing a reorganisation, and your job is being made redundant,' Moore remembered him saying.

'My job cannot be made redundant,' replied Moore. 'It is a regulatory requirement to have my job.'

'You lost the confidence of key executives and non-executives.'

'Who?' asked Moore.

'I don't have to explain myself to you,' said Crosby.

The subsequent fates of the two men encapsulate the perverse incentives the Western financial system offers. Moore left Crosby's office bewildered. 'It was a terrible shock. I felt absolutely devastated. I went outside on the street and just cried. A million thoughts going through my head. How am I going to tell my wife? How am I going to tell my kids? What are people going to think of me?'

HBOS paid him off. Not one headhunter phoned him to sound him out for a job, even though he was one of the most experienced risk managers in Britain. He had broken the *omertà* of a hierarchical culture, and rendered himself unemployable.

In his spare time, and he had plenty of spare time, Moore conducted a survey of 563 risk managers about the causes of the financial crisis. 'Most risk professionals saw the technical factors which might cause a crisis well in advance,' it concluded. 'These included easy availability of global capital, excessive leverage and accounting standards which permitted over-valuation of assets. The risks were reported, but senior executives chose to prioritise sales. That they did so is put down to individual or collective greed, fuelled by remuneration practices that encouraged excessive risk-taking. That they were allowed to do so is explained by inadequate oversight by non-executives and regulators, and organisational cultures which inhibited effective challenge to risk-taking.'

James Crosby went to Buckingham Palace to meet no less a personage than Her Majesty the Queen. Gordon Brown had instructed her to knight Crosby for his services to the financial industry, as he had asked her to knight Fred Goodwin and Alan Greenspan before him. Crosby's decision to sack Moore and carry on lending as before had been endorsed by his senior colleagues, auditors and the financial regulators. Trapped in the group-think of a bubble market, no one in a position of responsibility could guess how a strategy of borrowing on the whole-sale markets to fund an exponential growth in a bank's loan book could possibly go wrong. Fresh honours followed. Brown appointed Sir James, the manager who had sacked his risk manager for warning of risks, to the financial regulatory author-ity that was supposed to guard against risk. There Sir James remained until HBOS went bust in the crash, and Moore forced him to resign by going to Parliament to reveal all.

With millions in excessive debt and millions jobless, one might have expected a surge of protest against managerialism and hierarchy. By the autumn of 2011, the banks had received almost £1 trillion in subsidies in the form of cheap Bank of England loans and deposit and debt guarantees, given by the state on condition that they improved lending to British businesses. The banks took the money, but did not lend, because there were no easy profits or easy bonuses in business loans. The most unjustly rewarded executives in the world had wrecked Western econo-mies and shown no willingness to change their ways. Yet it never occurred to the supposedly liberal-left governments of Barack Obama and Gordon Brown to provide incentives to allow employees to speak up and speak truthfully, or to impose penal-ties on those who stayed silent. Governments did not promise to provide full compensation to bankers who revealed their corpo-rations' risky policies. They did not say that all bureaucracies, public as well as private, should allow elected workers' repre-sentatives on their boards, who might provide a fair hearing to those who suspected their managers were going haywire. They did not say that bailed-out banks should remain under account-able state control because the government could not do a worse job than the private sector. Nor was there irresistible public pressure on them to reform.

It was as if the citizens of the West did not want to know.

# *People Don't Want to Know*

For the last time, I will ask you whether you believe in freedom of speech. If you say that you do, you are in a distinct minority. In most cultures for most of history, speech has not been free. Criticise the state, and the state punished you. Break with the religion or defy the taboos of the tribe, and the tribe punished you. The powerful cannot afford to lose face, because as soon as they do, the authority of the state and the tribe begins to drain away.

The democrats of ancient Athens John Milton admired were among the few to escape from hierarchical control. Citizens exercised *parrhesia*, which translates as 'all speech', or sometimes 'true speech'. They had the right to say anything to anyone: to speak truth to power. Aristophanes mocked the city's generals and demagogic politicians. They responded with lawsuits alleging that he was slandering the *polis*. Their threats did not silence Aristophanes, but provoked him into producing more satires. It sounds stirring, until you remember that women and slaves did not enjoy the freedom allowed to male citizens, and liberty in Athens as elsewhere broke down in moments of crisis. Frightened after their defeat in the Peloponnesian War, Athenian citizens sentenced Socrates to death for corrupting the minds of the young and – inevitably, given the persistent link between religion and censorship – for refusing to honour the city's gods. For Xenophon and Plato, Socrates' nobility lay in his refusal to flee from prison when the opportunity presented itself. He preferred accepting his punishment to showing a fear of death, and died a free man.

By drinking the hemlock, Socrates was truer to the Athenian ideal than were his persecutors. 'To be happy means to be free and to be free means to be brave,' Pericles said in his oration for the Athenian war dead, as he emphasised that ancient ideas of free speech have a notion of courage behind them. Citizens of modern democracies, who are at liberty to talk about politics in whatever manner they please, may find the insistence on bravery puzzling, but if they think about how careful they are to 'respect' employers and religious militants they will understand the link.

Michel Foucault believed that speech was truly free only when the weak took a risk and used it against the strong: 'In *parrhesia*, the speaker uses his freedom and chooses frankness instead of persuasion, truth instead of falsehood or silence, the risk of death instead of life and security, criticism instead of flattery, and moral duty instead of self-interest and moral apathy.'

On Foucault's reading, the worker who criticises his boss uses *parrhesia*. The boss who shouts down his worker does not. The woman who challenges religious notions of her subordination is a *parrhesiastes*. The priest and her relatives who threaten her with ostracism or worse are not. In the ancient Chinese story, the mandarin who knows he must tell the emperor that his policies are foolish orders carpenters to build him a coffin and takes it with him to court. Pericles would have approved.

So far, so commonplace. For who does not admire the brave dissident, and who does not flatter themselves into believing that they would be equally brave in the same circumstances? It is one thing to admire, however, another to emulate. Anyone who has worked in a hierarchical organisation must have noticed that bravery is rarely on display when a superior enters the room.

The best proponents of freedom of speech do not just demand courage. They say we must not only tell truth to power, we must also tell truth to ourselves. John Stuart Mill was more concerned about the self-censorship imposed by the received opinion of Victorian Britain than by the small British state of the nineteenth century. When he says in *On Liberty* that 'If all mankind minus one, were of one opinion, and only one person were of the contrary opinion, mankind would be no more justified in silencing that one person, than he, if he had the power, would be justified in silencing mankind,' he sounds like an intellectual reducing his argument to absurdity. But Mill, who had to fight the religious conformity of his day as well as the self-satisfied culture of Britain at its imperial zenith, meant what he said. The majority had no right to use social pressure to silence arguments, because without argument it could never be sure if its opinions were true: 'Complete liberty of contradicting and disproving our opinion, is the very condition which justifies us in assuming its truth for purposes of action; and on no other terms can a being with human faculties have any rational assurance of being right.' If an argument is false, then exposure produces greater trust in truth. If it is true, or partially true, then there is no case for repressing it. Censorship was the enemy of human progress.

Mill's Victorian belief in progress strikes those who know the history of the twentieth century as naïve – although I note that parts of humanity have progressed in their treatment of women, homosexuals and the races Mill, to his shame, dismissed as 'inferior'. Victorian liberals had the advantage over us in one respect, however. Because they believed that humanity was moving forward, they had few relativist qualms about saying that liberal society was better than what had gone before, and could be better still. For Mill, the decisive argument against censorship was that 'ages are no more infallible than individuals'. Just as we now regard ideas that were the common sense of the past as false and ridiculous, so many opinions we now take for granted will strike the future as cruel and absurd. I believe that posterity will look back on our treatment of animals, and the insouciance with which we have presided over the sixth mass extinction of species in the earth's history, and shudder. Even if I am wrong, I can be certain that, for ill as well as good, the ideas that some small and derided groups of men and women are discussing now will one day be in the mainstream.

Nor was Mill's demand for openness utopian. Modern societies fit Mill's ideal in several respects. The scientific method demands that its practitioners must be prepared to accept that they are wrong. A Nobel laureate cannot rely on his status to protect him from ridicule. If the evidence does not support his theories, he must either lose face and admit his error, or exclude himself from the debate. At their best, science and the humanities follow Mill's dictum that 'The beliefs which we have most warrant for, have no safeguard to rest on, but a standing invitation to the whole world to prove them unfounded.' Democratic societies also expect their politicians to have thick skins. Elected leaders can rarely call out the police to punish those who subject them to criticism, even if their opponents are malicious, ill-informed and self-serving – as they often are. Nor, in most circumstances, can the citizens of democracies call on the law to punish those who produce arguments they regard as immoral, threatening, false or scandalous. *Parrhesia* brings many benefits. Democracy, science, intellectual excellence and the ability of citizens to live as autonomous adults depend on the right to criticise and accept criticism.

Let no one pretend that it is easy. Along with the bravery the Athenians recommended, which most people do not possess, Mill insists on an open mind, which most people do not possess either. We must not only be ready to make the powerful lose face, we must be prepared to lose face ourselves. We must not only run the risk that our country/tribe/confessional group will punish us for questioning its taboos. We must be ready to confront our own taboos, our idea of ourselves, and give people who may well be unhinged and spiteful a hearing. Few are prepared to do it. In Richard Landes' nice phrase, most societies regard self-criticism at an 'individual and collective level, as akin to chewing on broken glass', and 'have elaborate ways of enforcing silence'.

Beyond Mill lies Marx. Anyone who has engaged in political controversy will have experienced a moment of elation when they produce an argument that is so clear, so logical, so morally certain, so factually accurate and so elegantly presented that they cannot imagine how anyone could read it and fail to be convinced. It is best to get these delusions out of your system early in a writing career, because readers rarely accept arguments that challenge their interests. Even if they acknowledge at some level that there may be truth in what you say, they will blank out the unwelcome knowledge. By blanking out, I do not mean that they fall for one of the standard cognitive biases that push people into delusion and denial, simply that they decide that it is not advantageous to act on what you have said, even though they suspect that you may be right. Political information is not neutral. It always helps someone and hinders someone else. If you show that a conservative politician is corrupt or incompetent, conservatives worry that your work will help bring to power left-wing politicians who will raise their taxes. If you show that a left-wing politician is a charlatan, left-wing readers worry about the boost you are giving to conservatives who will reduce the welfare state on which they depend. During the Arab Spring, outsiders thought that once the subject peoples had risen up, the dictators would vanish like mist before the wind. As it turned out, the dictators had supporters, not just among servants of the regime who feared the loss of their jobs, but among those who preferred tyranny to chaos. China, the world's most populous country, and Russia, the world's largest country, are autocracies whose rulers convince a proportion of the population that it is better to blank out knowledge of their arbitrary abuses of power and concentrate instead on the deluge that could follow if their arbitrary power collapsed.

As we have seen, Westerners who know perfectly well that the God of the Torah, the Bible and the Koran is a fable nevertheless refuse to condemn the bigotry of the faithful for fear of provoking a violent reaction or laying themselves open to accusations of religious prejudice. Instead of denouncing oppression, they concentrate their energy on denouncing 'new atheists' and 'enlightenment fundamentalists' for voicing what they know to be true. Meanwhile, in any business or state bureaucracy, it is far from certain that a whistleblower will win the admiration of his or her colleagues. Even if their supposedly secret information is not false or is beside the point, even if they are not leaking commercially confidential information that an organisation has every right to keep private, their actions will damage their firm or institution. The scandal will delight its private or bureaucratic rivals, and in extreme cases threaten the whistleblowers' colleagues' income or jobs.

Employers, like kings, dictators, politicians, bishops, rabbis, imams, priests, civil servants, judges and censors, can urge their fellow citizens to shut up and forget for fear of the consequences. No one should be surprised at the lack of demand for free speech in the workplace. Seeing the arrogant brought down is very satisfying, but when the exposure of your boss entails the loss of your job, the pleasure soon wanes.

Given the political, cultural, psychological and economic forces ranged against freedom of speech and freedom of the press, the wonder of free societies is not that they are rare, but that they exist at all. In these circumstances, one might have hoped a country that boasted of being a bastion of liberty would have protected its precious inheritance.

# SIX

# A Town Called Sue

TOM CRUISE: *You made me look stupid! I'm gonna sue you too!*
STAN: *Well fine! Go ahead and sue me!*
TOM CRUISE: *I will! I'll sue you … in England!*

*SOUTH PARK,*
'TRAPPED IN THE CLOSET' (2005)

The threat of sexual violence hangs over *Chinatown*, the last film Roman Polanski was to make in Hollywood. Jack Nicholson plays Jake Gittes, a private detective who thinks he has seen it all. In the best *noir* tradition, a beautiful and mysterious woman comes to his office. Evelyn Mulwray says she wants to hire him to follow her husband, an official with the local water company. She suspects he is having an affair, and Gittes thinks he has a simple case. He realises that he does not when the real Evelyn Mulwray appears and tells him that the first woman was an impostor engaged by her husband's enemies – rich men, led by the monstrous Noah Cross, who are creating a desert in the mountain valleys east of LA by diverting the water supply. They intend to buy out the parched farmers cheaply, then turn on the sluices and enjoy possession of valuable real estate. They sent a fake Evelyn to the detective's office because they need to find and silence Mulwray, who knows too much about their plot.

Greed is not the only sin on display. Noah Cross is Evelyn Mulwray's father. She tells Gittes he raped her when she was fifteen, and left her pregnant. He now wants to find his daughter/granddaughter, and rape her too. In the dismal finale, despairing even by the standards of the post-Vietnam 'new Hollywood' of 1974, Gittes fails to expose the criminals or to save Evelyn's daughter. Cross seizes the child with the assistance of police officers, who shoot Evelyn Mulwray dead, and tell the powerless Gittes to forget what he has seen.

The film ends with a string of quotes that anticipate Polanski's later career, and the careers of men richer and nastier than Polanski. 'I don't blame myself,' Cross tells Gittes, as he admits to incest. 'You see, Mr Gittes, most people never have to face the fact that at the right time and the right place, they're capable of *anything.*'

Gittes plays with that thought. 'He's rich!' he says, as he begins to make sense of the corruption he is witnessing. 'Do you understand? He thinks he can get away with *anything.*'

Sex and money were pertinent themes in Polanski's life. Dandyish and talented, he enjoyed the Swinging Sixties. His marriage in 1968 to the beautiful actress Sharon Tate – star of his daft but appealing caper movie *The Fearless Vampire Killers* – was one of the great parties of the fashionable London of the day. If one had to fix a moment when the swinging stopped and the sixties turned rancid, the night of 9 August 1969, when Charles Manson's 'family' went berserk in Polanski's Hollywood home, could be it. Manson was a petty criminal who moved into Haight-Ashbury, San Francisco's bohemian quarter. He found that babbling about the joys of drugs and free love attracted a large following of counter-cultural drifters and that perennial type of middle-class girl whose revolt against parental authority consists of a search for more domineering masters than her parents had ever been. As well as worshipping big daddy and agreeing to subject themselves to his sexual demands, 'family' members ticked the boxes on the checklist of late-sixties radical chic. 'The Karma is turning, it's blackie's turn to be on top,' Manson told his followers. 'The cities are going to be mass hysteria, and the piggies won't know what to do, and the system will fall and the black man will take over.' Black power would be short-lived, however, because Manson, the true ruler of the world, would emerge from the chaos and 'scratch blackie's fuzzy head and kick him in the butt, and tell him to go pick cotton. It would be our world then. There would be no one else, except us and our black servants.'

As a prelude to Armageddon, Manson's followers went to Polanski's isolated mansion, cut the telephone lines and slaughtered everyone inside for no reason at all. The heavily pregnant Sharon Tate's last words were, 'Please, I don't want to die. I want to live. I want to have my baby. I want to have my baby.' Her killers showed her no mercy, and inscribed 'PIG' in her blood on the front door.

For conservatives, the Manson murders were an overdue comeuppance for everything they loathed about their permissive age. The police regarded Polanski as a suspect. The press treated him abysmally. Reporters asked him whether his wife was having an affair, and one suggested that he might have arranged her murder to ingratiate himself with occult friends. One newspaper ran the headline 'Live Freaky, Die Freaky'. The dead were not the victims of a psychopathic cult leader and his followers, but of their and Polanski's promiscuity.

After all that distress and humiliation, Polanski appeared to have known too much suffering. As a child he had survived the Kraków ghetto. He had grown up in the drab dictatorship of communist Poland. He had come to America and seen a jeering press blame him for the murder of his wife and unborn child. He was entitled to a little slack.

The forty-three-year-old Polanski began to pull on the rope when he had an affair with the fifteen-year-old Nastassja Kinski in 1976, and hosted 'children's parties' for his new love. Explaining himself later to Martin Amis, he said, 'Fucking, you see, and the young girls. Judges want to fuck young girls. Juries want to fuck young girls – *everyone* wants to fuck young girls!' He tugged harder when he decided to photograph 'sexy, pert' thirteen- and fourteen-year-olds for a 'gentlemen's magazine'. And he gave himself enough rope to hang himself when he raped a child in 1977.

Polanski met Samantha Gailey's mother in an LA nightclub, and offered to get her daughter into *Vogue*. When he had secured possession of the thirteen-year-old, he took her to Jack Nicholson's mansion. He gave her a glass of champagne and told her to take her top off. In her subsequent testimony to a California grand jury, she did not come across as a 'sexy, pert' Lolita but a frightened child, miles out of her depth.

Polanski gave her Quaaludes, a relaxant, and told her to go into a nearby bedroom and lie down, she told a grand jury.

'I was going, "No, I think I better go home," because I was afraid. So I just went and I sat down on the couch.'

'What were you afraid of?' asked the prosecutor.

'Him. He sat down beside me and asked me if I was OK.'

'What did you say, if anything?'

'No.'

'What did he say?'

'He goes, "Well, you'll be better." And I go, "No, I won't. I have to go home."'

'What happened then?'

'He reached over and he kissed me. And I was telling him, "No," you know, "Keep away."'

Polanski began to engage in oral sex. 'I was ready to cry. I was kind of – I was going, "No. Come on. Stop it." But I was afraid … he goes, "Are you on the pill?" And I went, "No." And he goes, "When did you last have your period?" And I said, "I don't know. A week or two. I'm not sure."'

'And what did he say?'

'He goes, "Come on. You have to remember." And I told him I didn't.'

Polanski had heard all he needed to know. The girl could not remember when she last had a period, and had told him she was not on the pill. So, she alleged, he decided to sodomise her.

If you happen to know any thirteen-year-old girls, the final scene is the most convincing. Instead of running away and raising the alarm, Samantha obediently returned to Polanski's car after the assault, and sat and cried while she waited for him to drive her home.

Polanski arrived and said, 'Don't tell your mother about this and don't tell your boyfriend either,' she told the jury. 'He said something like, "This is our secret."

'And I went, "Yeah."'

When Samantha's mother saw the pictures Polanski had taken of her semi-naked daughter, she called the police. A grand jury charged him with giving a drug to a minor, committing a lewd act upon a person less than fourteen, rape of a minor, rape by use of a drug, oral copulation and sodomy. As so often in rape cases, the victim did not want to testify. To spare her a cross-examination, and the coverage of the salivating media, the prosecution allowed Polanski to make a plea bargain. He would admit statutory rape of a minor in return for the state dropping the other five charges. The judge sent Polanski to prison for a psychiatric evaluation before sentencing. Once free, Polanski and his lawyers convinced themselves that the judge was preparing to give him a long sentence to appease a press that was running pictures of him chatting in bars with attractive women.

Christopher Sandford, Polanski's biographer, could find no evidence that the judge intended to renege on a deal to keep Polanski's sentence short, but Polanski did not trust the court, and other biographers have said that he had reason to be suspicious. Instead of returning to face his punishment, he fled to

France, where he had citizenship. The French would not extradite him. If, however, he entered a country with a stiffer extradition treaty with the United States, the local police could arrest and deport him to face the wrath of American judges, who are not at their most lenient when they sentence fugitives from justice.

Hollywood forgave him, and the French loved him. In his first days in France, 'when he strolled outside on the Champs-Élysées, a large crowd invariably gathered to applaud him. The men signified their approval by clapping. The women by jostling among themselves to touch his hem, and frequently much more.' *Le Matin* said Polanski was a victim of America's 'excessively prudish petite bourgeoisie'. Others compared him to Alexander Solzhenitsyn and Nelson Mandela.

Treated as a star and a victim, Polanski never showed regret for his crime. In 1988, Samantha Gailey sued him. He paid out a large sum, and in return she said that she wanted the case dropped so she could get on with her life. But the law does not allow the private resolution of criminal prosecutions. Polanski remained an exile from Hollywood. Whenever his name came up, he could count on someone saying that his considerable artistic merits notwithstanding, he remained a self-confessed rapist on the run from justice. There seemed to be no way he could escape his past and silence those who wanted to drag up the old unpleasantness in Jack Nicholson's mansion, until 2002, when *Vanity Fair* ran a long feature on Elaine's, the favourite restaurant of New York's artistic old guard. Among the stories regulars told about its good old days was an anecdote from Lewis Lapham, a left-wing essayist. What with its artistic clientèle, Lapham had learned to leave prudishness behind when he went through Elaine's doors. Still, a scene from 1969 stuck in his mind. Polanski had entered Elaine's shortly after the murder of Sharon Tate, Lapham remembered. He made a beeline for a 'Swedish beauty' sitting next to Lapham.

'Polanski pulled up a chair and inserted himself between us, immediately focusing his attention on the beauty, inundating her with his Polish charm. Fascinated by his performance, I watched as he slid his hand inside her thigh and began a long, honeyed spiel which ended with the promise, "And I will make another Sharon Tate out of you."'

Polanski had had enough of the attacks. He announced from France that he would sue *Vanity Fair* for libel.

But how could he? An important objection that I think only writers will grasp was that the magazine had not set out to attack Polanski. *Vanity Fair* buried the anecdote near the end of a long, star-struck piece about a fashionable New York restaurant. Polanski now wanted the legal system to focus on a few sentences – to magnify them as if they were bugs under a microscope – and ignore the likelihood that most readers would have skim-read them, if they had read them at all. Every fact in a work of non-fiction ought to be correct, but proving the veracity of an anecdote from a generation back is formidably hard. All a writer can say is that he or she checked with people who were there at the time. *Vanity Fair* should have checked with Polanski. But he would have denied it, as everyone denies unflattering stories.

A stronger objection was that the story may have been wrong, and Lapham's memory of the incident may have been false. He was certain that it was not, and another witness remembered the model asking Polanski to leave. *Vanity Fair* later admitted getting the date of the incident wrong – the alleged encounter with the blonde took place after Sharon Tate's funeral, not before it, as the magazine had said. More than thirty years after the event, the Swedish beauty said that all she could remember was that 'Roman Polanski came over to the table when I was eating and it was as if he tried to say something but he didn't ... He just stared at me for ages.'

In normal circumstances, falsely saying that a man propositioned a woman just after the murder of his wife would be a cruel slur, even if a journalist made it in a throwaway paragraph. The claimant would have the right to demand compensation for damage to his reputation and a correction. But Polanski later admitted that he had started having casual sex with women within a month of his wife's murder, so he could not claim that it was libellous to suggest that he would have made a pass at the time. In the end, it was not the alleged pass but the alleged chat-up line that was the sole defamatory issue at stake.

It may be a terrible thing to say of a bereaved husband that he used his dead wife's name to entice another woman into bed, but why was it such a terrible thing to say about Polanski? Libel law protects men and women of good reputation. How could a man who had pleaded guilty to the statutory rape of a minor, after a thirteen-year-old girl had accused him of getting her alone, giving her drinks and drugs and, after checking the date of her period, anally raping her, maintain that he had a reputation on matters sexual that was worthy of the law's protection? Any sensible judge would say that he could not possibly give Polanski damages. Even if the offending lines were false, Polanski had no good reputation to lose.

There was a further logistical difficulty. *Vanity Fair* published in New York. But if Polanski had gone to America to sue, the police would have arrested him as a fugitive from justice and sent him to face a vengeful judge in California.

His plan would have been hopeless, were there not one jurisdiction he could turn to. A legal system that strained its sinews and besmirched its country's good name to help rich men who thought they could get away with *anything*.

## Writing in Stilted English

Nothing destroys clichés about the gentle temperament of the British so thoroughly as reading what the British read. In political journalism, the British pick their side and line up their targets. Right-wingers inflame prejudices against gypsies, immigrants and all public-sector workers except the police and the armed forces. Left-wingers inflame prejudices against social conservatives, Jews, and all members of the upper and upper-middle classes except the public-sector great and good. Both suspect the white poor. The right regard them as scroungers, who steal the money of the middle classes, either by breaking into their homes or by taking their taxes in benefit cheques. The left regard them as sexist and racist homophobes.

The chavs or the toffs, the niggers or the yids – the thuggish British journalist never forgets that hate sells better than sex.

Away from politics, the popular press keeps millions happy with gossip, soft-core pornography, health scares and sport. Its journalists work with the sneer of the sadist on their lips. The *Daily Mail*, whose online paper is one of the most visited news sites in the world, specialises in running cruel examinations of women in the public eye. They can never do anything right. They are too fat or too thin, too old or too young, too pretty or too plain, too fertile or too barren, too promiscuous or too frigid. To find stories on celebrities or anyone else in the news, national papers hacked the phones of their targets. The main player in the criminal enterprise was Rupert Murdoch's News International, whose quasi-monopoly control of the privately owned media ensured that elected British leaders debased themselves and their country by bending the knee to the tycoon. Initially, the police backed away from mounting a full investigation into the hacking scandal that might have brought the perpetrators to justice. Some officers were frightened that Murdoch's papers would turn on them, and the suborned politicians would not defend the rule of law. Others were taking bribes from reporters in return for information. Yet more were dining with newspaper executives and looking forward to casual work with the Murdoch press after their retirement. The media company and the police got away with blaming the scandal on a 'rogue' royal correspondent of the *News of the World* and a private detective he hired. The police were forced to reopen the case by questions from Labour MPs, and dogged reporting of a story everyone else thought was dead by the *Guardian* – which I should say in the interests of transparency is the sister paper of my employers at the *Observer*. The truth began to trickle out that men in Murdoch's pay (and the employees of other newspapers) had hacked thousands of phones. No trick was too contemptible for them to pull. They hacked into the phones of the families of dead soldiers, the parents of murdered schoolgirls and of the victims of the 7/7 Islamist atrocity. When the *Guardian* revealed that they had hacked the phone of Milly Dowler, a teenage girl who had been abducted and murdered, and deleted voicemail messages that might have helped the police to identify her killer, the public outcry was such that Murdoch was forced to close the *News of the World* to save his wider business interests – which include the publishers of this book, I should add in the interests of further transparency.

The sincerity of the public's outrage was open to doubt. The *News of the World* had been Britain's most popular newspaper because it gave its audience what it wanted. When typical British readers tossed it aside to snuggle up with a good book, they did not bury their noses in works of moral improvement. Often they reached for one of the many detective novels that competed to give the nastiest accounts imaginable of the abuse of women. After reading fantasies of men imprisoning, binding, gagging, stringing up, raping, slicing, burning, blinding, beating, eating, starving, suffocating, stabbing, boiling and burying women alive, one critic on a London literary magazine gave up. She refused to review any more crime novels, because 'each psychopath is more sadistic than the last and his victims' sufferings are described in detail that becomes ever more explicit'. Popular non-fiction was little different. In the first decade of the 2000s, 'misery memoirs' were the surprise bestsellers of the book trade.

The purportedly true stories of abuse 'survivors' spared the reader nothing in their accounts of bestial violence against children.

Compare today's prurience with the gentility of the past. In the shock they caused and the voyeuristic interest they provoked, the British equivalent of the Manson murders of 1969 was the 'Moors murders' of 1963–65. On 7 May 1966, the morning after the jury convicted Myra Hindley and Ian Brady of murdering five children and burying their bodies in the hills outside Manchester, readers had to stare hard at the front page of *The Times* to find the news. The lead story was a less than gripping piece about the then Home Secretary visiting the US to discover what lessons, if any, he could learn about law enforcement. The second lead was an account of HM Government's difficulties with the white settler revolt in Rhodesia. Squeezed between them, and filling about half of one column of a seven-column broadsheet, was a curt summation of the case. *The Times* gave no details of the sadism involved. So disdainful was its editor of sensational journalism that he gave equal prominence to a speculative story on whether a ban by the Irish government on the movement of horses might hit the English racing season.

The popular press was more forthcoming, as you might expect. In the frantic search for a scoop, editors hired helicopters to follow the police investigation, and bought the stories of witnesses. But the reporting was restrained, almost refined, and written in better prose than journalists on most serious papers can manage today. The police had found a suitcase Hindley and Brady had hidden in a left-luggage locker, with pornographic pictures of Lesley Ann Downey, one of their victims, and a tape of the child pleading for her life. No one who heard it in court ever forgot the experience. The *News of the World* of the 1960s did not dwell on the horror. It confined itself to saying, 'There were sixteen minutes of tape with a child – her mother has said it was Lesley Ann's voice – screaming and whimpering and crying, "Please God, help me … please, please." And there was a woman's voice – Myra Hindley's say police who have heard her at interviews – saying "Shut up or I will forget myself and hit you one." Throughout these sixteen minutes there was not another sound in the court, not a cough, not a whisper.'

Beyond that description, there was no attempt to intrude on the girl's last moments. It never occurred to the paper to run the contents of the tape in full.

Reading the old clippings, I felt an ache for the lost age of popular literacy, when the *News of the World* could fit almost as many words onto a page as *The Times*, and expect its working-class audience to appreciate fine writing. Everyone at some point must feel an equal regret for the loss of British reticence and the coarsening of public life. The foul-mouthed celebrities on the television, the Peeping Toms of the tabloid press, the mob-raising screamers of talk radio and Twitter, and the emotionally incontinent blabbermouths who reveal their 'secrets' when they have nothing worth hiding, are representatives of the collapse of the values of the old Britain, which *The Times* and the *News of the World* once held to in their different ways.

The compensation for the decline in civility is the decline of deference. Investigative journalism did not exist in the 1960s. The colleagues of my first editor regarded him as a brave pioneer because he had revealed how detectives had beaten a confession out of a suspect. Local newspapers had never given the police such a hard time before. The rich of the day could operate without scrutiny. Business journalism consisted of bland reports on companies' results, rather than investigations into whether those results were genuine, while celebrities could present entirely false pictures of themselves to their fans.

Britons' automatic deference to monarchy, Parliament, Church and peerage has gone, and good riddance to it. We are meant to have become a more raucous and bawdy society, but a more honest society as well. So we are, in all respects except the one that matters most.

At their best, journalists expose the crimes of the powerful, and there were plenty of powerful people worthy of examination in the Britain of the early 2000s. London was awash with money, as it competed with Manhattan to be the hub of global finance. The despots challenged in the Arab Spring channelled their stolen wealth through the City. Oligarchs from around the world flocked to Britain because it offered them the rule of law, protection from assassins, luxury stores, art galleries, Georgian town houses, country estates and public schools that could train their sons in the gentlemanly style. If journalists tried to do what they should do and investigate them, Britain also gave them a further privilege: the power to enforce a censorship that the naïve supposed had vanished with the repressions of the old establishment. Among the many attractions London offered the oligarchs was a legal profession that served them as attentively as the shop girls in the Harrods food hall.

With an aristocratic prejudice against freedom of speech, the judges imposed costs and sanctions on investigative journalism which would have been hard to endure in the best of times, but were unbearable after the Internet had undermined the media's business models. Instead of aiming its guns at the worst of British writing, the law of libel aimed at the bravest.

The system the judges upheld had its roots in feudalism. Edward I, one of England's most barbarous kings, introduced the crime of *scandalum magnatum* while he colonised Wales, hammered the Scots and expelled the Jews. 'Henceforth none be so hardy to tell or publish any false News or Tales, whereby discord, or occasion of discord or slander may grow between the King and his People, or the Great Men of the Realm,' Edward declared in the Statute of Westminster of 1275. Although the statute fell into disuse, and was overtaken by the libel law Star

Chamber used in the 1630s, an element of the feudal concern to defend the mighty remains in English libel law and the laws of many former British colonies.

Contrary to natural justice and the Common Law, the burden of proof is on the defendant. Once a claimant has shown that the words in question are likely to provoke hatred, ridicule or contempt, the alleged libeller has to prove that what he or she has written is true, or a fair comment based on true information. English libel law, and the laws of Scotland, Ireland and all the former British colonies that take it as its guide, works on the assumption that a gentleman's word is his bond, and that anyone who impugns his honour must prove his case.

A second archaic quirk makes wealthy litigants appreciate English law all the more. The judiciary treat a gentleman's reputation as if it were his personal property, the defilement of which is a wrong in itself. Libel and trespass on land are the only torts the law says are actionable *per se*. A claimant does not have to prove that a writer has caused him to suffer financial loss or personal injury, any more than a landlord has to prove that a trespasser has damaged his land. The claimant can still sue even if no one has formed a bad opinion of him or read and remembered the offending words.

'The only purpose for which power can be rightfully exercised over any member of a civilized community, against his will, is to prevent harm to others,' said John Stuart Mill. The English law does not believe him. A litigant does not need to prove that he has been harmed. It is sufficient that the author has published the offending words in question, and that they *may* make a person or persons unknown think less of him.

The judges invoke a quasi-feudal precedent to justify compensating claimants. The Duke of Brunswick's Rule of 1849 states that every republication of an offending statement is actionable. It says much about how the dead hand of the past weighs on my country that I need to explain that twenty-first-century law takes its lead from the case of a corpulent and despised German princeling, whom the good people of Brunswick had had the sense to throw out in the revolutions of 1830. In 1849, while living in exile in Paris, the duke sent his servant to the offices of the *Weekly Dispatch* in London to get an old copy of the paper, which contained an unflattering article about him. The six-year time limit on bringing a libel action had long passed. The offending issue was gathering dust in an archive. But the helpful judiciary obliged His Grace by deciding that because his manservant had been able to purchase a back copy of a seventeen-year-old newspaper, the publishers had repeated the original libel, even though the duke himself had instigated the repetition of that libel by sending his manservant to buy the back copy in the first place. No precedent could be more dangerous in the age of the Internet, when readers can access blog posts, Twitter feeds, Facebook pages and online newspaper articles afresh with every new day. Because of a case from the 1840s, any one of the millions of people who have published on the Web could be sued for something they wrote years before.

To many onlookers, the law's biases seem reasonable. If writers produce a character assassination, what is wrong with the law requiring them to justify their words? As for putting a price on the value of a good reputation, who can measure the damage caused by smears and innuendos?

English lawyers are fond of quoting Iago's lines to Othello:

> Who steals my purse steals trash; 'tis something, nothing;
> 'Twas mine, 'tis his, and has been slave to thousands;
> But he that filches from me my good name
> Robs me of that which not enriches him,
> And makes me poor indeed.

They forget that Iago is a liar, and never admit that the English law does not confine itself to defending the reputation of men and women of good standing, but will come to the aid of any criminal who is not behind bars.

In the 1980s, the most fevered writ-generator was Robert Maxwell, a conceited and crooked media mogul. After fleeing to Britain from his native Czechoslovakia, he established business relationships with the communist dictators of the old Eastern Europe. In Britain, the Department of Trade and Industry said after one of his many dubious takeovers, 'he is not in our opinion a person who can be relied on to exercise proper stewardship of a publicly quoted company'. This condemnation, and his warm relations with tyrannies, did not prevent Maxwell from bombarding newspapers and book publishers with writs threatening to take anyone who impugned his reputation to the courts. 'His purpose was to make it impossible for any editor of a newspaper or book to consider writing about him critically without considering the enormous cost both financially and in time wasted that would entail,' said his unauthorised biographer Tom Bower. 'He would come down on them with the force of a bulldozer.' The scores of writs had their effect. When presented with leads, editors wondered whether they wanted the trouble and expense following them would entail. Those who took him on learned that sources from inside the Maxwell organisation, who had spoken to their reporters off the record, were too frightened of losing their jobs to appear in court, and that Maxwell was not above bribing witnesses outside his employ to change their testimony.

The law takes no account of the difficulty of getting on-the-record affidavits from sources in dictatorial corporations, and offers another benefit to litigants that Maxwell took full advantage of. The ordinary citizen might suppose that if a newspaper or a book publisher ran an unflattering portrait of a wealthy man, the wealthy man would sue the newspaper or book publisher. It was likely to have the resources to pay for damage to his fine reputation, after all. But nothing in English law stops the wealthy man suing the author personally, so his or her home and savings would be on the line unless they retract and grovel, or the shops that distribute books and newspapers. Maxwell calculated that the owners of bookshops or newsagents would not stock a controversial work if standing up for the freedom of publication might cost them money, and they had other titles to place on their shelves. His tactic of suing bookshops was not as violent a means of reprisal as the Islamists' tactic of hitting them with bombs, but the intent was the same.

Which is not to say that Maxwell eased up on his direct attacks on publishers. He targeted *Private Eye*, the most courageous British news magazine, and won colossal damages from the courts. The *Eye* had the distinction of receiving his last writ, in 1991, after it reported suspicions that Maxwell was 'gambling' with his employees' pensions. Sources in his corporation told its journalists that Maxwell was reducing their benefits and sacking those who spoke out. His lawyers maintained that it was outrageous to suggest that Maxwell was a criminal, who was raiding the employee pension fund to shore up the share price of his ailing businesses. Maxwell had 'suffered a very serious injury to his feelings and reputation', they said, as they demanded an apology with the usual damages.

A few weeks later, Maxwell either fell or jumped from his yacht. His businesses went bankrupt, and his employees found that he was indeed a criminal who had stolen £727 million from their pension fund.

The writs Maxwell issued against Tom Bower, *Private Eye*, the *Sunday Times*, the *Independent* and others were directed at stories covering his business activities. All those stories turned out to be true, or on the right lines. If they had a fault, it was that they were nowhere near as scathing as they should have been. The judges and law officers showed no regrets. They never paused to ask why the English law had punished investigations into a man who had never had a good name, and always deserved a worse one.

In 1998, the English judiciary hit its nadir when it allowed David Irving, one of Europe's leading neo-Nazis, to sue the American historian Deborah Lipstadt for saying that he manipulated evidence to 'prove' that the Holocaust had never happened. Penguin defended its author, as it had defended Salman Rushdie, and had to spend several million pounds, money it never recovered. After a full trial, the learned judge – one Mr Justice Gray – announced that in his considered opinion, and after weighing all the relevant evidence, he had concluded that the Nazis were indeed a bad lot who had gassed millions of Jews at Auschwitz and elsewhere, and that Irving and others who said they had not were likely to be liars.

Where would the English be without their lawyers to guide them?

The law's readiness to censor writers and order their publishers to pulp books and pay costs and fines weakens conservative claims that England and the rest of Europe are afflicted with an over-mighty 'liberal judiciary'. The judges are not true liberals, but the successors to the aristocratic Whigs of pre-democratic Britain. William Hazlitt defined a Whig as neither liberal nor conservative, but 'a coward to both sides of the question, who dare not be a knave nor an honest man, but is a sort of whiffling, shuffling, cunning, silly, contemptible, unmeaning negation of the two'. Modern judges prove Hazlitt's point for him. After presiding over the false convictions of the Birmingham Six, the Guildford Four and other innocent men and women in the terrorist trials of the 1970s, they were obliged to learn to uphold the rights of defendants to fair trials in the criminal courts. However, when citizens are not prisoners of the state, but are exercising their right to be full participants in the deliberations of society, they shut them up. British and European 'liberalism' is uncomfortable with freedom of speech. Liberal judges do not have the instinctive democratic belief that citizens in open societies should be free to argue without restraint. Instead, they think they have a duty to intervene in open arguments, invariably on the wrong side. They subvert the right to freedom of speech protected by the First Amendment of the American Constitution, sanctified by custom in Britain and enshrined in the European Convention on Human Rights, as they try to create a journalism that never runs the risk of provoking the anger of the wealthy.

A prissy nervousness afflicts writers when they tackle people who can afford to sue: plutocrats, banks and corporations; or those who have a reputation for using no-win, no-fee lawyers to sue even if they are not personally wealthy themselves: front organisations for Jamaat-e-Islami and the Muslim Brotherhood, alternative-health cranks and other vexatious litigants. The people writers ought to have gone into journalism to scrutinise are the very people the law requires them to treat with exaggerated caution. Instead of writing about them with the required vigour, we switch to stilted English and pepper our pieces with 'we are not suggesting thats' – when we want to suggest just that – 'allegedlys', 'could be saids', 'mays', 'seems', 'some may thinks' and 'appears', inside ugly sentences that are hacked back by lawyers; when, that is, they are published at all. In newspaper offices, lawyers are powerful figures who start to worry as soon as reporters mention a litigious man. Often they spike pieces, saying that no amount of cuts and caveats can avert the risk that a plutocrat will begin lengthy and expensive litigation before a hostile judiciary.

The service the courts provided the Dutch base metals and oil trading company Trafigura best illustrates the readiness of the legal profession to censor on behalf of the wealthy. Trafigura had hired a ship to deliver toxic waste to Amsterdam in July 2007. Waste-disposal companies tested the load, noted its foul stench, and refused to touch it unless Trafigura gave them a generous fee. Trafigura would not pay, and went round the world to find a country willing to take it. The Estonians and Nigerians turned the ship away. Finally, it docked in the poverty-stricken Ivory Coast, where dealers took the waste at a bargain rate, and did not treat it but dumped it. Many people became sick, and several died.

Trafigura said the waste could not have caused the suffering. When the BBC contradicted its account, Trafigura sued for libel. The BBC backed down, and withdrew any allegation that the toxic waste dumped in Africa had caused deaths. That would have been the end of the controversy in Britain, had not Trafigura had a draft internal report – the 'Minton Report' – whose authors said that on the 'limited information' they had received the harmful chemicals 'likely to be present' in the waste included sodium hydroxide, cobalt phthalocyanine sulphonate, coker naphtha, thiols, sodium alkanethiolate, sodium hydrosulphide, sodium sulphide, dialkyl disulphides and hydrogen sulphide.

The report was not the final word on the dumping. Other experts had reached different conclusions, as experts are wont to do. When the case for compensating the alleged victims came to court, lawyers for the sick Ivorians could not prove that the waste had harmed them, but Trafigura could not prove that it had not, and paid compensation without admitting liability. The contest between the two sides ended in a tie. Nevertheless, news organisations facing the prospect of legal action, and the families of the dead living with ongoing grief, would have liked to have read what the report's author had to say.

To stop the press publishing the findings, Trafigura hit the media with that ingenious legal invention, the super-injunction: a court order so secret it is a contempt of court to reveal that it even exists. Paul Farrelly, a Labour MP, ignored the judge's ruling and tabled a question in Parliament, which stated that Trafigura's solicitors had secured an injunction from the High

Court to prevent publication of the report on the 'alleged dumping of toxic waste in the Ivory Coast'. Trafigura's solicitors told
journalists that reporting what the MP had told Parliament, and
mentioning the 'existence of the injunction would, absent a vari-
ation to the order', place them in contempt of court.

It is worth pausing to contemplate how many principles the
English legal system was prepared to overturn. The civil wars of
the seventeenth century, in which John Milton and his contemporaries lined up, concluded with the settlement enshrined in
the 1689 Bill of Rights. It asserted that Members of Parliament
had absolute freedom of speech, and no monarch or court could
interfere with their proceedings. The radicals of the eighteenth
century fought and won a hard battle to allow the press to report
Parliament, so that MPs' constituents could know what their
supposedly accountable representatives were saying on their
behalf.

To no avail. Only a public outcry forced a U-turn, and pushed
Trafigura's lawyers into saying that the injunction had not 'been
obtained for the purpose of restricting publication of a report
of proceedings in Parliament'. Just all other reporting of the
Minton Report's contents.

The belief that 'If you are telling the truth, you have nothing
to fear' does not apply in England. The courts say that you are
guilty until you prove yourself innocent. They take no account
of the difficulty in persuading confidential sources to place their
careers at risk by taking the witness stand. They tell the claimant
that he does not need to prove that he has suffered damage or
harm. They do not consider whether the claimant has a good
reputation the law is obliged to defend. They are presided over
by judges drawn from the pseudo-liberal upper-middle class
who have no instinctive respect for freedom of speech or gut
understanding of its importance. The judges are willing to look
on as claimants go for individual writers, who cannot afford to
fight back, or retailers, who have no commercial interest in

fighting back. The single concession they make to the democratic age is the so-called 'Reynolds Defence', that allows editors
to defend statements they cannot prove are true, if they can
nevertheless prove that they acted responsibly and in the public
interest. I will not detain you with the details of how an editor can show he has acted in the public
interest. The Reynolds Defence carries so many conditions it is
as if the lawyers designed it to fail. The senior judiciary complain
that the judges in the libel courts disregard what protections it
offers, and few writers or defence lawyers think it worth their
while invoking its terms.

Scandalous though these barriers to justice are, they would
not be so intimidating if the English legal system had not given
a further and overwhelming advantage to the moneyed classes.
Civilised countries must find ways for citizens to take action
against poisonous writers who cause real harm. They must insist
on prominent corrections, and if editors refuse to carry them,
the law must punish them. But if justice is to be done, it must be
speedy, or the powerful will be able to close down stories for
years. And it must be cheap, otherwise most members of the
public will not be able to protect their reputations, and most
publishers will be unable to afford the risk of defending their
work, and will fall into silence.

In Britain, money buys silence. The cost of libel actions in
England and Wales is 140 times higher than the European average. If you lose a case, lawyers operating on a no-win, no-fee
contract force you to pay damages, your costs, your assailant's
costs, a 'success fee' for the victorious lawyers – which doubles
their real costs – and a payment to cover insurance bills. In 2010,
Lord Justice Jackson added these together, and estimated that
the costs of civil litigation in England could amount to ten times
the damages the court awarded.

A chill descended on English writing as publishers realised
that punitive costs could cripple them. Libel law became the

strangest branch of English jurisprudence. It was a law that lawyers hardly ever tested in court. Libel judges had to find other work for much of the year. The overwhelming majority of libel actions never ended in a hearing to determine if a work was true or its opinions fair, but remained hidden from public view. Publishers quietly settled, coughed up and withdrew offending material rather than run the risk of facing extortionate bills. Beyond these cases of censorship lay the unknowable number of writers and publishers who self-censored. As when you contemplate religious censorship, you must always think of the books that were never written, and the investigations that were never begun, because of the overweening power of money.

Lawyers began to wonder about the point of defamation law. The London media solicitor David Allen Green said, 'Almost all the statements which can actually damage a person's reputation – employers' references, credit searches, complaints to police and regulatory authorities – are covered by "qualified privilege".' The person making the statement was free to defame – regardless of the damage caused – 'as long as he or she is not being malicious'. Police officers could have records that falsely suggested that you were a child abuser, but you could not sue them. A credit agency could erroneously claim that you were a serial debt defaulter, and you could not sue them either, when a bank denied you an essential loan, unless the agency had acted with a negligent disregard for the truth. If a newspaper, academic journal, book publisher, blogger or TV station made any kind of accusation, you could sue them, and in all likelihood the case would never come to court because of the horrific costs of fighting and losing an action.

The denial of access to the courts was a final malign consequence of the English system. Censorship only made sense if judges weighed the evidence in a fair hearing. But cases rarely went to court. Therein lay the beauty of the English system for the rich litigant. He need not risk a trial in open court, where the defence could air the argument against him on the record. He could secure an apology through fear of financial loss, while sparing himself unwelcome publicity. Instead of being a means of establishing facts, the law became a device deployed by lawyers, who tellingly began to call themselves 'reputation managers'. A dubious businessman trying to make his way in English society would make a show of contributing to charities. He might buy some fine art, or donate to the opera, so he could pose as something more refined than a money-grubbing philistine. He would contribute to a political party in the hope, nearly always realised, of buying himself a peerage. And if anyone tried to query his philanthropic reputation, he could divert a small part of his fortune to a 'reputation manager' who would manage the offender with writs, and deter others from following the story.

In 2006, reporters on the Danish newspaper *Ekstra Bladet* decided to investigate the stunning rise of the Icelandic bank Kaupthing, which was buying assets across Denmark. How, they asked, had a bank from a volcanic island, without the resources to support a huge and voracious financial sector, become so powerful? The newsdesk decided they should concentrate on the links between the bank, Russian oligarchs and tax havens. Kaupthing was furious. It was accustomed to receiving praise from the financial press for the entrepreneurial dynamism of its managers. It threatened to sue *Ekstra Bladet* in Copenhagen, and at the same time filed a complaint with the Danish Press Council, which handled cases of breaches of press ethics.

The paper defended its journalism, and the Danish Press Council rejected the bank's complaint. Kaupthing withdrew its Danish lawsuit, and the argument seemed to be over until *Ekstra Bladet*'s bewildered editors heard that the bank was now suing them in London. The costs were beyond anything they had experienced before. In Denmark, lawyers consider a libel action that costs £25,000 expensive. In London, lawyers for Kaupthing and *Ekstra Bladet* ran up costs of close to £1 million *before* the case came to court. *Ekstra Bladet* could not run the risk of doubling, maybe trebling, the bill if it lost. It agreed to pay substantial damages to Kaupthing, cover its legal expenses and carry a formal apology on its website.

A few months later, Kaupthing, along with the other entre-preneurial, go-ahead Icelandic banks, collapsed. Iceland's GDP fell by 65 per cent, one third of the population said they were considering emigration, and the British and Dutch governments demanded compensation equivalent to the output of the entire Icelandic economy for the lost deposits of their citizens in Kaupthing and other banks.

Two points are worth flagging. The Danish journalists did not predict the collapse, but instead showed they had the nose for trouble that all good reporters possess. They could sense that there was something wrong with banks from a country with a population no larger than that of Coventry or Peoria, Illinois, buying overpriced foreign assets and acquiring the debts to match without having a government capable of acting as a lender of last resort in an emergency. Kaupthing went for the paper in England – not just because it wanted to kill the original story, but because it also wanted to deter others from spreading the idea that Iceland was not a safe place for investors. The English legal profession obliged. It placed the bank off-limits. Newspapers lawyers thought once, twice ... a hundred times before authorising critical stories. As events were to turn out, the English legal profession had also stopped the British investors who were to lose deposits worth $30 billion in Iceland from learning that there was a whiff of danger around the country's banks, although no lawyer showed any remorse about that.

A second point staggered foreigners. Even though Kaupthing was an Icelandic bank challenging a Danish newspaper, it was able to go to London and find a legal system willing and able to provide the coercive pressure it required. Most people would assume that what Danes wrote about Icelanders was none of England's business. England's lawyers thought differently. Their meddling did not shock all foreigners, however. Roman Polanski for one realised that England could give him what no other country would offer: a chance to sponge his reputation clean.

## Globalising Censorship (2)

On 21 July 2008, the United Nations declared that the practical application of English libel law 'has served to discourage critical media reporting on matters of serious public interest, adversely affecting the ability of scholars and journalists to publish their work'. England's authoritarianism was not a local concern, but created the global danger that one country's 'unduly restrictive libel law will affect freedom of expression worldwide on matters of valid public interest'.

Libel law was making England look like a pariah state. The Internet ensured that all online publications everywhere on the planet could be read in England. Thanks to the Duke of Brunswick and his obedient servant, a single view of a Web page in the UK constituted a publication of the libel in England, however old the offending words were. True, wealthy men could sue only if they had a reputation in England that critical reporting could damage. But as many oligarchs had a London home, or had business dealings in the City, they could overcome that obstacle with ease. The courts retained the option of saying that a rich man should sue in the country where the offending article was published, but the judges wanted to catch passing trade, and on most occasions welcomed plutocrats to the courts of old London town.

The first casualty was the British reading public, which could not buy works published in free America in their bookshops. The threat of legal action either banned or ensured the mutilation of Kitty Kelley's muckraking biography of the royal family, virtually every American discussion of the funding of Islamist terrorism, and *The Best Democracy Money Can Buy*, Greg Palast's account of the dark side of corporate life.

An admirably vulgar episode of *South Park* highlighted the absurdity of banning material in one part of the democratic world that was freely available elsewhere. In an episode entitled 'Trapped in the Closet', Scientologists decide that the child character Stan is the reincarnation of L. Ron Hubbard, the herder of credulous souls who founded a sci-fi cult in the 1950s. Celebrity Scientologists John Travolta and Tom Cruise join the crowd on Stan's lawn in South Park that has gathered to worship him. When Stan tells Cruise he does not think he's as good an actor as Leonardo DiCaprio, but is 'OK, I guess', the despairing Cruise buries his face in his hands. 'I'm nothing,' he says. 'I'm a failure in the eyes of the Prophet!' He runs into Stan's wardrobe and locks himself in, allowing assorted characters to shout, 'Tom Cruise, come out of the closet!' with all the false but funny innuendo that implied, for the rest of the show.

In the final scene, Stan refuses to become the Scientologists' new guru, and renounces L. Ron Hubbard and all his works. Hearing this blasphemy, Cruise comes out of the closet and cries, 'I'll sue you … *in England!*' To make the joke complete, the Scientology episode was the one episode of *South Park* British television managers dared not show, in case they were sued … *in England.*

English broadcasters' fear of the law spared the producers of *South Park* an experience common to human-rights campaigners and investigative journalists around the world: the bewilderment that came with receiving a letter threatening to initiate proceedings in the High Court in London. Far from being a beacon of liberty, a place where people from authoritarian regimes or working for authoritarian corporations could hear arguments about their masters aired, England was liberty's enemy. Saudis who could not investigate a petro-billionaire in

Riyadh for fear of punishment found that London punished exposés when they were printed elsewhere. Ukrainian and Russian journalists, who took no small risk when they confronted their native oligarchs, discovered that the English legal system was as willing as their native jurisdictions to punish them for insubordination.

I still recall the shame I felt when the legal director of Human Rights Watch in New York told me she spent more time worrying about legal action from England than from any other democratic country when she signed off reports on torture, political persecution and tyranny. In the late 1990s, her colleagues had collected eyewitness testimony and Rwandan government documents, and named those who played a role in the Rwandan genocide. In 2005, one of the men named in the report threatened a defamation suit in the UK, although only a few readers had accessed the report online from Britain. Her colleagues had to go back to Rwanda, reconfirm facts and relocate sources, and amend the report to avoid a full-blown legal case, even though the new Rwandan government was investigating the complainant and he had gone into hiding.

It was a familiar pattern. English judges allowed Boris Berezovsky to sue the American *Forbes* magazine for accusing him of being involved in the gangsterism that marked the arrival of Russian capitalism. The magazine sold around 780,000 copies in the United States, while readers accessed about six thousand copies in print or via the Net in the UK. Among the reasons the judges gave for allowing Berezovsky to avail himself of the services of the English rather than the Russian or American law was that his daughter was studying at Cambridge. *Forbes* retracted. The Ukrainian oligarch Rinat Akhmetov successfully pursued *Kyiv Post*, which had just a hundred British subscribers, and a Ukrainian website which did not even publish in English. The son of the ruler of the Republic of the Congo tried to sue Global Witness for a breach of privacy after it published details of how he was spending a fortune on luxury hotels and goods, while the country's inhabitants suffered from miserable poverty.

These were mere part-time litigants when set against the foreigner who exploited the reach of the English libel law more than any other: Sheikh Khalid bin Mahfouz, a Saudi banker, whom I think I can write about now because he is dead – and the dead cannot sue, not even in England.

'Behind every great fortune there is a great crime,' Balzac is meant to have said. And as with so many other oligarchs, bin Mahfouz's fortune had a whiff of the gutter about it. He was in charge of the National Commerce Bank of Saudi Arabia, and worked with the Bank of Credit and Commerce International. In 1992, after BCCI's spectacular collapse, the New York District Attorney indicted him as a front man for a 'Rent a Sheikh' fraud. Bin Mahfouz was a principal shareholder and director in the BCCI Group, whose presence on the board reassured trusting investors, the DA said. Without their knowledge, he withdrew his investment, an action that resulted 'in a gross misstatement of the true financial picture of the bank'. Luckless investors, who did not realise that bin Mahfouz had got out before the balloon went up, suffered 'larger losses when BCCI's worldwide Ponzi scheme finally collapsed'. Bin Mahfouz denied all allegations, but he agreed to pay a fine of $225 million, and accept a ban on any further activities in the American banking system. England did not hold it against him. When investigative journalists began to talk about his alleged links to al Qaeda, London lawyers pounded them with writs with a ferocity not seen since Robert Maxwell's day.

In one respect, however, bin Mahfouz differed from the old brute. He defended his 'reputation' in the English courts while not being a British citizen. Nor, somewhat surprisingly, was he a Saudi citizen. In 1990, the billionaire acquired Irish passports for himself and ten members of his family over a convivial lunch at the Shelbourne Hotel in Dublin with the Irish Taoiseach

Charles Haughey. Bin Mahfouz promised to invest in the country. Haughey promised him citizenship. A subsequent inquiry found that Haughey breached statutory procedures in the interest of pleasing bin Mahfouz.

Time and again, bin Mahfouz used the law or the threat of legal action to ban books which tied him to Islamist violence. It was not that he denied the charge in its entirety. He admitted that he had given money, but said it was only when Islamists were fighting the Soviets. Writers seeking to test his assertions, and see if there were grounds for the relatives of the dead of 9/11 naming him in their lawsuits, or the US Treasury Department treating him with suspicion, were clobbered. The serial litigant did not allow any disobliging reference to him, however hedged with lawyerly caveats, to go unpunished. Terrified publishers pulped rather than run the risk of a trial.

To be fair to the ghost of the billionaire, he could raise legitimate doubts about some of the claims against him. In a normal country, an argument would have taken place, freely and in the open, about the merits of the case. But in this respect, Britain was closer to Saudi Arabia than a free country, and bin Mahfouz was a man only *Private Eye* dared write about.

The legal actions went on without a hitch – he launched thirty-three suits – until bin Mahfouz lawyers issued a writ against *Funding Evil: How Terrorism is Financed and How to Stop It* by the American author Rachel Ehrenfeld. In truth, Ehrenfeld's was not the best book on the subject – that distinction belonged to *Charity and Terrorism in the Islamic World*, by J. Millard Burr, a former USAID relief coordinator in Sudan, and Robert O. Collins, a history professor, which the Cambridge University Press pulled to avoid a libel trial. Ehrenfeld's case stood out because of where her book was published rather than what she said. She published in New York, not London. No British publisher bought the rights for fear of the law, and that fear denied the British public yet another book others could read.

Bin Mahfouz still sued, because twenty-three copies reached Britain via Amazon.

Despite this paltry sale, the courts allowed his action to proceed, and ordered that Ehrenfeld should withdraw her book and pay him $225,000 even though bin Mahfouz was not English, Ehrenfeld was not English, and her book had not been published, publicised or reviewed in England. The imperialism of the English judiciary, its belief that it could punish books whose connection to England was virtually non-existent, finally made the world wake up to the danger London posed to freedom of speech. American writers, from leftists to neo-cons, realised that the availability of books on the Net was overriding their constitutional rights. English law 'constitutes a clear threat to the ability of the US press to vigorously investigate and publish news and information about the most crucial issues before the US public', said a coalition of American publishers. England was organising 'book burnings', added a Republican senator, not entirely hyperbolically, because chastened publishers withdrew defamatory books from the shelves and pulped them. Rory Lancman, a stout member of the New York State Assembly, stood on the steps of the New York Public Library and began a campaign to make English verdicts unenforceable in America with a magnificent speech: 'When American journalists and authors can be hauled into kangaroo courts on phoney-baloney libel charges in overseas jurisdictions who don't share our belief in freedom of speech or a free press,' he said, 'all of us are threatened.'

## Polanski Redux!

Naturally, England had no difficulty in satisfying Roman Polanski. *Vanity Fair* was an American magazine, but it sold in Britain, and that was enough to justify his action in London. There was the slight problem that if Polanski appeared at the Royal Courts of Justice to give evidence, the police would arrest him and deport him to America to face an overdue appointment with an angry judge. The judiciary spared him that indignity by saying that he did not need to give his evidence in person, but could deliver it via a video link from the safety of France. Just because he was a fugitive did not mean he was an 'outlaw' whose 'property and other rights could be breached with impunity', said the House of Lords, then the highest court in the land. Not one judge on its benches had the wit to realise that Polanski was not seeking to protect his property from theft or his body from torture, but asserting that he could still say he had a sexual reputation worth defending after his rape conviction, and demand damages from those who doubted it.

Polanski looked magnificent on the video link. The camera focused close on his face as he told the jury that the offending paragraph about the Scandinavian model was 'an abominable lie' which implied he possessed a 'callous indifference' to his wife's murder. He admitted under cross-examination, however, that a month after Sharon Tate's death he had been sleeping with other women. Mia Farrow added more stardust to the proceedings, by arriving in court to give evidence on Polanski's behalf. She said she had been with him on the night he went to Elaine's, and he could not possibly have made a pass at a strange woman because he was in no mood for seduction.

Even if the jury ultimately decided that the story as told in *Vanity Fair* was untrue, the magazine would have had a chance to reduce the damages, perhaps to vanishing point, if it had been allowed to show in court the full testimony of the girl Polanski had raped. 'The jury in London was permitted to hear only the outline of the formal conviction and not the background,' the editor recalled. 'The details could not be published in the UK during Polanski's suit against *Vanity Fair*; after the verdict, the reporting restrictions were lifted.'

The judge went on to tell the jury that 'We are not a court of morals. We are not here to judge Mr Polanski's personal lifestyle'

– even though others might have thought that the 'lifestyle' of a convicted sex offender had some bearing on the case. The jury found for Polanski, and the court awarded him damages of £50,000 and costs estimated at £1.5 million.

If Polanski was seeking to stop discussion of his crime, the 2005 libel action was a failure. Not all the lawyers in England could make the case go away. In 2010 he strayed into Switzerland, where the gendarmerie arrested and threatened to deport him. Nor did readers suffer: they could easily find the details the judge told the jury not to consider on the Web. His action seemed futile.

Yet you risk misunderstanding the nature of censorship if you assume it is always concerned with the obliteration of information. For a few years, Polanski could say that a court had considered the evidence about his sex life, and upheld his reputation and punished his detractors. And not just any court, but an *English* court, whose judgements in other areas of law were – correctly – respected.

Location matters as much in censorship as it does in property development. London gave the powerful something as useful as the suppression of secrets: it gave dignity and authority to their claims of innocence. Even if unwelcome information about them remained in circulation, rich claimants could tell all fair-minded people that an impartial legal process had vindicated their reputations and damned their critics as knaves, fools or liars. They could warn anyone who thought about repeating the allegations against them that the English courts would hit them with stupendous damages, and costs as well.

From Robert Maxwell onwards, they had the satisfaction of making their enemies learn that they could not criticise them without feeling the consequences. They taught their opponents a lesson in 'respect'; showed them that there were still punishments for offending the mighty. The cases they brought could consume their critics' lives, and threaten on occasion to bankrupt them, but they did not consume the lives of the oligarchs. They could hand the job of imposing retribution to their lawyers and reputation managers, and cover the costs of litigation from their loose change.

Censorship is not always about hiding secrets. Sometimes it is just an assertion of raw power.

# RULES FOR CENSORS (6):

## *Money Makes You a Member of a Master Race*

On 1 February 1960, four black students – Joe McNeil, Frank McCain, Dave Richmond and Ezell Blair – went to the lunch counter at Woolworth's in Greensboro, North Carolina, and ordered hot dogs and coffee, a courageous request to make at that time and in that place. Despite the US Supreme Court announcing that segregation was unconstitutional, white supremacists still ruled the American South. Most whites could vote, and most blacks could not – poll taxes, literacy tests and intimidation kept them off the electoral rolls. White Southern politicians did not just fail to represent black interests; they were the beneficiaries of a political system whose first purpose was to keep blacks disenfranchised. If they wanted to be re-elected, they knew they had to defend segregation or pay the political price. Political disenfranchisement had a further consequence. Because blacks were not on electoral rolls, they could not serve on juries, let alone aspire to be judges. They were at the mercy of racists in the legal system who could.

Segregation did not just mandate separate services for blacks and whites. Blacks' inferior political and legal status ensured that the services provided to them were in every respect shabbier and meaner. It is extraordinary that within a generation of the struggle against segregation, liberals and leftists could forget the importance of treating citizens without regard for their colour or creed, and embrace identity politics. In the Deep South, 'respecting difference' and 'celebrating diversity' meant that whites went to white schools and universities, and blacks went to underfunded black schools and universities. Whites drank at whites-only water fountains, and blacks at blacks-only fountains. Blacks had to sit at the back of buses, and could not use the 'white' seats at the front; and in Woolworth's and other dime stores they could shop, but they could not sit down at the whites-only counter and order a hot dog and a cup of coffee.

McCain ordered a hot dog and a cup of coffee. The waitress consulted the manager.

'Sorry, I can't serve you. We don't serve coloureds here.'

'But you do have hot dogs and coffee,' said McNeil, pointing at whites eating and drinking further down the counter.

'I can't serve you.'

The boys didn't argue, but they didn't move. They just sat at the counter until the store closed.

The next day twenty-seven black Greensboro students went to Woolworth's. The waitress wouldn't serve them either. So they just sat there too.

The sit-in movement spread across the American South. Blacks occupied whites-only beaches, parks and libraries as well as cafés and dime stores. In Nashville, Tennessee, eighty students put on their smartest clothes, picked up their textbooks and Bibles and divided into relay teams. The first fourteen sat down at a lunch counter.

'Right away the toughs started throwing things over us and putting out cigarette butts on our backs,' recalled Candice Carawan. 'I've got to say that didn't surprise me. What did surprise me is that when the police came they just watched. Finally, they turned to the students at the lunch counter: "OK nigras, get up from the lunch counter or we're going to arrest you." When nobody moved, they just peeled those people with their neat dresses and their Bibles right off their seats and carried them out to the paddy wagons. Before they were out of the store, another fourteen of us took their places at the counter. They got peeled off, and another fourteen sat down. By the end, eighty of us got arrested. Boy it was something!'

At no point did they resist. Christian pacifism and American idealism inspired the black Civil Rights movement of 1955 to 1968. When Carawan's white 'toughs' smeared food over blacks sitting at lunch counters, the blacks did not stand up and hit them. When white employers sacked black workers for trying to register to vote, the workers did not turn violent. When the police stood aside and gave the Ku Klux Klan fifteen minutes' free time to inflict ferocious injuries on 'freedom riders' trying to travel on the segregated buses of the Deep South, the protesters did not fight back. When the police inflicted injuries of their own on protesters in jail cells, the protesters did not retaliate. Even after white supremacists dynamited the Sixteenth Street Baptist Church in Birmingham, Alabama, and murdered four little girls, blacks did not bomb white churches in return.

At the start of the Civil Rights movement, Martin Luther King said that it would adhere to the tactics of non-violent civil disobedience. 'Don't let anyone compare our actions to the Ku Klux Klan. There will be no crosses burned. There will be no white persons pulled out of their homes and taken out on some distant road and murdered. If we protest courageously and with dignity, future generations of historians will pause and say, "There lived a great people, a black people, who injected new meaning and dignity into the veins of civilization."'

Civil disobedience against unjust laws or an occupying power is a hard tactic, that demands intelligence and courage. Only rarely does it work in full democracies. When there are iniquitous laws that have no popular mandate, and require popular cooperation, a mass refusal to obey can destroy them. Hundreds of thousands refused to pay Margaret Thatcher's poll tax, a naked piece of class legislation which said that a dustman must meet the same tax bill as a duke. As large parts of British society withdrew their consent for the tax, it collapsed, as did her premiership shortly afterwards. In most instances, however, the proponents of civil disobedience have to justify breaking the law rather than campaigning to change it. This is the catch that usually snags leftists in Western democracies when they feel the urge to turn militant. They rarely have a respectable answer to the question, 'If you say you have the right to break the law, why can't people you find repellent – racists, fascists – break the law too?'

Debates about the morality of law-breaking in a democracy did not concern the Civil Rights movement. The American South in 1960 was anything but a democracy. To the question, 'Why do you not use the ballot box to seek change?', blacks had the irrefutable answer that white supremacists stopped them voting.

The courage in civil disobedience comes from the dignified nature of the resistance. Protesters never sink to the level of their opponents. As well as refusing to meet violence with violence, true believers in civil disobedience respect the law as they break it. They do not try to escape arrest like common criminals, but use their trials to dramatise their cause and alert public opinion. It follows that peaceful civil disobedience can work in oppressive societies that nevertheless allow protesters to protest. The example Martin Luther King drew on was Gandhi's campaign of the 1930s and 1940s against British imperial rule in India. Like Gandhi, King directed his protests against a system that was repressive, but not so repressive as to make disobedience futile. If King had called on the masses to defy the law and take to the streets, and the masses had known the police would have gunned them down, the masses would have stayed at home.

Writing about Gandhi's belief that the victims of Nazism should arouse the conscience of the world by passively protesting, a sympathetic George Orwell said that Gandhi did not understand the impossibility of protest in totalitarian states. 'It is difficult to see how Gandhi's methods could be applied in a country where opponents of the regime disappear in the middle of the night and are never heard of again. Without a free press and the right of assembly, it is impossible not only to appeal to outside opinion, but to bring a mass movement into being, or even to make your intentions known to your adversary.'

A civil disobedience movement needs a civil society to agitate, and a free or at least half-free press to report its case. It uses the power of publicity against the power of the police baton, and cannot succeed if censorship stops domestic and international opinion from learning of its struggles.

In March 1960, the Committee to Defend Martin Luther King tried to use publicity to stir the conscience of America. It united Northern liberals, black Southern ministers and celebrities such as Harry Belafonte, Marlon Brando, Nat King Cole and Sidney Poitier, who risked losing income by challenging the prejudices of a large section of their audiences. They declared their solidarity with the sit-in movement in a two-page advertisement in the *New York Times*. Under the stirring headline 'Heed Their Rising Voices', they pledged their support to the American teenagers whose 'courage and amazing restraint have inspired millions and given a new dignity to the cause of freedom'.

The committee picked out details of the black struggle to heighten their readers' indignation. In Montgomery, Alabama, they said that after students sang the patriotic anthem 'My Country, 'Tis of Thee' on the State Capitol steps, 'their leaders were expelled from school, and truckloads of police armed with shotguns and tear-gas ringed the Alabama State College Campus. When the entire student body protested to state authorities by refusing to register, their dining hall was padlocked in an attempt to starve them into submission.' The committee went on to describe how the authorities harassed King. 'Again and again the Southern violators [of the US Constitution] have answered Dr. King's peaceful protests with intimidation and violence. They have bombed his home almost killing his wife and child. They have assaulted his person. They have arrested him seven times – for speeding, loitering, and similar offences. And now they have charged him with perjury – a felony under which they could imprison him for ten years. Obviously, their real purpose is to remove him physically as the leader to whom the students – and millions of others – look for guidance and support, and thereby to intimidate all leaders who may rise in the South.'

Not everything the liberals, ministers and celebrities endorsed in the advertisement was correct, for it is rare for every word in a piece of political writing to be true. Writers do their best, but even if we manage to fact-check everything, an argument is not a rendition of pure information. Unlike speak-your-weight machines, writers select facts, emphasise and arrange them. Critics and censors can always find reasons for offence if they put their minds to it, because there is always something – an unchecked fact, an unsupported innuendo – to object to.

The defenders of Martin Luther King knew two great truths, which no one could deny: racial oppression was everywhere in the United States; and the authorities were determined to use force to maintain the status quo. The detail did not bother them, and when they said that the police had arrested Martin Luther King seven times, they made a mistake. In fact the police had hauled him in four times. King said officers had assaulted him on one occasion. The officers denied it. Students had staged a demonstration on the State Capitol steps in Montgomery, as the advert stated, but they sang 'The Star-Spangled Banner', not 'My Country, 'Tis of Thee'. The State Board of Education had expelled nine students, but not for leading the demonstration at the Capitol, but for demanding service at a whites-only lunch counter in the Montgomery County Courthouse on another day. The defence committee also overestimated the extent of police complicity in subduing the protests. Although the state authorities deployed the police near the campus in large numbers, they did not at any time 'ring' the campus. Nor was there any attempt to 'starve' the students into submission.

These were undoubtedly blemishes. No writer who does not try to get his or her facts right can demand the trust of the reader. However, it was not the mistakes that infuriated Alabama's officials but the truths the campaigners were telling about the official harassment of the leaders of the Civil Rights movement, and the punishment of students asking for racial equality. That the proclamation of support for King appeared in a do-gooding Yankee newspaper written for the Confederacy's traditional enemies in the North did nothing to improve their temper. They wanted to stop publicity for the Civil Rights movement, because they understood that press coverage was putting pressure on a reluctant Kennedy administration to end the abuse of power.

But how could they stop it? America in 1960 did not have official censors to vet reports and send writers and editors to prison. Instead it had Thomas Jefferson and James Madison's First Amendment to the US Constitution, which guaranteed freedom of speech and freedom of religious conscience:

> Congress shall make no law respecting an establishment of religion, or prohibiting the free exercise thereof; or abridging the freedom of speech, or of the press; or the right of the people peaceably to assemble, and to petition the government for a redress of grievances.

But America had also inherited the English libel law, and the ideas of English judges became the tools of Southern politicians and bureaucrats as they sought to work their way around constitutional guarantees of freedom of the press.

On the face of it, no official appeared able to sue the *New York Times*, because it had not mentioned any official by name. But libel law covered whatever innuendos or suggestions the court could find, as well as the words on the page. The defenders of Martin Luther King had denounced the police's treatment of students and of King. Lawyers for L.B. Sullivan, Montgomery's police commissioner, decided that the *New York Times* was accusing him of answering 'Dr. King's peaceful protests with intimidation and violence'.

Libel law got round a further difficulty. Hardly anyone in Alabama read Yankee newspapers. In 1960, only 394 of the 650,000 copies the *New York Times* sold daily went to news-stands and subscribers in Alabama. But because libel, almost alone among civil torts, did not require the alleged victim to prove that he or she had suffered damage or financial loss, the fact that a mere few hundred people in Alabama had read the offending advert did not matter. If the *New York Times* had sold one copy in Alabama, that would have been sufficient.

Sullivan demanded a retraction. The *New York Times* refused, as the advertisement had not mentioned him. Sullivan sued. To give his action a local touch he included in his libel writ four black Alabama ministers who had put their names to the advert, and he took his case to an Alabama court. A white judge and jury heard the case and, naturally, found for Sullivan. They awarded him $500,000. Bailiffs seized the ministers' cars, while the court told the *New York Times* to find the equivalent of well over $3 million in today's money.

No newspaper could then or can now take many fines of that size. But the Southern courts had created the principle that criti-cism of a public body was a direct criticism of the person in charge of it, who could then sue for libel. The writs kept on coming. Alabama city commissioners sued the *New York Times* again, this time for $3 million, after its reporter Harrison Salisbury filed a piece that spared the reader nothing. Alabama's authorities, he wrote, had segregated everything from parks to taxis, and created an American Johannesburg. They even banned a book showing black rabbits and white rabbits playing together. 'Every channel of communication, every medium of mutual interest, every reasoned approach, every inch of middle ground has been fragmented by the emotional dynamite of racism, enforced by the whip, the razor, the gun, the bomb, the torch, the club, the knife, the mob, the police and many branches of the state's apparatus.'

The white legal system did not only target newspapers. Anthony Lewis, in his history of the struggle for civil rights and press freedom in America, tells the story of what happened to the publishers of a pamphlet issued by a citizens' committee which recounted how the police stopped a black man, forced him out of his car and shot him in the back. The FBI identified and charged a local policeman, but an all-white jury in a segregated court acquitted him. Alabama lawyers told the police they could sue the citizens' committee for criminal libel for suggesting that it had a racist killer in its ranks.

All sides realised what was at stake. The newspapers of the old Confederacy welcomed the prospect of libel law denying publicity to the Civil Rights movement. Sullivan's victory over the *New York Times*, said the *Alabama Journal*, 'could have the effect of causing reckless publishers of the North ... to make a re-survey of their habit of permitting anything detrimental to the South and its people to appear in their columns'. The South was 'libelled every day'. Now Southern lawyers were fighting back, and calling editors from hundreds of miles away to make them answerable to Alabama's courts. Or as the *Montgomery Advertiser* headlined the verdict: 'State Finds Formidable Legal Club to Swing at Out of State Press'.

The Civil Rights movement knew that the intimidation, the bombing of black churches, the attacks on black children going to white schools, had to be publicised if they were to be stopped. But as lawyers for Alabama's black ministers said after the Sullivan verdict, 'If the libel action is not struck down not only will the struggles of Southern negroes toward civil rights be impeded but Alabama will have been given permission to place a curtain of silence over its wrongful activities.'

The American Supreme Court intervened, and its decision in the 1964 case *New York Times Co. v. Sullivan* is one of those rare moments in history when freedom of speech made an unequivocal advance. Herbert Wechsler, the *New York Times*' lawyer, who had earned the right to be respected by prosecuting Nazi war criminals at Nuremberg, made a bold argument. He did not confine himself to saying that Alabama had no right to impose punishments on newspapers that sold only a few hundred copies in the state. Nor did he look at the racist nature of the Alabama legal system. Rather he examined the history of American liberty from the Revolution on, and argued that politicians and their officials should not be allowed to punish citizens in the libel courts for freely expressing their opinions, even if some of their facts were wrong and some of their views offensive.

No court had ruled that libel law was an attack on free speech before. Judges and legislators had exempted defamation, slander and calumny from protections for freedom of speech and freedom of the press. They reasoned that lies stuck, and the malicious could sully good reputations. Citizens needed protection from poison pens, and it was not a restriction on freedom to give it to them. But the *New York Times* argued that the law was not being used by citizens seeking to protect themselves from scurrilous journalists. Instead, it had become the chosen instrument for state officials and police chiefs seeking to punish citizens protesting about their abuses of power.

On its own, this argument was not enough. The English tradition of libel authorised the punishment of the 'seditious' who libelled the state and its officers. In 1704, Lord Chief Justice Holt ruled that 'It is very necessary for all governments that the people should have a good opinion of it. And nothing can be worse to any government than to endeavour to procure animosities, as to the management of it; this has always been looked on as a crime, and no government can be safe without it be punished.'

Ruling classes have always wanted to silence critics, and the rulers of America were no exception. Within a decade of Congress accepting the First Amendment, John Adams persuaded it to pass a Sedition Act, which punished the press for publishing 'false, scandalous, and malicious writing' against the government or its officials. The president wanted to muzzle press criticism of America's conflict with revolutionary France, whose seditious agents he saw everywhere. Among the dissidents the state arrested were Benjamin Franklin's grandson, who edited an anti-government newspaper, and a blunt citizen who saw townspeople in Massachusetts welcoming President Adams with a cannon salute and remarked to the man standing next to him that he would not mind if they fired the cannonball through the president's 'ass'.

The panic passed, and Congress repealed the authoritarian law. But the Supreme Court was packed with Adams's supporters, and it never declared the punishment of 'seditious' newspapers unconstitutional. It was still open for public officials to do what Sullivan had done, and haul his critics before the courts.

Wechsler and the *New York Times* showed that Adams' two immediate successors as president, Thomas Jefferson and James Madison, as well as many others, regarded Adams' political censorship of 'seditious' newspapers that criticised the state as a clear breach of the First Amendment and an attack on democracy. 'The censorial power is in the people over the Government,' said Madison, 'and not in the Government over the people.' Moreover, Wechsler could quote a string of rulings by American judges from succeeding decades who had defended freedom of speech and of the press against the state. (My favourite being from a judge in the 1940s, who dismissed contempt of court accusations against a union leader by saying, '[I]t is a prized

American privilege to speak one's mind, although not always with perfect good taste, on all public institutions.')

The Supreme Court agreed. Debate on public issues should be 'uninhibited, robust and wide-open', it ruled. If the government and its officials were on the receiving end of 'vehement, caustic and sometimes unpleasantly sharp attacks', that was the price they paid for exercising power in a democracy. They had to learn to live with it.

The judges did not force the American government to reveal all, and leave it powerless to punish those who leaked its secrets. Instead they established new rules for the conduct of public debate. They were careful not to allow absolute liberty. Private citizens can sue as easily in America as anywhere else, if writers attack them without good grounds. Poison pens are still punished, and individual reputations are still protected. If, however, a private citizen is engaged in a public debate, it is not enough for him or her to prove that what a writer says is false and defamatory. They must prove that the writer behaved 'negligently'. The judiciary protects public debates, the Supreme Court said in 1974, because 'under the First Amendment, there is no such thing as a false idea. However pernicious an opinion may seem, we depend for its correction not on the conscience of judges but on the competition of other ideas.'

Finally, the judges showed no regard for the feelings of politicians and other public figures. They must prove that a writer was motivated by 'actual malice' before they could succeed in court. The public figure must show that the writer knew that what he or she wrote was a lie, or wrote with a reckless disregard for the truth. Unlike in Britain, the burden of proof was with the accuser, not the accused.

The US today is not a free-speech utopia. Various states have had to pass laws against SLAPP actions – 'strategic lawsuits against public participation'. The corporations which brought cases of libel, breach of confidence, invasion of privacy or conspiracy did not expect to win, but to slap down protesters with expensive litigation that could drag on for years. But the black students who sat in their best suits and dresses at whites-only lunch counters could still claim a victory. They had opened up American society, and forced the judiciary to recognise a paradox. Free societies living under the rule of law can only be free if the law's reach is limited. As with religion, the political arguments of a democracy are too important to allow the courts to police them.

If the disputes of 1960s America feel like ancient history, think about the similarities between yesterday's white supremacists and today's super-rich.

- The racist expected deference because he was in a superior position. To his mind, the colour of his skin should guarantee that others 'respect' him or face punishment. Flatterers surround today's wealthy, whether they are subordinate employees, supplicants looking for favours or politicians looking for campaign donations. They spend large parts of their professional lives hearing deferential voices, and regard criticism when it comes as an assault on their dignity.
- A white politician or bureaucrat in the 1960s upheld a segregationist political order and knew that the political order would protect him if he played the game. A critic could not take a case against him to any regulatory institution – the Alabama courts, the state police or the state legislature. If you attacked one part of the system, you attacked it all. A modern employer knows that rival firms will refuse to employ a whistleblower if he fires him. Even if the information the whistleblower releases is in the public interest or to the benefit of shareholders, an attack on one employer is an attack on every employer.
- In the courts of the old South, a white skin conferred an overwhelming advantage. In the British courts, money confers an

overwhelming advantage. In neither instance do the courts accept that the powerful and wealthy have the means to refute or rebut criticism without the need for legal sanctions.

The most striking continuity, however, lies in the failure to look at the wider interests of society. For it takes an almighty effort to make an established order recognise that free debate, even hurtful, raucous, inaccurate and disrespectful debate, causes less harm than the bludgeon suppression.

# *John Stuart Mill and the Struggle to Speak Your Mind*

John Stuart Mill is an easy philosopher to love, but a hard one to follow. On first reading, his harm principle, that the 'only purpose for which power can be rightfully exercised over any member of a civilized community, against his will, is to prevent harm to others', seems mild when set against the vast systems of the Continental philosophers. While his nineteenth-century contemporary Karl Marx dreamed that the workers would free themselves from wage slavery, and unleashed the slavery of revolutionary tyranny as a consequence, Mill dreamed of allowing people to do as they pleased as long as they did not harm others. What could be more polite – more English – than his injunction to mind your own business? Do not be deceived by the apparent modesty. Mill's ideas are at the root of more revolutions in human behaviour than Marx and all his followers managed.

Mill's father, the utilitarian philosopher James Mill, brought up his son to be a genius. Young John could speak Greek by the time he was three. By the age of eight, he was reading Plato's dialogues, and by thirteen he was helping his father compose a treatise on political economy. His autobiography describes the mental breakdown his hothouse childhood induced, and hints with Victorian reticence at how he fell for Harriet Taylor, a married woman, who was the love of his life and his salvation.

Under her influence, he became the first British Member of Parliament to make a case for the emancipation of women. If men should have the freedom to express themselves and experiment with their lives as long as they did not harm others, Mill argued, why should not women enjoy the same rights? He dismissed the objection that women's natures meant that they were not fit to exercise freedom. Under the condition of oppression, women could not reveal their true nature; and until equality came, 'no one can possibly assess the natural differences between women and men, distorted as they have been'. Nor would he allow the customs of the past to dictate the future, if custom did more harm than good. The religious fanaticism of our time devotes much of its energy to keeping women down. Its bombs and thunderous declarations are an attempt to silence Mill's argument that nature and tradition cannot justify the suffering caused by male oppression.

The fight for homosexual equality is also a Millian struggle. His harm principle held that what consenting adults did in private was no business of the state. Even if the rest of society disapproved of pre-marital, promiscuous or gay sex, even if it thought that homosexual love harmed homosexuals, it had no right to intervene. Notice how broadly Mill set his harm principle. It is not enough to say that people who hate the idea of homosexuality suffer mental distress at the knowledge that it is legal. They must suffer actual harm, and as they do not, they cannot prohibit it. His most glaring failure was one that the colonial subjects of Queen Victoria would have noticed at once. Mill gave freedom to people in the 'maturity of their faculties', and did not include blacks and Asians as full adults. Just as Milton could not extend liberty to Catholics, so Mill could not extend it to the subject peoples of the British Empire.

If today's governments took Mill seriously, they would end the 'war on drugs'. They would remove restrictions on all pornography apart from child pornography, whose producers by definition harm children, who cannot give informed consent. They would have to allow incest between consenting adults – although I think we could rely on instinctive human revulsion to prevent it – and they would have no argument against public nudity. As I mentioned, Mill is not an easy philosopher to follow, but look at the misery and corruption caused by the war on drugs before you are tempted to dismiss him.

Mill did not believe in absolute freedom of speech – no one can, because it denies man's nature as a social animal – instead he argued for the limits on censorship to be set as broadly as possible. He and Harriet Taylor went over the arguments in *On Liberty* repeatedly before publication, and chose their example of where the boundary should be set with care. If agitators claim that corn dealers starve the poor, they said, the law has no right to punish them. Only if they say the same to an angry mob gathered outside a corn dealer's home, or hand placards to the mob denouncing the corn dealers' wickedness, can the state intervene. Mill does not say that the law should punish the incitement of hatred against corn dealers. Even if their critics made their neighbours despise them as rapacious capitalists, even if the criticism was unfair and caused them financial harm, corn dealers could not go to court. The law should restrict itself to punishing speech that directly provokes crime – incitement to murder, incitement to violence or incitement to arson. It should not punish incitement to hatred, because it is not a crime to hate people, any more than it is to envy them or to lust after them.

The enemies of Mill's liberalism were once on the right, and in many parts of the world they still are. Conservatives said Mill could not brush aside the views of the societies, tribes and communities just because individuals seeking to break with taboos were not harming others. When Britain discussed legalising homosexual acts between consenting adults in the 1950s, on the Millian grounds that what gays did in the privacy of their bedrooms was no one's business but their own, the conservative jurist Patrick Devlin said that the law was still entitled to punish them. 'Invisible bonds of common thought' held society together, he argued, and individual homosexuals must accept legal penalties because no one could live apart from society. Opponents of social conservatives make a mistake when they think they can ignore these objections or overcome them without effort. The conservative may well suspect that his God is a fabrication and his holy book is a fable, but he will none the less fear for the future if the traditions and taboos his society holds are cast aside. The best liberal response is to reassure conservatives that change will not be as bad as they think – in all likelihood their daughters will not run off with the first man they meet, and their sons will not start trying on their wives' dresses. If they look as if they might, social conservatives remain free to try to persuade them that they are wrong. All that is forbidden to them is the argument that if a majority in a society finds the law's tolerance of gay lovemaking or women's emancipation revolting, the majority is entitled to demand retribution. If the knowledge that others are engaging in taboo behaviours inflicts a psychic wound and provokes the deepest feelings of revulsion, that's tough. Conservatives just have to learn to live with it.

Today's liberals lack the self-confidence to say the same about intellectual freedom, and have become as keen on censorship as conservatives once were. They want to silence those who pose no direct harm comparable to Mill's rabble-rouser urging on the mob outside the corn dealer's home. Like homophobic conservatives, who worry that if societies' taboos go, the promotion of homosexuality will turn young people gay, they worry that if the law allows unpalatable views to escape unpunished, hatred will turn to violence. Hence, they support laws against incitement to racial and religious hatred in Britain and across Europe, against Holocaust denial in Germany and Austria, and against Holocaust denial *and* denial of the Armenian genocide in France. Hence, they enforce speech codes that mandate the punishment of transgressors in the workplace and the universities. Few liberals have the confidence to say that free speech, like sexual freedom, would not create a terrible society, because they do not trust their fellow citizens. They do not realise that most people in modern democracies do not harbour secret fascist fantasies, and that the best way to respond to those who do is to meet their bad arguments with better arguments.

In trying to find the best argument against censorship, John Stuart Mill wanted to be true to his father's utilitarianism – that happiness is the only good and pain the only evil – and to his own respect for intellectual freedom. He could not do both. His formulation that we should allow the widest possible freedom to argue because it is 'Better to be Socrates dissatisfied than a fool satisfied' may affirm the desirability of knowing thyself and knowing as much as you can about the world, but it is not a utilitarian calculation. Fools may well be happier in their ignorance than wise people are in their knowledge; certainly, there is no way of proving that they are not. Removing censorship and challenging taboos allows people to live as autonomous adults. Such liberations may be desirable – in my view, they are essential – but they are not always happy or free from pain.

Mill is more convincing when he moves from happiness to harm. We lack the certainty of the Victorians that the world can be made better, but we know that it can be made worse. Breaking with Mill's insistence on the widest possible freedom for individuals is one of the surest ways of doing it.

We are relearning a lesson we ought never to have forgotten: you cannot be a little bit free. You cannot have one law for civilised people who read the *New York Times* and know the difference between a Bordeaux and a Burgundy, and another for beer-swilling bigots who watch Fox News. Saul Bellow explained why when he said, 'Everybody knows there is no fineness or accuracy of suppression; if you hold down one thing, you hold down the adjoining.'

Equality before the law means what it says. As Bellow understood, those who demand the suppression of others must expect to be suppressed themselves. Naïve liberals were once comfortable with punishing expressions of racism, homophobia and misogyny. Whereas Mill would only allow the police to arrest a demagogue whipping up a mob outside a mosque or a gay bar, they wanted to regulate writing and speech which did not directly cause crime. To use the phrase of the philosopher Joel Feinberg, they replaced Mill's harm principle with an 'offence principle', which held that societies are allowed to punish speech that people find exceptionally offensive.

Leave aside if you can the sensible objection that the offence principle justifies courts censoring political debates – for do not many politically committed people find the views of their opponents 'exceptionally offensive'? – and instead look at the boomerang that has whirled back through the air and smacked the children of the 1960s in the face.

They knew that racists, homophobes and misogynists were bad people with terrible ideas, and too few worried about the ground they were conceding when they accepted excessive restrictions on free speech. They ought to know better now. Because they decided that they must do more than fight bad ideas with better ideas, and allowed 'offence' to a faith or racial group, rather than actual harm, to be grounds for censorship, they could not defend liberal principles against Islamists who were also racists, homophobes and misogynists. The same failure to look at wider consequences bedevils the other examples of censorship discussed in these pages. There are many excellent reasons for maintaining corporate secrecy, but the excessive faith in managerial command and control has led to criticism being silenced, and left us with half-ruined societies that still do not dare think about new ways to bring transparency to the workplace. The feudal assumptions behind libel laws are not all bad. Judges have punished newspapers which deserved chastisement, and deterred editors from publishing nasty and worthless work. If democracies in Europe and beyond were to import the principles of the US First Amendment, the amount of rubbishy and 'exceptionally offensive' work in circulation would grow. Preventing its publication by maintaining current laws seems as worthy as banning hate speech or preventing the publication of commercial secrets, until you remember Bellow's warning that truth and falsehood, the moral and the immoral, do not come in separate packages but are mixed together. You cannot hold down one without holding down the other.

## The Inaccuracy of Suppression

Of all the notions least worthy of legal protection, the idea that a chiropractic therapist can cure a patient's sickness by pounding his joints with low-amplitude, high-velocity thrusts must be close to the top of the list. The therapy is as rough as it sounds – to imagine a chiropractor at work on a joint, hold your hand flat as if you are a waiter carrying a tray of drinks, bend it backwards below the horizontal as far as you can, then hit it with your free hand. The theory behind the treatment is equally disquieting.

Daniel David Palmer already had an interest in spiritual and magnetic healing when he moved from Canada to Iowa in the 1860s. Once established in the US, he invented his own form of the laying on of hands. In September 1895, he met a deaf janitor by the name of Harvey Lillard. Palmer noticed that Lillard had a vertebra racked from its normal position in his spine. Lillard roused Palmer's amateur curiosity when he told him that he had lost his hearing seventeen years before, when he had bent over and heard something pop in his back. 'I reasoned that if that vertebra was replaced, the man's hearing should be restored. With this object in view, a half hour's talk persuaded Mr Lillard to allow me to replace it. I racked it into position by using the spinous process as a lever and soon the man could hear as before.'

Palmer had performed the founding miracle of the chiropractic faith, a wonder his disciples venerate to this day. With typical bombast, he said that if all he had achieved was the healing of the janitor, 'This of itself, should have been hailed with delight.' But new wonders kept on coming. As Palmer manipulated joints and shoved backs, he convinced himself that he had found a cure for deafness, heart disease and just about everything else. Displaced vertebrae caused 95 per cent of all diseases, he announced. Viruses and bacteria were irrelevant. The key to the cure of all sicknesses lay in the back. To be specific, he concluded that 'innate intelligence' – a substance unknown to science – flowed up and down the spine. A chiropractor who manipulated its joints could therefore heal the body and for good measure 'correct abnormalities of the intellect as well'.

'I am the originator, the Fountain Head,' he bragged. 'It was I who combined the science and art and developed the principles thereof. I have answered the time-worn question – what is life?' He compared himself to Muhammad, Jesus and Martin Luther, and built the Palmer School of Chiropractic in Davenport, Iowa, in 1897 to spread his new religion.

Midwestern doctors were outraged, and had the courts send him to jail for failing to pay a fine for practising medicine without a licence. Far from convincing his followers that he was a fraud, the sentence persuaded them that he was a martyr persecuted by the bullies of conventional medicine. His son Bartlett moved into the family business, and made so much money from trusting patients that he was able to buy the first car Davenport, Iowa, had seen. Alas, in 1913 he used it to run down his father on the day of the Palmer School of Chiropractic's homecoming parade. Daniel died in hospital a few weeks later.

His death may not have been an accident. Father and son had fought for control of the movement, and Bartlett had many reasons to loathe Daniel. His father's violent therapy had its antecedents in the violent treatment of his children. He had pummelled them when they were young, and thrown them onto the street when they were eighteen, telling them to make their own way in the world. 'All three of us got beatings with straps, for which father was often arrested and spent nights in jail,' recalled Bartlett.

Once he was filling his father's shoes, Bartlett Palmer proved himself an astute huckster. He sold expensive, if medically worthless, equipment to muscular initiates to the back-racking trade, established his own radio station to promote it, and pushed the chiropractic empire into Europe.

Doctors scoffed at the chiropractors' belief that they could channel the mysterious force of innate intelligence. Along with satirists and journalists, they laid into the therapy without restraint. The alternative practitioners joined the argument by fighting among themselves. All mystical movements are prone to schism, and believers in the chiropractic gospel were no exception. Therapists who made a fleeting contact with reality began to doubt the movement's claims to provide a cure for all sicknesses. They still believed that chiropractic therapy could treat musculoskeletal problems, but they doubted it was a panacea, and rejected the concept of innate intelligence. They called themselves 'mixers', because they accepted elements of conventional medicine. The 'straights', on the other hand, remained committed to the belief that chiropractic therapy could treat almost any condition. The arguments between the two sects added to the commotion. At no point did a court feel that it was its business to silence anyone taking part in the debate.

Scientists examining the therapy faced a special difficulty, which those who laughed at Palmer did not readily appreciate. Just because he was a violent mystic, with a mind clouded by ignorant mumbo-jumbo and egotistical self-delusion, that did not mean his treatments were necessarily worthless. His therapy could provide the right results for the wrong reasons; be effective in practice although ludicrous in theory. The scientific method insisted that it was not sufficient to say that an alternative therapist walked like a quack and talked like a quack – critics had to demonstrate that his treatments were quackery.

The task of doing so fell to a free-ranging researcher called Edzard Ernst. He was a professor at Vienna University's medical school, whose prolific research record might have allowed him to take a job in the grandest of universities anywhere in the world. Instead, he decided in 1993 to become the world's first professor of complementary medicine, at Exeter University, a fine institution, but something of a backwater in the opinion of his fellow academics.

Ernst's decision was not so eccentric. Although alternative or complementary medicine was a neglected scientific subject, establishing what merit, if any, it possessed was of pressing public importance. Ernst estimated that the global spend on alternative health care stood at £40 billion in 2008. The pseudo-science of homeopathy generates the largest profits, because the cost of the raw material for homeopathic 'remedies' is so low. Homeopaths believe, on the basis of no evidence at all, that the smaller the proportion of an allegedly beneficial substance in a 'remedy', the more effective that remedy becomes. Their theory ensures that the most valuable animal on the planet is not a rare Chinese panda or endangered Siberian tiger, but a common French duck. Every year, functionaries working for a French homeopathic firm kill one. They extract its heart and liver, then dilute them with water to a ratio of $1:100^{200}$ – that is, 1 part duck to 1 plus two thousand zeroes of water. Not a molecule of the offal survives the drenching; water is all that remains. The company drips it into sugar pills, and in keeping with homeopathic orthodoxy, claims that a 'memory' of the dead duck lingers in the medicine. Its remembrance of the unfortunate *canard* gives the sugar pills curative powers. From one bird, they produce warehouses-full of 'medicines' that they sell for millions of dollars.

Ernst resisted the temptation to dismiss the popularity of alternative medicine as the product of the silly obsessions of the rich world's 'worried well'. There are thousands of homeopaths in Britain, but hundreds of thousands in India, he noted. In the poor world as well as the rich, not just homeopaths and chiropractic therapists but the sellers of aromatherapy, hypnotherapy, magnet therapy, massage therapy, flower and crystal remedies, acupuncture, feng shui and colonic irrigation claim that there is no need for modern drugs. They offer 'natural', 'herbal', 'holistic' and 'traditional' remedies to desperate people with little money to waste on useless treatments as well as to the wealthy.

Ernst understood that practitioners of alternative medicine pose two dangers to rich and poor alike. First, their treatments may not cause actual harm, but because patients believe in the remedy and trust the therapist, they fail to visit clinicians who might actually help them. Second, the treatments may cause actual harm, while still deterring patients from visiting competent clinicians.

In the case of chiropractic therapy, Ernst and his colleagues conducted systematic reviews and meta-analyses of the available clinical trials. They showed that spinal manipulation could do nothing to relieve headaches, period pains, colic, asthma, allergies and all the other conditions therapists claimed to be able to treat. This was not a startling finding. If there were anything in the 'straight' version of chiropractic claims, trouble with the back would bring on a host of apparently unrelated medical problems. No one has been able to show that it has. For neck pain, the evidence was more mixed. Two reviews concluded that spinal manipulation was futile. A third found its effects were more beneficial, although Ernst pointed out that the lead reviewer in this case was a chiropractic therapist. There was more of a scientific consensus that spinal manipulation was as effective in treating back pain as conventional physiotherapy and anti-inflammatory drugs. But there's the rub – no variety of back rubbing, conventional or alternative, does much to relieve back pain: they are all equally ineffective.

A credulous patient who believes that chiropractic treatment can cure or alleviate illnesses that have nothing to do with musculoskeletal conditions may well avoid seeking trustworthy advice, and suffer the consequences. Believers in the efficacy of nearly all other alternative treatments run the same risk – a traveller who believes that homeopathic treatments can protect her from malaria, for example, risks her life if she refuses to take conventional medicines as well. As for the further risk that the patient could suffer positive harm at the hands of the alternative therapists, chiropractic therapy stands out as one of the few alternative treatments that are dangerous in themselves. In 2001, a systematic review of five studies revealed that roughly half of all chiropractic patients experienced temporary adverse effects, such as pain, numbness, stiffness, dizziness and headaches. Patients put themselves in jeopardy when they allowed therapists to execute high-velocity, low-amplitude thrust on their necks – one of the most vulnerable parts of the body, as hangmen know.

Manipulating the neck risks attacking the arteries that carry the blood to the brain. Because there is usually a delay between damage to the arteries and the blockage of blood to the brain, the link between chiropractic treatment and strokes went unnoticed for many years. Typical of the suffering Ernst revealed was the case of a twenty-year-old Canadian waitress who visited a chiropractor twenty-one times between 1997 and 1998 to relieve pain in her lower back. On her penultimate visit, she complained of stiffness in her neck. That evening she began dropping plates at the restaurant, so she returned to the chiropractor. As the chiropractor manipulated her neck, she began to cry, her eyes started to roll, she foamed at the mouth and her body began to convulse. She slipped into a coma and died three days later. At the inquest, the coroner declared that she died of a 'ruptured vertebral artery', which occurred in association with a chiropractic manipulation of the neck'. Hers was not an isolated case. A 2001 study by the Association of British Neurologists found thirty-five cases of neurological complications, including nine strokes, occurring within twenty-four hours of neck manipulation.

Conventional medicine can have fatal consequences. But medical regulators assess drugs before allowing them on the market, and doctors monitor their effects and seek the informed consent of patients. Neither of the first two checks exists in chiropractic treatment, and a 2005 study of British chiropractors found that 77 per cent did not seek informed consent.

Ernst did not start with a prejudice against alternative medicine – he had trained in herbalism, homoeopathy, massage therapy and spinal manipulation – but the good scientific principle of basing beliefs on evidence shook him out of his complacency. The Exeter University researchers found that 95 per cent of alternative medical treatments had no reliable evidence to support claims for their effectiveness, and suggested that we dropped terms like 'alternative', 'complementary' and 'conventional' medicine, and instead tried 'medicines that work' and 'medicines that do not work'.

Leaving all medical questions to one side, Ernst's research was a great story. The British alone spend £1.6 billion a year on alternative treatments that do not work except as placebos, and there was a pool of potential readers who wanted to know why. Ernst teamed up with Simon Singh, one of the best modern science writers, to bring his work to a wider audience. Singh trained as a scientist at Cambridge University. He completed his PhD at the CERN laboratory, where he learned about the demands of the scientific method. Before his colleagues would allow him to put a scientific paper into the public domain, they tore into his ideas, challenging his premises, doubting his methods and questioning his ability. It never occurred to Singh that he could sue a critic of his work, even if the criticism was damaging to his reputation or wholly misguided. If the criticisms were wrong, he could expose their falsity. If they were right, they would stop him making a mistake. It tells us something about our times that I need to labour this point, but freedom to speak includes the freedom to be wrong. In science, as in any other intellectual pursuit, free debate without fear of the consequences is the only way of allowing facts to be established and arguments to be tested. As Carl Sagan beautifully explained, 'At the heart of science is an essential balance between two seemingly contradictory attitudes – an openness to new ideas, no matter how bizarre or counterintuitive, and the most ruthlessly sceptical scrutiny of all ideas, old and new. This is how deep truths are winnowed from deep nonsense.'

Singh had written acclaimed books on the history of code-breaking and the efforts of generations of mathematicians to find a proof for Fermat's last theorem. He explained scientific ideas to a lay audience without glossing over difficulties the reader needed to understand – one of the hardest forms of prose writing there is, in my opinion.

In 2008, Singh and Ernst released *Trick or Treatment,* a history of how the various alternative therapies came about, why they once seemed plausible, and why patients and governments should now reject most of them. A few months after the book was published, the British Chiropractic Association held National Chiropractic Awareness Week. Singh noted that it offered its members' services to the anxious parents of sick children, and wrote an article for the *Guardian,* 'Beware the Spinal Trap'. He began by saying that readers would be surprised to learn that the therapy was the creation of a man who thought that displaced vertebrae caused virtually all diseases. A proportion of modern chiropractors still believed in Palmer's 'quite wacky' ideas, as the British Chiropractic Association was proving by claiming that its members could treat children with colic, sleeping and feeding problems, frequent ear infections, asthma and prolonged crying. There was 'not a jot of evidence' that these treatments worked, said Singh. 'This organisation is the respectable face of the chiropractic profession and yet it happily promotes bogus treatments.' He went on to explain that he could label the treatment as 'bogus' because Ernst had examined seventy trials exploring the benefits of chiropractic therapy in conditions unrelated to the back, and found no evidence to suggest that chiropractors could treat them.

By the standards of polemic, it was an even-tempered piece; far angrier articles have been written with less cause. Singh was warning that parents would be wasting their money if they took children to chiropractors, and could risk harming them too. He backed up his comments with reliable evidence, and concluded that 'If spinal manipulation were a drug with such serious adverse effects and so little demonstrable benefit, then it would almost certainly have been taken off the market.' This unexceptionable thought was no more than a statement of the obvious.

On the offence principle, one could see why chiropractors would find Singh's argument extremely offensive, even if it were true or mainly true. According to the harm principle, there was no reason to punish him even if his argument was not supported by strong evidence but was false. On the contrary, John Stuart Mill believed that if all reasonable people thought an opinion was false, they still had no right to suppress it. They must allow the debate to run its course. The courts of his native country turned Mill's idea on its head. Instead of praising Singh for contributing to a debate on children's health that all reasonable people should welcome, the judges allowed the British Chiropractic Association to sue him for libel.

## The March of the Nerds

On a wet evening in 2009, I addressed a meeting in a London pub close to the law courts. I gave a speech along the lines I have presented in this book. I warned that the Internet was opening up the possibility of extra-territorial censorship, and that authoritarian jurisdictions could ban books, impose fines and use international agreements to enforce their verdicts. British judges were the worst offenders in the democratic world, I continued. They allowed sex offenders to sue. They allowed criminals to collect damages, and did not reform the law when their criminality was exposed. They presided over a system that was so biased and so expensive it compelled honest men and women to deny what they knew to be true. Suing scientists engaged in essential arguments about public health was the logical continuation of a policy of suppression.

Simon Singh's case was not unique. The American health conglomerate NMT sued the British doctor Peter Wilmshurst in London for criticising its treatments in an online American scientific journal. Another pharmaceutical company was to go after a Danish radiologist after he alleged at a scientific conference in Britain that there was evidence of a link between one of its treatments and a rare and crippling muscular condition. The editors of medical journals were admitting that they refused to print or censored scientific papers they feared might bring them to the attention of the courts. A vitamin salesman sued Ben Goldacre, Britain's pre-eminent demystifier of pseudo-science, after Goldacre condemned him in the *Guardian* for peddling his pills to sufferers from Aids in southern Africa, and telling them that retro-viral drugs were poisons. The libel action failed, but for more than a year all British newspapers, and all foreign newspapers the vitamin salesman might sue in London, risked a writ if they talked about his sales techniques.

My glum account of English oppression was a warm-up act for Singh, who was preparing to take the microphone and announce whether he was prepared to fight the libel writ.

The chiropractors had not sued the *Guardian*, but had gone for Singh personally, hoping that the threat of financial ruin would force him to grovel. The *Guardian* withdrew his article from their website, thus lessening any 'offence' caused, and offered the chiropractors the right of reply, so they could tell their side of the story and convince readers by argument rather than by threats that Singh was in the wrong.

The chiropractors carried on suing Singh, and demanded that he pay them damages and apologise. Singh did not see why he should, considering he was reporting reputable evidence that chiropractic therapy was the invention of a faith healer, whose claims that his mystical method could cure sicknesses that had nothing to do with backache were nonsense. At a preliminary hearing to determine the 'meaning' of Singh's article, the judiciary soon showed why English law was feared and despised across the free world. Determined to draw him into the law's clutches, the judge put the worst possible construction on Singh's words.

He ruled that because Singh had said 'there is not a jot of evidence' that chiropractic therapists could cure colic, sleeping and feeding problems, frequent ear infections, asthma and prolonged crying, the courts would at enormous expense see if they could find one piece of evidence, however small, to support the chiropractors. Maybe if a child stood up in court and breathlessly announced that a chiropractor had cured her, that would be a jot. Maybe if the judge could find a smidgeon of doubt in one of the studies, Singh would have to pay for a phrase that may have been ever so slightly inaccurate.

If Singh could prove that no such doubt existed, he would still not be free of the law. The judge ruled that when Singh said of the British Chiropractic Association, 'This organisation is the respectable face of the chiropractic profession and yet it happily promotes bogus treatments,' he was accusing it of dishonesty. It seemed clear to those of us who did not have the benefit of a legal training that he was doing no such thing. In his article, Singh said that chiropractic therapists had 'wacky ideas', and accused the hard-line among them of being 'fundamentalists'. In normal English usage, to describe someone as a fundamentalist who holds wacky ideas is to accuse him of folly, not of mendacity.

Not according to the judge. In his role as a definer of hidden meanings, he ruled that when Singh wrote 'happily promotes', he did not mean that chiropractors 'carelessly' promoted bogus therapies without a thought for the available evidence, or 'stupidly' promoted them because they did not understand the findings of clinical trials. No. Singh was accusing therapists of deliberately and fraudulently promoting quack remedies they knew to be worthless. 'That is in my judgement the plainest allegation of dishonesty and indeed it accuses them of thoroughly disreputable conduct,' the judge told Singh.

Proving whether a believer in magical medicine, the 'faked' moon landings, the 'truth' about Obama's birth certificate or any other mystical or paranoid theory is a fool or a liar is a next to impossible task. The most disturbing thing about fantasists is that they are often sincere. Yet on the ruling of the English courts, a writer who described a neo-Nazi or an Islamist as 'happily promoting bogus conspiracy theories' about the global reach of the Elders of Zion, for which there is 'not a jot of evidence', could be sued for libel in London. And unless the writer could prove that the object of the critique was a liar instead of a fool, the writer would lose.

After hearing the judge's ruling, Singh's friends, his lawyers and everyone else who had his best interests at heart advised him to get out of the madhouse of the law while he still could. He had already risked £100,000 of his own money. If he fought the case, it would obsess his every waking moment for a year, possibly longer, and he could lose ten times that amount if the verdict went against him. Even if he won, he would still lose, because another peculiarity of the English law is that the victor cannot recoup his full costs. It was as if the judiciary had put Singh in a devil's version of *Who Wants to be a Millionaire?*

Singh's wife, the BBC journalist Anita Anand, understood the principle at stake, and backed her husband. Whatever happened, she said, the case would not divide them. But the question remained for Singh, how far could he go before deciding that the risk to his family's finances was too great? To cap it all, the judge had come up with a reading of Singh's words that made a defence impossible.

No one would have blamed him for backing down. There would have been no dishonour in withdrawing from the fray. Thousands of publishers and writers in England and beyond have looked at the cost and biases of the English law and thought surrender the only option. Singh said that if he were a twenty-five-year-old with no money he would have apologised. But his bestselling books had given him financial independence. He resolved to refuse to put his name to a lie by authorising an apology. He knew what his enemies would do with it. Ernst and Singh had spent years investigating alternative medicine. No potential patient would spend more than a few days doing the same. If he apologised, chiropractic therapists would wave his retraction at potential patients, and say that Singh had admitted that their philosophy was not gibberish, and their claims to treat children were not bogus. As shamefully, an apology would also make Singh complicit in silencing other journalists, scientists and editors, who would think hard before challenging alternative therapists after seeing how the law had forced him to retract.

From Stalin in his show trials to oligarchs suing investigative journalists, censors want recantations as well as exemplary punishments. I have seen billionaires, including convicted criminals, extract admissions of guilt from British newspapers too poor or too frightened to fight, and use them to convince journalists and politicians around the world that legitimate criticisms of their actions were groundless. Singh did not wish to join such sorry company.

He told the audience in the pub that night that he cared about health and the health of children, and thought that his article was fair and reasonable. He had spoken to his lawyers, and they had promised to try to find a way to appeal the judge's ruling. 'I should be able to write about scientific issues without the fear of being intimidated,' he said. 'It's about more than just me. Bloggers, journalists and scientists … we should all have the right to write about important issues without fear of being intimidated. It's not just about science. It's about all journalists being able to write fairly and reasonably.'

The audience who had gathered to hear him were science bloggers, members of the 'skeptic' movement the Internet had empowered to argue for evidence-based politics and against official toleration of superstition. They did not need newspaper editors or broadcasters to give their views a hearing. They knew that they could reach any interested reader with access to a computer anywhere in the world, and revelled in the new opportunities the Web had opened up.

The normal response of the British to a speaker's description of an abuse of power is to say 'Tut-tut,' often quite sternly. But instead of shrugging their shoulders and muttering, 'It's a bad business but what can we do?', Singh's audience of Net-literate skeptics turned into a heaving mass of whooping, hollering geeks. They roared their defiance as a red mist descended over their spectacles, and vowed they would not rest until they had brought the rotten system of English censorship crashing to the ground.

Shocked and awed, I said to Ben Goldacre, 'The nerds are on the march. I wouldn't like to be standing in their way.'

An uncharacteristically spiritual look passed over the great debunker's face. 'Yes,' he said. 'Strike us down, we shall become more powerful than you could possibly imagine.'

I realised this was what Obi-Wan Kenobi said to Darth Vader in *Star Wars*, and mockingly commented that the skeptic movement's highest cultural reference point was a 1970s sci-fi movie.

I should have been more courteous.

Goldacre was right about this, as so much else. The 'Streisand effect' kicked in with a vengeance. Dozens of websites reprinted Singh's original article. What had been a small piece on the comment pages of a British newspaper became a global phenomenon read by anyone with an interest in science and free debate. Although newspapers and broadcasters were careful about what they said for fear the chiropractors would sue them too, bloggers were uninhibited. They seemed beyond the control of the censors. Individually, each writer or tweeter appeared too small to go after. Collectively, there were too many of them. Because skeptics were informed readers of science blogs, Singh's solicitor Robert Dougans, a brilliant young lawyer on his first big case, and Adrienne Page, his QC, found they could call on the knowledge of hundreds of scientists just by logging on to the Net and crowd-sourcing their appeal.

The chiropractors produced pleadings for the court that said there was reliable evidence that they could cure sick children. Bloggers put them up, and their readers picked them apart. The chiropractors claimed that a study suggested that they could cure babies with colic. One online commentator noticed, 'There was no control group at all. It simply follows 316 babies and found that most of them eventually got better. Well, they do, don't they?' The chiropractors said a second study found that their treatments worked. The bloggers said that this study consisted of 'two case reports and they refer to use of a mechanical device, not the usual chiropractic manipulation'. Computer-literate scientists, who understood the investigative power of the

Net, tracked down six hundred chiropractic therapists in Britain who claimed they could treat childhood illnesses, and reported them for breaching advertising standards requirements. The regulators at the General Chiropractic Council were so over-whelmed with complaints that they had to take on more staff. At one point in 2010, one in four chiropractors was under investigation.

A justifiable paranoia descended on British chiropractic therapists. Their trade associations warned them to take down their websites and to refuse to talk to strangers, who might be undercover skeptics. If they had leaflets 'that state you treat whiplash, colic or other childhood problems in your clinic or at any other site where they might be displayed with your contact details on them. DO NOT USE them until further notice.'

The Singh case brought home to English law the interactive possibility of the Net. It was not just that the courts could no longer stop an article being read, or that their threat of censor-ship turned readers into active citizens who could help Singh and his lawyers in building a defence. Libel law had created a virtual community that was ready to turn into the most success-ful British free-speech movement since the campaign fifty years previously against the obscenity laws the state used to prosecute Penguin Books for publishing *Lady Chatterley's Lover*.

On the one hand, the legal establishment faced a traditional reform campaign which William Wilberforce would have recog-nised. Sense about Science, Index on Censorship and English PEN mobilised elite scientific, media and political figures. Running alongside the traditional reformers was the exuberant and anarchic reform campaign on the Web, which Wilberforce could never have imagined.

The judiciary backed down. Faced with growing alarm from politicians and courtrooms packed with protesters, and maybe the dim realisation that they were sitting on the benches of a democracy, the judges of the Court of Appeal reversed all previous rulings. The legal reasoning they used was technical – when Singh said there was 'not a jot' of evidence to support the therapists' claims, the judges decided he was making a 'fair comment' based on facts truly stated rather than stating a plain fact. It seemed to outsiders to be a distinction without a difference, but the ruling meant that the chiropractors now faced fearsome difficulties in pressing forward with their case. They dropped their action, and Singh, and all the campaign groups and Net activists who stood by him, savoured a rare triumph.

Those of us who thought that English judges did not know the difference between John Milton and Milton Keynes listened with wonder as the Lord Chief Justice remembered which country he came from, and aligned himself with its best traditions. 'To compel an author to prove in court what he has asserted by way of argument is to invite the court to become an Orwellian ministry of truth,' he said, and then quoted the passage from the *Areopagitica* where Milton recalled meeting the persecuted Galileo in Florence in 1638. 'I have sat among their learned men', Milton said of the Italians who entertained him, and 'for that honour I had, and been counted happy to be born in such a place of philosophic freedom, as they supposed England was, while themselves did nothing but bemoan the servile condition into which learning among them was brought; ... that nothing had been there written now these many years but flattery and fustian. There it was that I found and visited the famous Galileo, grown old a prisoner of the Inquisition, for thinking in astronomy otherwise than the Franciscan and Dominican licensers thought.'

The judge did not quite say that English libel law was as great a threat to scientific thought as the Inquisition's order to Galileo to recant his belief that the earth went round the sun. But he saw a valid comparison, and said 'that is a pass to which we ought not to come again'.

Modern culture despises politicians. In newsrooms or on satire shows, no lawyer stops journalists and comedians from mocking them, because politicians generally don't sue. Most have thick skins, and those who do not know they will look ridiculous in the eyes of their voters if they go to court. In my experience, politicians are more open than the supposedly liberal judiciary. They are certainly more protective of the reputation of their country. The United Nations had condemned Britain. After the Saudi plutocrat Khalid bin Mahfouz used English law to attack books that American houses had not even published in England, President Obama signed a law that stated that the US courts should not enforce the orders of English judges against American authors. Now scientists were telling the judges that lawyers for cranks and pharmaceutical corporations were threatening free debate about public health.

Politicians honoured Simon Singh's bloody-minded refusal to bow before pressure by agreeing to reform. In the run-up to the general election of 2010, all three main political parties made a manifesto commitment to reforming the libel laws, after fifty thousand voters signed a petition defending free speech and free enquiry. The victorious Conservative/Liberal coalition government honoured its promises and proposed making it far harder for libel tourists to use the London courts to punish their critics. Ministers also wanted a strengthening of the defences available to writers, and in a nod to John Stuart Mill, they added that claimants must prove they had suffered substantial harm before they could sue. Even if the draft Bill becomes law, it has many gaps. The presumption of guilt still lies on the accused, and more seriously, the cost of libel actions looks as if it will remain formidably high.

At the time this book went to the printers, it was not certain that Parliament would pass the measure into law. Even if it does, the most striking feature of the reform campaign was its timidity. English radicals are remarkably conservative, and the reformers did not ask Parliament to adopt the American system and allow citizens to say and write what they pleased about public figures, as long as they did so without a negligent disregard for the truth. The police and credit reference agencies can pass on false information and the citizen cannot sue them for libel unless they act with malice, yet the law continues to demand that the public debates of a democracy must be constrained.

If reformers had been braver, they might have argued that giving primacy to freedom of speech would not allow the worst aspects of American culture to implant themselves in Britain. The First Amendment did not permit radio shock jocks and Fox News to flourish in the US. On the contrary, the courts had ruled that America's 'fairness doctrine' – which required broadcasters to cover matters of public importance and to give airtime to contrasting views – was compatible with constitutional protections for freedom of speech. The judges held that because only a limited number of stations could fit onto the broadcast spectrum, the state had a right to prevent their owners from delivering unbalanced or propagandistic journalism. 'There is nothing in the First Amendment which prevents the Government from requiring a licensee to share his frequency with others,' the Supreme Court said in 1969. 'It is the right of the viewers and listeners, not the right of the broadcasters, which is paramount.'

Free-speech legislation did not undermine the fairness doctrine, rather in the 1980s the American political right, led by officials in the Reagan administration, began the task of dismantling the regulatory controls which required broadcasters to air balanced journalism. Today's European broadcasters who yearn to deliver similarly hectoring and prejudiced journalism say that cable television and the Internet have destroyed the reasons for legally enforced impartiality. Technological advance has removed the spectrum scarcity which limited the number of channels, so how can countries like Britain justify restricting what they broadcast? But even though cable and the Web have created a space for every type of political view, one can still argue that television and radio broadcasters should be treated as special cases.

In everyday life we accept differing standards in differing circumstances. We have a right to swear when we are at home or with friends. If an employer were to dismiss us for swearing at customers or clients, we would not say that he or she was infringing our rights to freedom of speech. There is no public-interest defence for swearing at customers, and we could still swear in other circumstances. Similarly, society is entitled to say that there should be a corner in the marketplace of ideas where journalists and their managers and owners must respect notions of fairness and balance, particularly when radio and television stations continue to be controlled by the state or by wealthy individuals and corporations.

A more dangerous American development has been the ability of lobbyists to use free-speech legislation to overturn restrictions that had existed since the early twentieth century on corporations and trade unions funding attack ads during elections. A US Supreme Court decision passed by a margin of 5–4 in 2010 effectively gave every organisation the right to sponsor propaganda. At first glance the ruling appeared logical: why should corporations not enjoy the same rights as individuals, newspapers and bloggers to say what they wanted in an election debate? Its logic fell apart under closer examination, and the perverse verdict is ripe for overturning. Corporations and trade unions are not individuals but collectives, which is why the law should never allow them to sue for libel. They cannot vote or run for office, and corporations may be controlled by foreigners who cannot vote or run for office either. It is unlikely that every shareholder, customer or employee of a company, or every member of a trade union, will agree with the political stance the controllers of the collective take in an election campaign. When a company board or a trade-union committee takes a political stance, it forces dissenters to pay a de facto tax to subsidise views with which they profoundly disagree.

The US Supreme Court ignored the distorting effects of big money on debate. Or as Justice John Stevens said when he dissented from the view of the majority of his fellow judges, 'At bottom, the Court's opinion is a rejection of the common sense of the American people, who have recognized a need to prevent corporations from undermining self-government since the founding, and who have fought against the distinctive corrupting potential of corporate electioneering since the days of Theodore Roosevelt. It is a strange time to repudiate that common sense. While American democracy is imperfect, few outside the majority of this Court would have thought its flaws included a dearth of corporate money in politics.'

Arguments about the distorting effects of special interests on democracy are as old as representative government. The novelty of the present lies in the new argument that we no longer need to worry about the power of religion, money or the state. The Singh case and many battles like it appeared to prove that the Web had made the old debates about restrictions on freedom of speech redundant. Singh's supporters, like the supporters of so many other modern causes, had used the new technologies to circumvent legal restrictions. Optimists could say that their success showed that we were moving into a new world, whose liberalism would make past generations blink with astonishment. All of a sudden, debates about blasphemy, libel, electoral laws, campaign finance and constitutional protections appeared leftovers from the analogue age. The wonder of the Web had dispatched the concerns of the past to the dustbin of history. Now we could write what we wanted, and no one could stop us.

# PART THREE

# *State*

*In our age there is no such thing as 'keeping out of politics'. All issues are political issues.*

GEORGE ORWELL, 1946

## SEVEN

# *The Internet and the Revolution*

*Tyranny's new nightmare: Twitter*

*LOS ANGELES TIMES*, 24 JUNE 2009

If I had been writing a book on censorship before the invention of the Internet, I would have concentrated on two subjects that have hardly featured in these pages: the power of the state in its dictatorial and democratic forms to suppress criticism; and the power of private and public media conglomerates to control debate. They dominated thinking about freedom of speech in the twentieth century, but by the twenty-first appeared less important than at any time since the highpoint of Victorian liberalism.

To understand how the culture has changed, look at what George Orwell wrote about censorship after he attended a meeting in 1944 to commemorate the tercentenary of the publication of Milton's *Aeropagitica*. At that time, the dominant mood in intellectual London was one of sympathy for Stalin's Soviet Union. Although Milton had argued for freedom of thought, Orwell found that communists and their fellow travellers at the celebration adopted the Marxist position that bourgeois freedoms were illusions, and intellectual honesty was a form of anti-social selfishness: 'Out of this concourse of several hundred people, perhaps half of whom were directly connected with the writing trade, there was not a single one who could point out that freedom of the press, if it means anything at all, means the freedom to criticise and oppose.'

Democratic Britain imposed its own censorship during the war and before it: through direct state controls on what writers and reporters might say, and more circuitously through the informal pressure publishers put on writers to say nothing that might undermine the nation's struggle against its enemies. The pressure was subtle but unremitting, and Orwell sighed that no one had been able to escape the 'continuous war atmosphere of the past ten years'.

He was as depressed by the economic constraints on writers as the ideological pressures. 'In our age, the idea of intellectual liberty is under attack from two directions. On the one side are its theoretical enemies, the apologists of totalitarianism, and on the other its immediate, practical enemies, monopoly and bureaucracy.' The unwillingness of the public to buy books meant that if writers wished to see their work published, they had to seek work in newspaper offices or film studios, which were in the hands of a few rich men, or at the stations of the publicly owned BBC radio monopoly. The alternative was to sell themselves as propagandists and draw wages from the Ministry of Information or the British Council, 'which help the writer to keep alive but also waste his time and dictate his opinions'. 'Everything in our age conspires to turn the writer and every other kind of artist as well, into a minor official, working on themes handed down from above and never telling what seems to him the whole of the truth.'

The tight-fisted public is as unwilling to buy books as ever, but much else about Orwell's description feels dated. Although Western troops have been fighting since 9/11, Orwell's 'war atmosphere' has not intimidated writers as varied as investigative reporters trying to find the truth about the second Iraq war, and malign fantasists peddling conspiracy theories. Far from fearing or respecting war leaders, journalists have treated them with the utmost contempt. As they did, they illustrated an unacknowledged truth about contemporary writing: reporters, editors and artists in Britain, America and most of Europe are not afraid of politicians. They are frightened of Islamists, and do not run cartoons that might offend them. They are frightened of oligarchs and CEOs, and worry about libel and the ability of the wealthy to bend the ear of their proprietors. But they are not frightened about leaking the secrets or criticising the actions of elected governments. One can map the shift of power from the state by tracing journalists' fears as the twentieth century progressed. In 1936, all British newspaper proprietors reached a 'gentlemen's agreement' not to mention Edward VIII's affair with Wallis Simpson for fear of offending the monarchy. In 2006, all British newspaper editors made an unspoken agreement not to run the Danish cartoons for fear of offending Islamists. In the 1930s, the public woke up to discover that their king was about to abdicate because he was determined to marry a divorcee, without their media forewarning them. In our time, the public woke up to discover that their banking system was about to collapse, without their media forewarning them.

In Western countries, the power of the state to intimidate its civil servants was little greater than the power of businesses to enforce silence on their employees. America and Israel were the exceptions, as so often, and clung on to the traditions of the old nation state that were fading in Europe. The Israeli courts imprisoned a soldier who leaked military secrets which suggested the army followed an illegal shoot-to-kill policy. Meanwhile, when the American soldier Bradley Manning passed thousands of cables from the US State Department to WikiLeaks, a vindictive Pentagon held him in solitary confinement. But even the American authorities made no attempt to stop US newspapers publishing the WikiLeaks secrets. The cases of two British civil servants who released batches of secrets provided a better guide to the weakness of the twenty-first-century democratic state. In 2003 Katherine Gun revealed how the British intelligence services were bugging the United Nations at the behest of the Americans in the run-up to the second Iraq war, and in 2006 Derek Pasquill showed how his employers at the Foreign Office were allowing the Muslim Brotherhood to influence British policy. In both instances, the government threatened to teach its servants not to embarrass their masters in wartime by prosecuting them for breaking the Official Secrets Act. In both instances, it dropped the threat of trial and imprisonment for fear that jurors would show how unimpressed the public was by the 'continuous war atmosphere' by acquitting them.

Warriors in the War on Terror attempted to attack freedom of speech, although nearly all the arrests were in Russia, China and the Arab dictatorships, who used the war as another excuse for clampdowns they would have authorised anyway. The British Labour Party tried to enforce a new offence that would punish anyone who 'glorifies, exalts or celebrates the commission, preparation or instigation (whether in the past, in the future or generally) of acts of terrorism'. Prosecutors might have used it legitimately against people who were directly inciting murder, or illegitimately against citizens who expressed sympathy with terrorists. As it was, they did little worth recording. Politicians in the 1997–2010 Labour government became notorious for issuing bloodcurdling threats to please press and public, and then doing nothing. Their attempt to restrict freedom of speech in wartime was no exception to the rule. The handful of cases where the state attempted to censor alleged Islamist sympathisers showed only how far Britain was from martial law.

Managers at Nottingham University reported a student to the police for downloading an al Qaeda training manual. It turned out that the material was freely available in the US, and that the suspect was researching rather than practising terrorism. He was released without charge, and successfully sued the police for false arrest. The courts jailed five men from Bradford who had down-loaded pro-jihadi sermons featuring all the usual hatreds. The Court of Appeal freed them on the Millian grounds that in England the state should prosecute you for what you did, not for what you read. The strangest case was that of a young Muslim woman who worked at Heathrow Airport, a likely terrorist target. She collected books on how to poison, shoot and bomb, and wrote poems in praise of murder. In 'How to Behead', she said:

> No doubt that the punk will twitch and scream
> But ignore the donkey's ass
> And continue to slice back and forth
> You'll feel the knife hit the wind and food pipe
> But don't stop
> Continue with all your might.

She was in love with death, but there was no evidence that she was involved in terrorism, and the court gave her a suspended prison sentence. Her mild punishment, which was subsequently overturned by the Court of Appeal, stood out because sentences for any kind of anti-government speech were so rare. Western democracies managed to fight without imposing restrictions on freedom of speech. Instead of Orwell's 'war atmosphere', there was an anti-war atmosphere. If the government had wanted to charge those who said that Islamist violence had nothing to do with Islamist ideology and was solely a response to Western provocation, it would have had to arrest a quarter of the public and three-quarters of the intelligentsia.

Meanwhile, Orwell's world of media monoliths that writers must appease if they wished to be published vanished. The BBC's monopoly was broken in the 1950s. By the 2000s, there were hundreds of TV channels and radio stations. If a writer, producer, journalist or actor crossed the BBC, it no longer meant an end to a broadcasting career. Newspapers remained under the control of corporations and plutocrats, but the

Internet so undermined what power they had that by the 2010s media commentators were wondering if the 'dead tree' or 'legacy' press could survive.

The Net achieved more than that. For all his fame as a futurologist, Orwell never predicted a final change. Enthusiasts hailed the Internet as the most important advance in communications technology since the invention of movable type in the 1450s. They may have been right, although it is too early to say. When they went on to announce, however, that the new age of transparency would free humanity from the constraints imposed by political power, they endorsed a faith as utopian as the communism that Orwell opposed.

## Welcome to Utopia

In 1996, as the jubilation about the possibilities of the new technology was building, John Perry Barlow, a former lyricist for the Grateful Dead, stood as defiantly as Martin Luther and issued a thunderous manifesto. His audience was not a revolutionary crowd outside a dictator's palace, but the politicians and CEOs meeting at the global elite's annual beanfeast at Davos in the Swiss Alps. The object of his protest was as bewildering as its location: a proposal from the Clinton administration to deregulate the telecommunications industry.

The president was as prepared to annul America's old controls on cross-media ownership, as he was willing to shred the old restrictions on bank ownership. But Barlow had no complaints about corporations funding the politicians who passed the laws that increased corporate control of the airwaves. What stirred his passion and ignited his radical rage was a rider to the main Bill. Christian conservatives had insisted that there should be provisions to control the circulation of indecent material on the Internet. Their protests were ludicrous posturings to please the Christian core vote. As they must have known, their planned censorship conflicted with the First Amendment. The Supreme Court duly stuck down the measure as unconstitutional. But Congress's suggestion that democratic legislatures might regulate the Internet, even though in this instance they could not, provoked Barlow to issue a ferocious denunciation of the futility of state regulation, which must have pleased the bankers and executives enjoying the Alpine air.

'Governments of the Industrial World,' his Declaration of Independence of Cyberspace began, 'you weary giants of flesh and steel, I come from Cyberspace, the new home of Mind. On behalf of the future, I ask you of the past to leave us alone. You are not welcome among us. You have no sovereignty where we gather … We are creating a world that all may enter without privilege or prejudice accorded by race, economic power, military force, or station of birth. We are creating a world where anyone, anywhere may express his or her beliefs, no matter how singular, without fear of being coerced into silence or conformity. I declare the global social space we are building to be naturally independent of the tyrannies you seek to impose on us. You have no moral right to rule us nor do you possess any methods of enforcement we have true reason to fear.'

Barlow cut a ridiculous figure: 'a Deadhead in Davos' who dressed an argument for unregulated markets in the clothes of red revolution. 'Barlow may have sounded like an alienated counter-culturist as he railed against the Telecoms Act,' wrote the left-wing American critic Thomas Frank, 'but he essentially agreed with the suit-and-tie media execs on the big issue – that markets enjoyed some mystic, organic connection to the people, while governments were fundamentally illegitimate.'

Everyone with knowledge of recent history now realises that Clinton's deregulation of the banks led to a disaster, and new controls are essential. But most people who think about censorship agree with Barlow that attempting to censor what appears on the Net is not only pernicious but pointless.

What seemed in the mid-1990s to be the burblings of the plutocracy's pet hippy is the conventional wisdom of our day. The Internet had rendered traditional diplomacy obsolete, declared a wide-eyed Parag Khanna of the New America Foundation, a think tank for futurologists. There is no point worrying about old-style foreign policy, because non-governmental organisations and ad hoc networks linked by social media will soon replace it. Networking will achieve 'universal liberation' – no less – 'through exponentially expanding and voluntary interconnections'. The liberators will not be philosophers, the radicalised masses or political leaders, but celebrities, who 'possess one of the core ingredients of diplomatic success: prestige'. He held out the example of Madonna to convince doubters: 'Her resilience and tirelessness [are] the reasons why she remains at the top of her game. Regular diplomats should learn from her staying power.' Gordon Brown said that the new technologies ensured that 'foreign policy can no longer be the province of just a few elites'. The world was becoming a global village, where 'you cannot have Rwanda again because information would come out far more quickly about what is actually going on and public opinion would grow to the point where action would need to be taken'. It never occurred to Brown that a genocide comparable to Rwanda had taken place in Darfur in western Sudan in 2003, and the wired world had done nothing to stop it. Hillary Clinton and many others believed that dictatorships would soon go the way of genocidal militias. If a despotic regime censored the Net, its businesses would not have access to global sources of news, and their trade would suffer, she argued. They must allow the free flow of information or pay the economic price, because 'from an economic standpoint, there is no distinction between censoring political speech and commercial speech'.

The Internet inspires such ecstatic visions because it feels as if it has rolled all previous communications technologies into one. The experience of using it crosses all the old boundaries.

The reader becomes a writer by commenting on other people's work. The writer becomes a reader by looking at other people's comments. One minute the audience is passive, as if it were reading an old-fashioned book or watching a twentieth-century film, music video or television programme; the next it is active: intervening, copying, linking and recommending. Readers who are writers and writers who are readers can speak to each other personally, as if they were using a telephone. But they can extend their range of contacts beyond the possibilities of ordinary social life on social-network sites. Through trawling personal blogs, Facebook or Twitter they can listen in to private conversations between friends as if they were spies tapping a phone. Yet if they stumble across an obscure piece of writing, or a video that interests them, they can make the private public by linking to it. If enough people copy their link, they will have created a viral phenomenon, as if they were an A&R man discovering a new talent. Because they can copy and upload information painlessly, they can build sites in a day with more words than a Victorian novelist could produce in a lifetime. Because they can allow crowd sourcing and Wiki editing, they can gather more opinions than the compilers of the *Oxford English Dictionary* or the *Encyclopaedia Britannia* had at their disposal.

No wonder the new technologies went to people's heads, and they began to believe that the citizen was 'no longer a passive consumer of political information and occasional voter, but an active player monitoring what governments and politicians were doing and demanding a seat at the table'.

Beyond these attractions lay a wonderful gift: working on the Net was no more expensive than the price of a laptop or a session in an Internet café. The communist-influenced intelligentsia Orwell despised may have denied some of the greatest mass murders in history, lied so often it no longer understood the difference between truth and falsehood, and disgraced socialist politics irredeemably, but it had one good argument: freedom of the press was a hollow ideal when freedom came at such a high price. Only wealthy men and corporations with access to capital, or governments with access to taxes, could afford to run a newspaper, television or radio station. Only they could hire professional journalists, with the skills required to deliver news in the limited time and space available, and the star performers who could attract a mass audience. Like the joke about capitalist freedom guaranteeing everyone an equal right to book a room at the Ritz, freedom of the press meant freedom for Orwell's private tycoons and state-funded broadcasters.

Now the costs of publication were effectively nothing, the space available was effectively limitless, and the potential audience was an ever-increasing proportion of the world's population. Journalists felt as obsolete as blacksmiths – the products of an outdated technology which required a now-redundant professional caste. Blogging, online videos and podcasts meant that everybody could be a journalist, broadcaster or artist. If they produced material the public wanted to read or see, they did not, in theory, need a promotional budget to attract attention – search engines and links would direct readers to them. If they wanted to share their interest in a hobby or an obscure political cause they did not need to buy special-interest magazines, because the same processes allowed them to connect to others. No one needed an editor or a proprietor's permission to publish. No gatekeepers kept out innovators or writers. Even if conglomerates such as Apple are beginning to restrict what the public can read on the Net, they do not for the time being have anything like the influence of the old press barons.

Supporters and opponents alike overestimated proprietors' power to sway the electorate even in the media moguls' heyday, but what influence proprietors had became negligible when the new technologies subverted their business plans and smashed their control of the news agenda. The economic facts of publishing life were on the side of the many, not the few. In every advanced country, millions of people could scrutinise elected and unelected power with an intensity the old media could not manage, and publish their findings.

Consider how the terms of trade for investigative journalism had changed. In the twentieth century, journalists who tried to persuade state or corporate officials to give them classified documents faced many obstacles that still exist. Then as now, they had to convince them to risk their careers. They had to prove to them that they were worthy of their trust, and would protect their anonymity in all circumstances. But computer processing power has rendered a fearsome logistical difficulty irrelevant. Until the 1990s, journalist and informant faced the physical problem of copying. Suppose, in the late twentieth century, a source in the British House of Commons had wanted to leak approximately 1.2 million receipts to the *Daily Telegraph* that revealed how MPs were claiming expenses for everything from the cost of cleaning their moats to duckhouses for their ponds. Or think of a disillusioned soldier in the American military who wanted to leak 251,287 documents recounting the conversations between the US State Department and its embassies. Even in the unlikely event of the information all being in one building that the source had access to, he would still have to go through dozens of filing cabinets without arousing suspicion. He would have to photocopy on site or 'borrow' every piece of paper, and again hope that his colleagues did not begin to suspect what he intended to do with the information. Even if he fooled them, either he would need a truck to move the documents out of the building in one go, or he would have to divide them into manageable batches and walk past police officers or military guards hundreds of times. In both cases, the likelihood of them stopping and checking his load would be so high as to be a deterrent in itself.

Suppose he overcame his fear, duped everyone in his building and transported his documents to a newspaper office. Its editors would be able to publish just a small part of what he had given them in an old-fashioned print newspaper – assuming, that is, the authorities allowed the editor to publish, and did not threaten the paper with court action or worse.

Before the Net, just one information dump made it from behind the security fence to the press: the Pentagon Papers, a secret study prepared by the US Defense Department which Daniel Ellsberg leaked in 1971 to show how the Johnson administration of the 1960s had lied about the course of its disastrous Vietnam War. The papers made up forty-seven volumes. Their two million words filled four thousand pages of original documents and three thousand pages of analysis. The US government was so conscious of the damage the secret history of the war could do, it had printed just fifteen copies. Fortunately for Ellsberg, he could target a copy that was not in the Pentagon or another heavily guarded military base, but was kept at the offices of the RAND Corporation, a think tank where he worked. Ellsberg had access to the papers, and with the help of a friend spent three months in the autumn of 1971 carrying documents in his briefcase to a safe flat, and returning them before anyone noticed their absence. The task of copying them was so lengthy he co-opted his children to help. If he had leaked secret information of comparable sensitivity in any other major power in the 1970s, he would never have seen it published. The Russians and the Chinese would have shot him and the journalists who helped him. The French and the British would have arrested them. As it was, the editors of the *New York Times* and other American papers who ran his stories had to fight in court to assert the rights of the free press that the First Amendment to the US Constitution guaranteed. Now, if you have security clearance or can hack a system, you can simply copy documents to a memory stick and slip it in your pocket.

The traditional enemies of freedom of thought could attempt to manage information when it came via a few publishers and broadcasters with assets to seize, and editors and publishers they could fine and imprison. If the *Daily News* published an attack on its government in the twentieth century, the authorities knew before they knew anything else that it had originated in the offices of the *Daily News*, and that they could hold the paper to account. Mass-circulation titles had to deliver millions of copies overnight. They had to publish in the countries they covered, and submit to the jurisdiction of national authorities.

Today, if the law stops you publishing in your own country, you can publish abroad and still reach your target audience. WikiLeaks based itself in Sweden because of that country's exceptionally strong legal protections for journalists, and was well aware that the constraints of geography no longer limited its ability to distribute news. It installed military-grade encryption on its laptops to prevent secret services breaking into its systems, and instructed its workers to speak to each other on protected Skype networks. To say that journalists in the twentieth century did not enjoy such advantages is to understate the case. The CIA and the KGB did not enjoy them either. When John Perry Barlow announced in the 1990s that governments did not 'possess any methods of enforcement we have true reason to fear', he appeared to have seen beyond the constraints governments placed on the writers of the time to a free future.

Nor did twentieth-century reporters enjoy the advantages of unrestricted space. Thirty years ago, a news programme would rarely devote more than a couple of minutes to a subject, while a broadsheet newspaper rarely had the space to reproduce more than three or four pages from a stash of leaked documents. The editors would decide what was significant, and would make the wrong decisions on occasion. On the Net, you can run all the footage or reproduce all the documents in searchable format online, and leave it to thousands of readers, in some cases hundreds of thousands of readers, to examine every detail and look for significant facts and damning connections the best of editors or reporters might have missed.

The importance of viewing evidence can never be underestimated. Politicians worry more about video footage that makes them look ridiculous or a document that incriminates than the most scathing polemics, because they understand that direct evidence is more damning than any critical review. The Web allows more evidence to be presented to the court of public opinion than ever before.

Before I get to work, I should add that just because the Net inspires techno-utopian fantasies it does not mean the fantasies are always mistaken. To talk of a 'Twitter revolution' in Iran is to be wrong on both counts: Twitter had just twenty thousand subscribers in Iran in 2009, and the disgusting brutality of the clerical regime ensured there was no revolution. But when those same neophiliacs talked of the Arab Spring being made up of 'Facebook revolutions', they were not wholly deluded. Ahmed Maher, who launched the April 6 Youth Facebook group in Egypt, which linked bloggers and activists, did not create a mass movement on the Net. There were not enough users of Facebook in Egypt to form a mass movement. If you wanted to belittle April 6's achievements, you might say that the millions attracted to groups supporting fashionable causes in the West made the support the movement attracted seem paltry. But as an astute writer for *Wired* magazine said before the revolution, you cannot use the number of people from a democracy who click on an 'I like' button to damn the efforts of dissidents in dictatorships. 'In places like Egypt, these virtual gatherings are a big deal. Although freedom of speech and freedom of religion may be democracy's headliners, it's the less sexy-sounding freedom of assembly that, when prohibited, can effectively asphyxiate political organization. Uniting seventy thousand people is no easy feat in a country where collective action is so risky. Social networking has changed that. In turn, it is changing the dynamics of political dissent.'

The youth movement in Egypt was a new opposition force the regime did not understand. It had not been able to infiltrate its ranks or buy off its members, as it had always done with its traditional opponents. It understood the danger of individual bloggers, and arrested them, then tortured and sodomised them in prison. But it could not cope with a new form of political association which could mobilise demonstrators. In Syria, the heartbreaking bravery of the activists who risked their lives as they filmed the atrocities of the Ba'athist death squads would have counted for nothing if the Web had not allowed them to publish their videos. There, as in Iran and Egypt, the Web broke the dictatorship's illusion of omnipotence. Once dissenters sat in jails tormented by the knowledge that not only could their captors murder them, but the secret police could erase most of the records of their movements' struggles. The Web provides a space where no censor can wipe them from the record of history.

When the first popular hero of the revolution against the Egyptian dictatorship was Wael Ghonim, a Google executive, persecuted by the police for running a Facebook campaign of an opposition candidate, those who doubt the power of the Web have some explaining to do.

Clay Shirky, a typically can-do American optimist and the most engaging of the cyber-utopians, picked on the example of Belarus as he explored the apparently limitless possibilities for human freedom the Net had opened. This small country, squeezed between Russia and Poland, had experienced the worst the twentieth century could offer: Tsarism with its persecution of non-Russian minorities, most notably the Jews; the First World War and the terrible battles on the Eastern Front; the Russian Revolution; the civil war that followed it; Lenin's terror; Stalin's terror; Hitler's invasion and its massacres; the Holocaust; the terrible battles of the Soviet reconquest; and the return of Stalin's terror once the war was over. After Stalin's death, there was only a modest respite: the life-denying rulers of late-vintage Soviet communism governed the unlucky land.

The fall of the Berlin Wall liberated Eastern Europe, but not

Belarus. It broke away from Russia, but the local strongman Alexander Grigoryevich Lukashenko maintained a Brezhnevian state. He ruled 'the last dictatorship in Europe' by censoring the press, killing opposition leaders and rigging elections. The United States and the European Union protested, but what could they do? If the men with the guns do not want democratic change, it takes other men with guns to make them change their minds. The West was not going to invade. Russia, the regional superpower, tolerated the dictator, and there was no domestic military force capable of organising a revolution.

The Web appeared to lift the dead weight of history from the shoulders of the oppressed. 'The use of flash mobs as a tool of political protest has reached its zenith in Belarus,' Shirky said as he explained how citizens could organise against oppression in the most unpromising circumstances. The ability of Belarusian dissidents to arrange fast, spontaneous protests via online chatrooms and the community pages of LiveJournal inspired him. In 2006, after Lukashenko 'won' his third term with another rigged election, an anonymous activist working under the name of 'by_mob' proposed a demonstration. Instead of urging opponents of the regime to chant slogans, he suggested that they show up in central Minsk and eat ice cream. The police arrested them, as they arrested anyone engaged in unauthorised public gatherings. Activists retaliated by posting pictures on the Web of the cops leading away citizens for the anti-state crime of eating ice cream in a public place. Other flash mobs followed, and demonstrators caught the overreactions of the authorities on camera and posted them to an international audience. Before the gift of new technology, the state-controlled media would not publicise protests, nor would it report on them accurately afterwards – if at all. The local public and international observers need never know they had happened.

The new technology blew away the old advantages the state's media monopoly gave it. Anonymous bloggers could arrange demonstrations without revealing their identities. Anyone on the Net could read about them and come along, or read accounts of the protest afterwards and see pictures and videos taken with mobile phones. Meanwhile, Shirky thought, the knowledge that electronic eyes were monitoring them limited the brutality of the secret police. Understandably impressed, he said that the Belarusian protesters were showing us that the Web was delivering freedoms that men and women once needed liberal constitutions and democratic governments to guarantee. 'To speak online is to publish, and to publish online is to connect with others. With the arrival of globally accessible publishing, freedom of speech is now the freedom of the press and freedom of the press is freedom of assembly. Naturally the changes occasioned by new sources of freedom are most significant in a less free environment.'

He could not have been more wrong. The Net, like all previous revolutions in communications technology, will change the world. But, like all previous revolutions in communications technology, it will give advantages to those who already enjoy power and wealth. As well as empowering the citizens of democracies and dissidents in dictatorships, it empowers elected governments, dictatorial regimes, police forces, spies, employers, blackmailers, frauds, fanatics and terrorists. Meanwhile the ideology of the Net activists who command attention and admiration in the West can be a sly and parochial creed which actively works against the interests of Belarusian dissidents and all others living with oppression. Worst of all, those who claimed that the 'Age of Transparency' had dawned did not think about how censorship works. If they had, they would have grasped that those 'weary giants of flesh and steel' are tougher than they look. For there is one prediction about the next decade that one can make with certainty: after watching protests from the Belarus flash mobs to the Arab Spring, no dictatorship will make the mistake of ignoring social networking again.

# RULES FOR CENSORS (7):

## *Look to the Past/Think of the Future*

Cyber-utopians do not study history. If they did, they would not be utopians. The one story from the past they love to recall is the tale from the Middle Ages of Johannes Trithemius, Abbot of Sponheim near Bad Kreuznach in the Rhineland, and his unintentionally revealing polemic against Gutenberg's new printing presses.

The abbot venerated the traditions of the medieval scribes. With skill and persistence, they preserved the culture and the religious doctrines of medieval Europe by copying manuscripts which would otherwise have rotted away. Their labour was arduous, and their manuscripts were expensive; only the wealthiest individuals and institutions could afford a library. Gutenberg's movable type destroyed the scribes' monopoly and rendered their skills obsolete. For the first time, printers could make a copy of a book in less time than it took to read it. Like the Internet, the new presses of the 1450s were a revolution in communications technology, massively increasing the ability to view the written word.

The loss of his old culture appalled the abbot. Rude mechanicals with elementary skills were supplanting holy men who had studied for years to master the art of producing illuminated manuscripts. The abbot's polemic against the new technology, *De Laude Scriptorum* ('In Praise of Scribes'), dwelt on the producer interest of the scribes. The wider interests of readers and authors did not concern him. He did not write about how movable type allowed an explosion in the number of books and the number of writers who could reach an audience. He did not praise the printing press for allowing readers to purchase books at a fraction of the cost of illuminated manuscripts, or for encouraging the spread of literacy. Instead the abbot praised the art of copying for allowing monks to spend their time enlightening their minds and lifting their hearts as they painfully transcribed the scriptures in monastic solitude.

To the delight of all who tell the story, the abbot did not send his manuscript to the monks so that they might labour in their cells scratching out copies by candlelight. He wanted as many people as possible to read his denunciation of the new technology. So naturally, when he completed his manuscript in 1492, he sent it to the printers, who set it in movable type so he could produce his book denouncing the press and praising scribes quickly and cheaply, and ensure that everyone who wanted to read it could obtain a copy.

A merry little tale the abbot's hypocrisy has made. Enthusiasts for the Web use it to mock the 'reactionary cant' of today's gatekeepers as they try to resist the new expressions of democratic will and personal fulfilment Web 2.0 brings. As a putdown for practitioners of my grubby trade of journalism, I accept that it is hard to better. But I notice that the excursion into history stops almost as soon as it begins. No one goes on to say what happened to Europe after Gutenberg's presses began to roll.

Let me attempt to fill in the gaps. Try to imagine a fifteenth-century Clay Shirky or Julian Assange. Suppose he is a young monk at Sponheim, and is so enthused by the promise of the new presses that he blows a raspberry at the abbot and renounces holy orders to join the 'Gutenberg revolution' that is promising to bring 'a new age of transparency' to late-medieval Europe. If he predicted that printing would vastly increase the number of people who could write books, the subjects they could cover and the size of their potential audience, he would have been stating the obvious. If he imitated today's Net boosters, and predicted that generals would be less likely to massacre civilians because the new technology would spread word of their crimes, later events would disappoint him. The slaughters of the post-Gutenberg wars of religion between Catholics and Protestants in the sixteenth and seventeenth centuries were catastrophic crimes against humanity that foreshadowed the barbarism of the total wars of the twentieth century. They tore the heart out of Europe, killing perhaps a quarter of all Germans and laying waste to areas of Central Europe to such a degree that many towns never recovered. Although printing helped the Protestant cause by allowing Bibles to be distributed in native tongues, countries that saw Protestantism triumph at the wars' end did not experience a blossoming of free speech or a flowering of civilised values. In Oliver Cromwell's England and John Calvin's Geneva, Protestants were as censorious as the Catholic monarchies in France and Spain, and equally determined to persecute heretics, witches and dissenters.

And if our neophiliac monk had been so foolish as to think that print would encourage political liberty, he would have been history's fool. The most striking feature of Europe from the fifteenth to the eighteenth centuries was the rise of royal absolutism in France, Castile, Prussia and Russia, and the emasculation or abolition of the medieval estates and parliaments. France had a revolution in 1789, but the Jacobin terror and the Napoleonic Empire followed. You cannot say that France achieved anything resembling a stable, liberal democracy that protected free speech until 1871. Most of Western Europe did not achieve that goal until 1945. Eastern Europe was not free until 1989. Russia is still waiting. Our freedoms are an exception, not a norm.

Absolute monarchs could live with the printing press. They could censor opponents of the established order by licensing printers or sending critics to jail for their uncomfortably enlightened views, and – here is where everyone gets the radical possibilities of new technologies hopelessly wrong – they could *use* the presses to produce propaganda on behalf of the monarchical order and its religion. The works of political and religious dissenters could still be smuggled into the country, but as long as their circulation was small, monarchs were secure.

Nazism, communism and George Orwell's depiction of Airstrip One in *Nineteen Eighty-Four* have such a hold on our minds that we forget that most dictatorships do not want *total* control, but *effective* control. Their modus operandi is closer to France under Louis XIV or Russia under Nicholas I than to the Soviet Union or Nazi Germany. As in the Europe of the absolute monarchs, most modern dictatorships effectively license publishers, broadcasters and Internet service providers. They tell them they can make money as long as they protect the interests of the regime. Material from dissidents circulates, but its authors and publishers must live with continual harassment.

Vladimir Putin's Russia is typical of dictatorships old and new. It does not try to censor everything. The regime understands that the total control of communism failed because it suppressed too much. On a personal level, the men at the top in the Kremlin do not want to go back to a time when the bribes they received were worth little because the luxuries of capitalism were on the other side of an iron curtain. Their underlings, meanwhile, have no nostalgia for the 1930s and '40s, when Stalin murdered loyal apparatchiks who were working in jobs that look disturbingly like theirs. The elite wants a safe and profitable autocracy, and will tolerate dissent as long as its effects are limited.

Opposition journalists in Russia can find work, and the Net provides an important space for critical thought. But the Kremlin controls the main sources of information, and never lets its critics forget that freedom of thought comes at a price. As in England and the old American South, libel is used to intimidate the enemies of the powerful – Art Troitsky, the country's bravest music critic, faced defamation suits that could cost him millions of roubles and his liberty for mocking police officers who cover up the crimes of the oligarchs and artists who suck up to the governing clique. As in Western Europe, apparently liberal laws the authorities say are aimed against the hate crimes of extremists suffocate wider debates. Edward Lucas, a historian of the return of Russian autocracy, described their potential to harass thus:

> The radio station Ekho Moskvy has maintained its feisty journalistic tone. Its editor, Aleksei Venediktov, says that he will fire any staff he sees practising self-censorship. It broadcasts interviews with hated figures such as the American-educated president of Estonia, and opposition leaders. It is a refuge for independent-minded journalists who would scarcely gain airtime elsewhere. But in just two months of 2007, Ekho Moskvy received fifteen letters from prosecutors invoking the extremism law. Why was the station carrying interviews with such provocative figures? Even an editor as gutsy as Mr Venediktov, a hippy-like workaholic with a burning faith in press freedom, may not withstand such pressure for long.

As in democratic countries, a corporation that wants government favours makes sure its newspapers and its websites do not offend the mighty. The difference between Russia and a free society is that there is no prospect of the government changing, and the Kremlin's ability to punish businesses that cross it includes the seizing of its assets and the jailing of its journalists. Businesses with close links to the Kremlin buy critical TV stations. The new owners sideline the old editors, and the coverage becomes a lot less critical. *New Times*, one of the few independent weeklies left in Russia, hired an editor the Kremlin disapproved of. The regime made its feelings clear to the proprietor. She refused to find an acceptable replacement, but advertisers rewarded her stand on principle by taking their custom elsewhere. Once the authorities had made their unhappiness plain, giving *New Times* money 'would be commercial suicide in a business climate where official disfavour means harassment by every state agency, followed usually by bankruptcy'. The feminists of Pussy Riot can perform punk protests until Church and state decide to silence them. If they had been in a totalitarian regime, the authorities would have arrested them at their first performance. It is an advance, I suppose, but not a decisive one. As well as punishing punk feminists who protest in cathedrals against the Orthodox Church's collusion with the Kremlin, the regime has passed laws that ban 'propaganda for homosexuality', and imposed a criminal liability for libel. It has treated non-governmental organisations which receive funds from abroad as potential foreign agents, and mandated punishments for the vague offence of 'threatening the Russian Federation's interests'.

In these conditions, the best one can say about the existence of opposition websites and newspapers is that they are an advance on the blanket repression of the communist era. To exaggerate their importance is to ignore the fact that supporters of the Kremlin so dominate the old and the new media that no opposition candidate can reach a mass audience. Worse, it is to misunderstand the nature of modern censorship.

Putin and his mafia friends do not worry overmuch that their opponents can publish somewhere in cyberspace or in a few highbrow journals, as long as they cannot break away from the fringe and reach the mainstream. State harassment, up to and including the murder of journalists, ensures that dissidents know the consequences of 'going too far'. Similarly, Bashar Assad's Syria, Hosni Mubarak's Egypt and the Islamists they supported did not care that anyone with access to the Net could find the Danish cartoons of 2005 with the click of a mouse. It was enough that newspapers and book publishers refused to run them, and that other artists and writers who might have satirised religion thought again before doing so. The persecutors of Ayaan Hirsi Ali wanted to silence her dissenting voice permanently. When they failed, they too were prepared to settle for warning Muslim and ex-Muslim women of the high price they might pay if they spoke out against misogyny. Go back to Roman Polanski and the Russian, Ukrainian and Saudi oligarchs England's wretched legal profession welcomed to the High Court in London. They would, if they could, have wiped every unflattering word about them from the Web. A few tried, but for the rest the readiness of the English judiciary to punish their critics and announce that they were men of good reputation was compensation enough.

Writers in the West have already found that the Web does not set them free. Like the Gutenberg press, the Web has hugely expanded the number who can publish – and shown that while it is not true that everyone has a book inside them, they most certainly have a blog. But to reach an audience you must find a way of making yourself heard above the cacophony of millions of competing voices, and understand the importance of putting your name to your work.

An anonymous blogger can print a leaked document or run a denunciation of an abuse of power. But if the abuse is to be tackled, then the blogger or the people who have read his or her work must go out and campaign for change in public. Those who throw off the coward's cloak of anonymity find the law of the land applies as much to them as to anyone else. If they live in a dictatorship, they run into the secret police. If they live in a democracy, they face legal constraints, and find that all the old arguments about what the law should allow or punish acquire a pressing importance.

A refrain heard in the Ryan Giggs and Simon Singh affairs was that individually, each writer or tweeter is too small to go after. Collectively, there are too many of them. That has not been true in all cases. In Britain, libel lawyers use Google alerts to flag every mention of their clients. As soon as Google draws their attention to unfavourable coverage by bloggers, they threaten critics with writs. The costs of English libel law are beyond the means of many newspapers, let alone individual bloggers, and in all but two of the many examples I know of, the blogger has retracted rather than run the risk of litigation.

The Net gives writers in democracies new tools, but it does not spare them the burden of campaigning, lobbying and enlisting support that their predecessors in the analogue age had to carry. As they try to organise reform movements, they may find that the decline of the old media is not wholly benign. The Net's advantages are palpable. Online communities can devote more space to airing grievances than television stations and newspapers ever could. The achievements of Web-based campaigns against corruption in India and child abuse in the Catholic Church speak for themselves. Mass-circulation newspapers and national television stations in free countries, however, can put a country's political class under overwhelming pressure. That power is fading. Replacing gatekeepers' quasi-monopolies with the myriad of sites on the Net also means replacing one knock-out punch with hundreds of jabs. The powerful of the future may find it easier to ignore the pinpricks of little websites than the bludgeon of the mass media.

Meanwhile, politically active Westerners can find that the Web seduces them away from the public they need to influence. It gives them unrestricted freedom, and then denies them the audience that makes freedom effective. The Web has made it easier for them to write than ever before – and easier still to be ignored. Potentially, anyone writing on the Web can reach a global audience. In practice, hardly anyone ever does.

The Web keeps the politically committed on sites which confirm their prejudices, and never forces them to tackle a wider society that has little interest in or knowledge of their political ideas. As for wider society, when there were only a few television channels, the mass audience had little choice but to watch national news programmes. Now they can surf the multi-media world, and avoid all contact with current-affairs journalism. The Web and satellite television risk confining interest in the vital concerns of the day to a minority of politically engaged hobbyists.

Evgeny Morozov, the most bracing critic of modern optimism, emphasises the anaesthetising effects of perpetual amusement. People use new means of communication not to engage in political activism, but to find entertainment. The Net is no exception, and has increased the opportunities for the masses to find pleasing diversions to a level that no one had previously imagined possible. In Russia, China, Vietnam and the other formerly puritan communist countries, the decision by the new market-orientated regimes to allow Western-style media to provide high-quality escapism, sport, dating and gossip sites was a smart move that made their control of the masses more effective. In Belarus, Morozov discovered Internet service providers that were offering free downloads of pirated movies and music. The dictatorship 'could easily put an end to such practices, [but] prefers to look the other way and may even be encouraging them'. Unlike so many who write about the Net, Morozov was brought up in a dictatorship – Belarus, as it happens – and the knowledge that freedom is hard to win explains his impatience with wishful thinking.

I hope I am not making the insulting error of pretending that democracies are as oppressive as dictatorships – such comparisons are the self-pitying and self-dramatising whines of spoilt Western children. I am merely saying that the Web cannot free individuals from the need to challenge the constraints of politics, law and popular indifference, whatever system governs their country. Writers in democracies have fewer constraints, and for that we should be more grateful than we are. But if we want to achieve political change, the new possibilities of reaching and talking to people are offset by the difficulties in breaking out of the ghetto and preaching to the unconverted.

Meanwhile, the Net-induced death of dictatorial systems is far from certain, or even likely. They can adapt, as absolutist regimes have always adapted. They may indeed find the task of controlling easier, because of one benefit the Net brings that none of the old communications systems offered.

With the exception of North Korea, modern dictatorships are not as oppressive as the Stalinist state Orwell dissected in the 1940s. On one point, though, he almost predicted the future. Every reader of *Nineteen Eighty-Four* remembers the 'telescreens' the party installed in homes, that had the potential to watch every movement and record every sound.

Early in the novel, Winston Smith half-heartedly attempts the mandatory morning exercises. He assumes that no one is watching him, and allows his mind to wander, when:

> 'Smith!' screamed the shrewish voice from the telescreen. '6079 Smith W.! Yes, YOU! Bend lower, please! You can do better than that. You're not trying. Lower, please! THAT'S better, comrade. Now stand at ease, the whole squad, and watch me.'

Orwell's image of a dictatorship that could turn televisions into spies in the home never became a reality.

Computers, on the other hand …

# EIGHT

# The Internet and the Counter-Revolution

*Polish border guards were put on alert when they received orders to detain a runaway herd of several hundred cows, which swam across the Bug River from Belarus to Poland. Belarusian authorities now plan to build a fence to prevent livestock from crossing the EU's longest eastern border into Poland.*

RADIO POLONIA, OCTOBER 2006

In the summer of 2010, actors from the Belarus Free Theatre landed in London looking like time travellers from another century. They were dressed in shabby clothes. They smoked cigarettes, and wondered why people tutted so. Their hosts were old-timers too, with records of solidarity with those struggling against dictatorship that stretched back into the Cold War. Index on Censorship, an organisation Stephen Spender founded in 1972 to help dissidents in the old Soviet bloc, greeted them. Tom Stoppard, who had written some of his finest plays about communist oppression, praised their bravery. It was as if nothing had changed since Stoppard was defending Václav Havel in the 1970s.

The stories the company told had an equally traditional feel. Natalia Koliada, its founder, described how the secret police had threatened her and her husband, and forced the company to perform in private houses or in the woods before audiences she had to vet to ensure they did not contain informers. Koliada had an ironic intelligence and an open heart. Even as she talked about her family's suffering, she could not stay glum for long. The absurdity of the dictatorship matched its cruelty, and she was soon bursting into astonished laughter. The company rejoiced in the story of how a herd of Belarusian cows had made a mass break for freedom and swum the River Bug to escape to Poland. Polish border guards had captured and deported the beasts back across the frontier, and the Belarusian authorities had promised to build a fence to keep them in. The human parallels the story offered of an unconcerned world cooperating with a dictatorship were too good for the theatre's writers to miss.

Koliada said that I should never forget that even in Russia the regime renamed the KGB the 'FSB' because of the unfortunate memories the old initials aroused. 'Not so in Belarus. Our dictator still calls our secret police the KGB. The nature of their job has not changed, why change the name? At least he's honest.'

That was the only honesty on offer. The censors and the censored had to play elaborate games, in which neither could admit their true motives. The actors had to pretend they wished to stage a work for artistic reasons, and not because they wanted to criticise the regime. The censors had to pretend that there were no reasons why any rational Belarusian would wish to criticise the regime, and yet find reasons for banning the work anyway.

One of the first plays the company tried to perform was *4.48 Psychosis* by Sarah Kane, a wrenching dramatisation of depression the British playwright completed just before she committed suicide in 1999, at the age of twenty-eight. (4.48 a.m. was the time her night terrors awoke her.)

The censor was in a quandary. He knew why the Free Theatre was drawn to Kane, and why the audience would appreciate the work. Along with prostitution and industrial injuries, mental illness stands at an extremely high level in Belarus. But as a functionary of Lukashenko's dictatorship, the censor could not accuse the company of trying to highlight a social evil the regime presided over, because that would mean admitting that mental illness *was* at an extremely high level in Belarus. He thought hard before passing judgement.

'You can't show it, because there is no depression in Belarus.'

'We're not saying there is,' the actors replied sweetly. 'Sarah Kane was British, so if any government is being criticised it is the British government.'

The logic of their argument stumped the censor for a moment. Then he rallied.

'Ah, but people who see the play may *think* that there is depression in Belarus – even though there isn't – so I'm still banning it.'

Andrei Sannikov, whose good manners and carefully chosen words signalled that he had once worked as a diplomat, accompanied the actors to London. He was preparing to stand as an opposition candidate in the December 2010 elections, and was trying to mobilise indifferent European publics to the Belarusian opposition's cause. He and his friends acknowledged that the Internet helped the opposition at home and abroad. It hosted their websites, and allowed them to mobilise domestic and international support. On occasion hundreds of thousands of people read articles on the Charter 97 dissident site. The Free Theatre told audiences of upcoming performances through blogs. The flash mobs which so impressed Westerners also inconvenienced the police. I will not pretend that the Net made no difference. For the Belarusian as for the Arab opposition, it gave them a new and welcome advantage. When the crunch came, however, it was as if it had never been invented. Belarusians learned the hard way that it takes a little more than flash mobs to shift a tyranny.

Before the election campaign began, Sannikov's press secretary committed suicide by hanging himself. Or that is what the police said. Sannikov did not believe a word of it. There was no suicide note, and his friend had not been depressed in the days before his death, but was looking forward to the coming struggle. Opponents of the regime had a habit of 'disappearing', and Sannikov had good reasons for fearing the worst.

The regime rigged the December 2010 election, and demonstrators came out onto the streets. A ferocious police response met them. Contrary to the predictions of Net utopians, phones that could upload to YouTube in no way inhibited the police, or caused them to worry about what outsiders might think, any more than they restrained the behaviour of the forces of the clerical regime in Iran or the Ba'athist regime in Syria when they turned on the revolutionaries. The police set on every demonstrator they could find. They arrested the entire staff of Charter 97, along with a thousand others. They marched Natalia Koliada to a prison van – 'a kind of mobile jail' – where they made her lie face-down. 'It was dark inside, and I couldn't see a thing. The guard said, "My only dream is to kill you; if you so much as move you'll feel my baton all over your body, you animal." Then he threatened to rape me.' In every corridor of the jail they took her to 'men were standing facing the walls with their hands behind their backs. It was like a scene out of films about fascism.' Perhaps the regime did not realise that it had captured a prize target – either that or a KGB clerk bungled the paperwork. When they arraigned Koliada in court the next day, they charged her under someone else's name with a minor offence. She escaped with a fine, and got out of the country.

They made no mistakes with Andrei Sannikov. The police picked him out at the post-election demonstration. They beat him with truncheons, and held the crowd back so it could not come to his aid. The KGB took his wife too, and once they were in jail they worked out a bestial way to destroy their sanity. The couple had left their three-year-old son with his grandparents. The police threatened to snatch the child and put him into state care, a tactic they had tried previously with Koliada's twelve-year-old daughter.

When they sentenced Sannikov to five years' hard labour for 'organising mass disturbances', spectators in the courtroom cried out, 'Andrei, you are our president!' Battered but dignified, Sannikov declared his support for democracy, the rule of law and enforceable international standards of behaviour from the dock: 'We all want one thing – to live in our own country, participate in fair elections and not to fear for our lives or the lives of our loved ones. That's exactly why we are being tried today, facing fabricated evidence from those who ignored the law. I want to warn all those who neglected the law today – you are bound to appear in court and incur deserved punishment. What's worse – you will inevitably have to look into the eyes of your children.'

They will have to look into the eyes of their children. Whether they will receive the punishments they so well deserve is an open question, whose answer depends on political calculations. Will the growing economic crisis push the populace into revolt? Will Russia abandon its support for the dictator? Whatever scenario one imagines, it is hard to imagine the Net making a decisive difference. As in democracies, the new technologies do not just allow citizens of dictatorships to expand their knowledge. They also help the authorities control the population. With people as with cattle, electric fences can always contain them.

## Welcome to Dystopia

An age of revolution provokes counter-revolution, as elites fight to hold on to power. Their success in crushing democratic movements ought to destroy the whimsical notion that technology determines political freedom. The Iranian and Belarusian regimes suppressed the opposition with the utmost brutality – and survived the revolt. The Syrian and Bahraini governments taught demonstrators that if they took to the streets they would kill them. In Libya, the revolutionaries required the support of the full force of NATO air power before they could overthrow the dictatorship. If in Egypt the Muslim Brotherhood and the army unite to form a common reactionary front, the Egyptians will find that revolution has replaced a bad regime with a worse one – as the Russians found after 1917 and the Iranians after 1979.

Liberals have been able to use the Internet in the struggles of our time. Like the printing presses, it has opened novel possibilities. But the Net does not make democratic change inevitable, because liberalism's enemies can use it as well. As with all other advances in communications technology, the Net adds to the influence of those who already possess it.

Dissidents in China, like dissidents in dictatorial regimes everywhere, welcome the Web. It allows environmental campaigns and protests against official incompetence that would once have been impossible – although it is worth noting that liberal bloggers avoid full-frontal attacks on the Communist Party.

The most popular sites in China offer entertainment, not politics, however, and the authorities see no reason to stop the masses losing themselves in escapism and fantasy. Overwhelmingly, those sites that cater for the niche current affairs market are not written by liberal bloggers, but by nationalists and authoritarian party-liners. They criticise the government not for denying human rights, but for not asserting China's interests with sufficient ruthlessness. The most sinister sites target dissidents. When a professor complained that the cult of Mao in China venerated a tyrant, who killed more people in the twentieth century than any other dictator, the hard-line Utopia website responded by collecting ten thousand signatures demanding that the police prosecute him for subversion. Utopia called him a 'capitalist running dog', 'cow ghost' and 'snake spirit' – insults that outsiders found quaint but that Chinese readers recognised as anathemas the party used to describe Mao's enemies when he began the massacres of the Cultural Revolution. Pro-regime websites, like pro-regime novelists, artists and journalists, face none of the harassment the state metes out to its political and religious opponents.

Liberals regarded China as an oddity after the fall of the Berlin Wall. History was over, and if the Chinese Communist Party wanted to continue to see its country grow, it would have to accept the democratic reforms that Westerners assumed the expanding middle class was bound to demand. When China grew into the world's second largest economic power, without the middle class demanding or the Communist Party granting democratic reforms, the deterministic argument changed. The Internet would now undermine communist rule, and the rule of all other repressive regimes. If dictatorial states tried to restrict and censor it, they would see their economies shrink as open societies reaped the economic benefit of free speech in cyberspace. The crash of 2008 ought to have thrown a bucket of cold water over the excited futurologists. Open societies suffered far more than closed regimes. A member of the Central Committee of the Chinese Communist Party was entitled to wonder why Americans were telling him he must allow free speech when China was booming and the First Amendment had not stopped debt-laden America going through a deep recession.

On a technical level, controlling the Net caused the party few headaches. From the beginning, the Chinese state had been able to dominate the medium, shape its growth, control its structure and limit its users' access to the rest of the world. With the co-operation of every large Western Web company except Google, China blocks the addresses of dissident sites or hijacks users' sessions when they search for suspicious words – 'Tibet' and

'Tiananmen' to name two. The state requires online censors – 'Big Mamas' – to remove politically sensitive postings in chat forums. (The cosy name for the not-so-cosy job comes from the title Chinese families accord to the wife of the eldest uncle, who has the responsibility of guiding and taking care of everyone else.)

Net censorship in China and elsewhere is a private–public partnership. After human-rights groups accused the American communications corporation Cisco of helping China construct firewalls and keyword-searching facilities, a bland spokeswoman was entirely unconcerned. 'Our customers determine the specific uses for the capabilities of these products,' she said. The company was doing what all good businesses must do, and keeping the customer satisfied. When Google pulled out of China after it found that hackers had broken into dissidents' accounts, presumably with state approval, no other Western technology company followed it. They were content to abide by the 'pledge of self-discipline' for the Chinese Internet industry, and to 'refrain from producing, posting or disseminating pernicious information that may jeopardize state security and disrupt social stability' in return for the chance of making money. China licenses Internet service and content providers in the same manner that authoritarian seventeenth-century governments licensed printers. The effects are the same. An official for Sohu. com, a Chinese search engine and content provider, admitted in the early days of the Net that his company was 'very much self-censoring', and would not link to news that might anger the Party.

Attacks on the complicity of Western corporations with censorship came regularly from human-rights groups, and only Google took notice. How long Westerners will have even a minimal capacity to influence decision-making in China and other authoritarian states is open to doubt. Western dominance of the Net cannot last. The speed with which the Chinese economy is growing will ensure that new censorship technologies are developed in an environment where human-rights groups are banned rather than politely ignored.

Authoritarian regimes and organisations do not just censor the Net – they mine it for information. On a scale greater than any other communications technology, the Net offers states the power to spy and to entrap. A traditional secret service that wanted to watch a target could tap his phone and open his mail. The technology was cheap, but listening to every call and reading every letter required agencies to employ teams of eavesdroppers, at considerable expense. If they wanted to hear private conversations, they needed to break into homes and bug them, and send trained agents to shadow the dissident to discover the identities of his contacts.

Now they can simply watch how suspects use the Web. If they can hack into their accounts, they can access all their contacts by monitoring their emails, Facebook friends and Twitter followers. 'Informants and covert surveillance are no longer required when we have vast databases, telecommunications companies, and Internet service providers who accumulate information on our political interests, hobbies, loves, hates, and fetishes,' concluded one security specialist as he looked at the new possibilities opening up for intelligence-gathering. Information is not scattered around in dusty filing cabinets, but collected in easily accessible and searchable files. You might object that true underground dissidents would act like al Qaeda terrorists, and send encrypted emails. The main targets of oppressive regimes are not always psychopaths or potential revolutionary leaders, however. Ordinary citizens concern them as much. Letting them fear that they are under surveillance has as much of a chilling effect on their engagement in political debate as punishments for dissident writers. The knowledge that the state is watching you, or might be watching you, is a powerful deterrent against activism.

The misnamed 'Twitter revolution' in Iran displayed the oppressive power of the new technologies. The authorities posted pictures of protesters on the Net, and asked supporters of the regime to identify them and hunt them down. They used text messages and email to warn Iranians of the dire consequences of 'being influenced by the destabilising propaganda which the media affiliated with foreign countries have been disseminating. In case of any illegal action and contact with foreign media, you will be charged as a criminal consistent with the Islamic Punishment Act.' At Tehran airport, passport control questioned Iranians who were leaving the country – maybe to go into political exile – about Facebook, and went onto their pages to note down the names of their friends.

In Belarus the state's agents have developed their own intimidatory techniques. They write threats beneath politically incorrect posts to spread fear, and act as agents provocateurs on the Web. 'It's very dangerous to be a blogger who writes against the regime,' says Natalia Koliada. 'The Belarusian regime has a special department of people who work at the KGB and Belarusian Republican Union of Youth to monitor the Net.'

Western companies that have supplied China with technology that can track dissidents justify themselves by saying that they sell the same technology to Western governments and organisations. Their implication that the power of the new surveillance technologies knows no borders is correct. In the free and unfree worlds alike, snoopers can accumulate information with a thoroughness that would have made their predecessors salivate.

## A Janus-Faced Technology

Let a small incident, which seems trivial when set against the clashes in Belarus, China, the Arab world and Iran, illustrate the Janus-faced nature of the new technologies.

Paul Chambers worked in a car-parts factory in the north of England, and tweeted in his idle moments. His friends and the friends of a young woman from Northern Ireland overlapped. The two did not know each other, and lived far apart. They probably would never have met had not the social network brought them together. Their friends organised a Twitter party in a London pub to which everyone in the ad hoc network was invited. Boy met girl, and boy and girl liked each other very much. Chambers arranged to fly from Robin Hood airport in the East Midlands to see her in Belfast.

Technological advances allow sexual advances. The invention of the bicycle expanded the gene pool of many a remote region, as it allowed young men to cycle beyond their villages to find mates. In the 1950s, teenage couples appreciated the value of cars that took them away from their parents' homes more than any other demographic. At times today, the sole point of the Web seems to be to allow the dissemination of pornography or, in the case of social network sites, the arrangement of assignations. Chambers was embarking on a romance that Twitter had nurtured and enabled. Just as previously isolated dissidents in Belarus, Iran, Russia, the Middle East and China found that the Web allowed them to make previously impossible connections with political sympathisers, so Chambers found that the Web allowed him to form a connection with a woman he would otherwise never have met.

The joy the Web spread appears plain. But consider the sequel. Before he flew to Belfast, Chambers saw a news report that snow had grounded all flights. 'Robin Hood airport is closed,' he tweeted. 'You've got a week and a bit to get your shit together, otherwise I'm blowing the airport sky high!!'

I should not need to explain that he was joking; engaging in the mock-bombast people use in private conversation all the time. When a woman says to her friends, 'I'll strangle my boyfriend if he hasn't done the washing up,' or one man tells another, 'I'll kill my boss if he makes me work late and miss the match,' they are not announcing a murder. The forces of law and order can rest easy. They do not mean it.

Staff at Robin Hood airport once had to patrol its precincts looking out for unattended baggage, and liaise with the police about credible terrorist threats. The Net gave them new sources of information, and they began to search Twitter for mentions of the airport's name. When a manager came across Chambers' tweet, he passed it to security officers. They saw no reason to panic. They realised that Chambers had not posted a 'credible' threat. But the procedures stated that every 'threat' must be referred up the line, and the airport staff had to obey orders.

A plain-clothes detective arrived at Chambers' workplace and arrested him under anti-terrorist legislation. A posse of four more anti-terrorist officers was waiting in reception.

'Do you have any weapons in your car?' they asked.

'I said I had some golf clubs in the boot,' Chambers said. 'But they didn't think it was funny. I kept wondering, "When are they going to slap my wrists and let me go?" Instead, they hauled me into a police car while my colleagues watched.'

The sight of detectives arresting Chambers scandalised his employers. They sacked him. The police realised that he wasn't a terrorist, just a guy who wanted to see his girl. State prosecutors could not let the matter rest, however, and decided to charge him with sending menacing messages over a public telecommunications network, even though no one took the message seriously, and business had carried on at the airport as usual. The magistrate did not allow common sense to make one of its rare appearances in an English courtroom, and ordered Chambers to pay £1,000 in costs and fines.

Shaken but still determined to give the new relationship a try, Chambers eventually reached Northern Ireland. He and his new friend got on so well that he found work in Belfast and they settled down as a couple. But the case did not go away. The ham-fisted behaviour of the authorities caused outrage on the Web. Friends and strangers came together to urge him to appeal. The week before the case went back to court, he told his new employers in Northern Ireland that there could be renewed press interest in the bomb threat that never was when the hearing began. All they heard were the words 'bomb' and 'threat'. They fired him too.

Paul Chambers' story has become a *cause célèbre* in Britain, because it would once have been unimaginable for a man to lose two jobs for making one lame joke. Security guards at airports could not have listened in to the conversations of random members of the public who had given no reason to arouse suspicion, and would never have wanted to do so. Their employers would never have told them to hang around bars on the off-chance that they might hear someone say, 'If it doesn't get its shit together, I am going to blow the airport sky high,' in a moment of mock rage. Security guards might have spent a lifetime eavesdropping and never heard the offending words uttered.

Suddenly, technology had made the impossible possible, and the possible has a nasty habit of becoming mandatory.

The blessings and curses the Net bestowed on Paul Chambers serve as a wider metaphor. The future may be one of greater information-sharing and informed collective action as people exploit new resources, or one of suspicion as people understand the growing likelihood of surveillance. What happens will depend on where you live, what rights you have, and how persistently you and your fellow citizens engage in political struggles to defend or expand those rights.

All new forms of technology change societies, but how they change them depends on the limits the politics of those societies set.

# The Primacy of Politics

Democratic governments are the natural targets for Net activists. It is easier to find and publish information in free societies that offer legal protections for press freedom. Rights to trial by jury ensure that even those writers who have broken the law can be spared punishment if they have taken on the state in the public interest. Sensible jurors do not like their rulers getting ideas above their station, and will acquit the technically guilty rather than do the state's bidding.

At the most basic level of protecting a writer's personal safety, democratic countries offer a further advantage. If you steal hundreds of thousands of documents from the Russian state and put them online, the FSB will try to kill you. Steal American secrets, and the CIA will not.

This mismatch between the coercive powers of democracies and dictators produces many morbid symptoms. The most prominent is the tendency of democratic elites to succumb to dictator-envy. Rather than despising their opponents, they despise the free traditions of their own countries. How, they wonder, can their decadent, flabby, argumentative societies defeat an enemy who fights to win and lets nothing stand in his way? They think that they can beat their enemy by imitating him, and do not realise that when they become their opponents they defeat themselves. A craving by the US government to have the same ability Islamist militias and Saddam Hussein possessed to torture suspects and hold them outside the Geneva Convention is the shortest and best explanation for the moral and political disasters of extraordinary rendition and Guantánamo Bay.

On the left side of the argument, Western radicals fall for an equally inane error. Because it is easier to expose abuses of power in democracies, and because Western radicals are most concerned about abuses of power in their own countries, they assume that democratic abuses are the major or only abuses of power worth protesting about. Their parochial reasoning leads to the most characteristic of left-wing betrayals. Radicals either dismiss crimes committed by anti-Western forces as the inventions of Western propagandists or excuse them as the inevitable, if regrettably blood-spattered, consequences of Western provocation. The narcissism behind their reasoning is too glaring to waste time on. (In their minds, Western societies, their corporations and foreign policies remain responsible for the ills of the world half a century on from the end of colonialism. This myopic vision has the flattering consequence of making them – the brave Western opposition – humanity's dearest friends, because they, and only they, can take on hegemonic power in its Western citadels.)

The duplicity the illusion sanctions ought to be a true cause for liberal guilt. Because they believe the real enemy is at home, Western radicals ignore the victims of dictatorial states and movements, and provide excuses for their oppressors. They see dissidents in countries like Belarus as tainted, because their sufferings cannot be blamed on the West. At their worst, Western leftists will follow through the logic of their position and collaborate with the oppressors.

Given the persistence of the old pathology, no one should have been surprised that the supposedly radical movement for Net 'transparency' turned on the victims of oppression.

Transparency purports to be a depoliticised ideal. Its supporters say they want information on what governments are doing and on who is trying to influence them. When they obtain it, they wish to use the Net's processing power and crowd-sourcing techniques to root out corruption. On a more elevated level, they hope that transparency will create a more democratic system that enables citizens to participate in the decision-making of previously secretive bureaucracies, as governments put data on the Net and allow the public to analyse it. They do not say what decisions citizens should reach once they have the data. They do not discuss wider political questions – how should a good society share its wealth, deal with the rest of the world, protect its environment, care for its sick and educate its children? More pertinently, they reveal their privileged background by taking the democratic state for granted. They assume that the public they address is already living in a society where freedom of information and open government are at least possible, and spend too little time thinking about all those living in countries without democratic rights.

Transparency campaigners accept that their aims are narrow. They make a virtue of their limited and depoliticised ambitions by saying that all they are doing is 'allowing people to make their own minds up'. They carry no responsibilities for what happens next. Outsiders can judge others by how they use the information they provide, but they cannot judge them. They are the enablers of debates. Where those debates go once transparency has been achieved, and what conclusions the participants reach, is no concern of theirs.

I do not mean 'depoliticised' as an insult, and there is much that is admirable about demands for transparency. Democracy and freedom of information go together, because if the electorate does not know what has been done in its name, it cannot pass a fair verdict on its rulers. Democracy's advantage over other systems is that it allows countries to replace rulers without violence. But electorates cannot 'throw the scoundrels out' if censorship prevents them from learning that the scoundrels are scoundrels in the first place. The limiting of state corruption, meanwhile, is also an ambition that is beyond conventional politics, because it is a universal human aspiration that everyone who has experienced the insolence of office shares.

The emptiness of the transparency movement does not lie in its limited aims, but in the phoniness of its claim that it has escaped politics. WikiLeaks, the supposed source of sunlight for the twenty-first century, which ignorant celebrities and unprincipled activists instructed 'everyone who believes in the power of transparency' to 'stand up for', had a political programme that allowed it to intervene on the side of the world's darkest forces. To quote him for the last time, the transparency movement amply proved the truth of Orwell's remark that 'So much of left-wing thought is a kind of playing with fire by people who don't even know that fire is hot.'

WikiLeaks could not leave the Belarusian dissidents alone. They did not fit into the narrow mentality of modern radicalism. The American and European governments offered the Belarusian opposition nominal support, as they offered support to the opponents of the Taliban, the Iranian mullahs and other anti-Western dictatorships. To a certain type of Western radical, Belarusian dissidents were therefore suspect and tainted. They had collaborated with the great satan. They were not real dissidents at all. So, in Belarus WikiLeaks' conduit was a believer in the fascist conspiracy theory who wished to help former communists fight the democratic opposition. Julian Assange's chosen emissary was Israel Shamir, a renegade Russian Jew who converted to Greek Orthodoxy and embraced every variety of contemporary anti-Semitism. A French court convicted him in his absence of stirring up racial hatred. His published writing showed him to be a Holocaust denier who believed that a secret conspiracy of Jews controlled the world.

The dalliances of the 'radical' WikiLeaks with a proponent of neo-Nazi thought are not as surprising as they once would have been. If you believe that Western democracies are the sole or prime source of oppression, then you are wide open to the seduction of fascistic ideologies, because they come from a radical anti-democratic tradition that echoes your own. If you think that Israel or the West is the sole or prime source of conflict in the Middle East, your defences against anti-Semitism are down, and ready to be overrun.

Assange made Shamir WikiLeaks' associate in Russia. Shamir gave the KGB in Belarus information it could use when he printed WikiLeaks documents that told the dictatorship there had been conversations between the opposition and the US. Shamir went to Belarus, praised the rigged elections and compared Natalia Koliada and her friends to football hooligans. Whether he handed over a batch of US cables without blacking out the names of Belarusian political activists who had spoken to American officials was an open question. The Russian Interfax news agency said Shamir 'confirmed the existence of the Belarus dossier'. The Belarusian state media added that he had allowed the KGB to 'show the background of what happened, to name the organizers, instigators and rioters, including foreign ones, without compromise, as well as to disclose the financing scheme of the destructive organizations'. Given Shamir's record, it was prudent to fear the worst.

WikiLeaks said in public that Shamir had never worked for it, and that Assange and his colleagues did not endorse his writings. Privately, Assange told Shamir that he could avoid controversy and continue to assist WikiLeaks by working under an assumed name. When the BBC revealed Assange's double-dealing, his lawyers accused it of using stolen documents to expose their client – a priceless accusation for the apostle of openness to level after he had received 250,000 stolen US cables.

WikiLeaks then sunk lower. For all my liberalism, I cannot think of one honourable reason why governments should not be allowed to keep information secret that might be used by the Taliban to compile a death list. Yet a death list was what the founder of WikiLeaks appeared ready to give men who would crush freedom of speech and every other human right. The US State Department cables Bradley Manning leaked to Julian Assange contained the names of Afghans who had helped allied forces fight the Taliban. One of the histories of WikiLeaks describes how journalists took Assange to a London restaurant in 2010. The Taliban had massacred religious minorities, murdered teachers for the 'crime' of teaching girls to read and write, and confined women to darkened rooms where passing men could not see them. Aware of its record, the reporters wondered whether Assange would endanger Afghans who had helped the Americans if he put their names online. 'Well, they're informants,' he replied. 'So, if they get killed, they've got it coming to them. They deserve it.'

No man is under oath when the wine is flowing at a restaurant table. Assange denied at a public meeting that the conversation had taken place. His actions justified his assertions. Like a journalist who realises he has a moral obligation to protect confidential sources, he carefully suppressed documents that named Afghans the Taliban would want to kill. His decent behaviour did not last. In late 2011 WikiLeaks put all the US State Department cables on the Net, unedited, unredacted, with the names of better and braver people than Assange could ever be in Afghanistan, China, Ethiopia and Belarus for their dictatorial enemies to find and charge with collaboration with the US.

As I said at the beginning of this book, all the enemies of liberalism are essentially the same. Opposing them requires not just a naïve faith in technology, but a political commitment to expand the rights that we possess to meet changing circumstances, and a determination to extend them to the billions of people from Afghanistan to Zimbabwe who do not enjoy our good fortune.

## HOW TO FIGHT BACK:

## *Advice for Free-Speaking Citizens*

### 1 The political is not personal

The private life of civilised society is built on white lies. Everyone except sociopaths self-censors when talking to friends and strangers. Our relations with others would break down if we did not restrain free speech and treat them with respect. No one, however, should demand respect for public ideas that have the power to oppress others as long as criticism is not a direct incitement to crime. Religious and political ideas are too important to protect with polite deceits, because their adherents can seek to control all aspects of public and private life.

### 2 The personal is not political

However hard journalists find it to argue for the suppression of the truth, demands for a right to privacy are justifiable. They will grow as the Net replaces the anonymity of the twentieth-century city, which was so well suited to anonymous liaisons, with a global village. As in all villages, tell-tales, Peeping Toms and poison pens will proliferate. The Net makes ineradicable proofs of past indiscretions available to every cyber-bully and Net-spy with a search engine. As it opens up previously unavailable information to employers, police forces, corporations, democratic governments and dictatorial states, many will realise that the new technologies are a secret policeman's dream, and ask for the law's protection.

It is symptomatic of the banality of what ought to be a complicated debate that the only argument we hear about privacy is the argument between celebrities' lawyers and tabloid editors – a struggle which recalls the joke about the Iran–Iraq war that 'It's a pity they can't both lose.' As we must deal with celebrities before we can move on, the best solution would be for the courts to offer public figures protection, but to override their privacy rights and allow publication if there is a public interest, even a small public interest, in their exposure. To do that we need judges who instinctively value free debate and are alert to the dangers of the powerful and wealthy manipulating the law. If such judges are impossible to find – and they may be, as we have seen – we should restrict privacy rights for all public figures, as the Americans do.

### 3 Respect is the enemy of tolerance
The loud calls from the religious for censorship in the name of 'respect' reveal the fatuity of modern faith. The religious do not say that they are defending the truth from libellous attack, because in their hearts they know that the truth of the holy books cannot be defended. Instead, like celebrities' lawyers trying to hide secrets, they threaten the gains made in the struggle for religious toleration by saying that those who ask searching questions of religion must be punished for invading the privacy of the pious.

Religious toleration freed men and women from the blasphemy laws and religious tests for office that Church and state enforced. It allowed argument, apostasy, free-thinking, satire, science and fearless criticism – freedom of religion and freedom from religion. The demand to 'respect' religion is an attempt to push back the gains of the Enlightenment by forbidding the essential arguments that religious toleration allowed.

**4 If you are frightened, at least have the guts to say so**
Once one did not write the word 'liberal' and add 'hypocrite'.
Since the Rushdie Affair, the reflex has become automatic. The
worst aspect of the fear the ayatollahs spread was that Western
intellectuals were afraid of admitting that they were afraid. If
they had been honest, they would have forced society to confront
the fact of censorship. As it was, their silence made the enemies
of liberalism stronger.

**5 Once you have paid him the Danegeld, you never get rid
of the Dane**
The slide from religious fanatics calling for the murder of
Salman Rushdie because he had written a blasphemous novel,
to murdering Salmaan Taseer merely for opposing the death
penalty for blasphemy, shows how appeasement feeds the beast
it seeks to tame. All dictatorial systems, secular and religious,
have a capacity to go postal: to move from attacks on their
enemies which can be rationally explained to random, almost
meaningless assaults on the smallest transgressions. It is best to
stop them before they get started.

**6 If you have the chance to enact one law ...**
... make it the First Amendment. For all the crimes and corruptions of American democracy, the stipulation that 'Congress
shall make no law respecting an establishment of religion, or
prohibiting the free exercise thereof; or abridging the freedom
of speech, or of the press; or the right of the people peaceably to
assemble, and to petition the Government for a redress of grievances' is the best guarantor of freedom yet written.

**7 Democracy does not end at the office door**
Demands for elected worker-directors and stronger protections
for whistleblowers are always justifiable, because they restrict
the power of the plutocracy. The banking crisis revealed that

they could also protect national security. Sensible countries should treat banks as if they were hostile foreign powers, and enable, protect and honour those who reveal the threats they pose to wider society.

## 8 The wealthy have means enough to defend themselves, they do not need the law to add to them

Free speech has advanced by a process of declaring subjects too important for states to censor. The American revolutionaries of 1776 said the law had no right to interfere in religious debates. The victories of liberalism and the struggle against the European dictatorships led to the acceptance by democracies that no one should regulate political ideas. The battles of the Civil Rights movement in the American South established that public figures in the United States could not seek the law's protection unless they were victims of 'malicious' attack – that is, of assaults from critics who showed a reckless disregard for the truth. Europe should import that protection, and ensure it covers business as well as politics. Given the power of plutocratic wealth and the dangers the financial system poses to modern democracies, the law should not allow CEOs, corporations and financiers the right to use their considerable wealth to limit free discussion of their affairs.

## 9 Free-speaking societies are rare …

… so protect them, and seek to extend the liberties they offer. Do not imitate the Dutch state and the liberal intellectuals who turned on Ayaan Hirsi Ali for speaking her mind, or the readiness of WikiLeaks to aid the Belarusian dictatorship. If rights are good enough for you, then they are good enough for everyone else.

## 10 Beware of anyone who begins a sentence with, 'There's no such thing as absolute free speech, so …'

… for they will end it by saying something scandalous. There are legitimate limits on free speech. Governments and companies are entitled to keep secrets, as are individuals. There is a need for a libel law, although on American not English lines, and laws against direct incitement to crimes, rather than vague charges against the incitements of various hatreds. But John Stuart Mill's principle that censorship should be applied only in extreme circumstances remains the best guide to follow. The example of the British legal profession's assault on scientists shows that when society gives censors wide and vague powers they never confine themselves to deserving targets. They are not snipers but machine-gunners. Allow them to fire at will, and they will hit anything that moves.

## 11 Location, location, location

It is not what you say, but where you say it. Most who try to censor want total control, but will settle for the effective control brought by isolating and punishing critics. The freedom the Net brings is illusory if it confines writers to working under pseudonyms in obscure corners of the Web. Writers who wish to be heard must break from the fringe into the mainstream by arguing for their ideas in the open. If they live in a dictatorship or a democracy with oppressive laws, they will find that on their own the new technologies offer few ways around the old restrictions on free debate.

## 12 The Net cannot set you free

Only politics can do that.

# ACKNOWLEDGEMENTS

I owe debts to many people. First and foremost to Christopher Hitchens, who gave me permission to dedicate this book to him. I do so with affection and gratitude. Ophelia Benson of Butterflies and Wheels, who combines broad sympathies with a narrow insistence on accuracy, read the proofs and helped at every stage along the way. Padraig Reidy and Michael Harris of Index on Censorship treated my repeated enquiries with patience and good humour.

This book has on occasion had hard words to say about the English legal profession. I must add in mitigation that Robert Dougans of Bryan Cave, David Buckle of Cubism Law, David Allen Green of Preiskel & Co. and Joanne Cash of One Brick Court found the time to break away from their busy practices to provide me with legal advice. If you are ever in trouble with the law, I commend them to you. I am equally appreciative of the informed advice of Anna Beer on John Milton, Klara Chlupata on Internet censorship, Chris Dillow on managerialism and its discontents, Edzard Ernst on the scientific study of pseudo-science, Ghaffar Hussain on the difference between Islam and Islamism, Natalia Koliada on the long struggle for Belarusian freedom, Naomi McAuliffe on corporate lawyers, Christopher Mitchell on M.F. Husain, Douglas Murray on the silencing of dissident Muslim and ex-Muslim voices, Gita Sahgal on the Rushdie protests, Jean Seaton on media history, Simon Singh on fighting the law and winning, Jeremy Stangroom on identity politics, and Salil Tripathi on Hindu nationalism. Many of my colleagues offered me the benefit of their experience, including Tim Adams, Peter Beaumont, Henry Porter and Mark Townsend of the *Observer*; David Leigh and Luke Harding of the *Guardian*; Hilary Lowinger, Ian Hislop and Francis Wheen of *Private Eye*; Heidi Plougsgaard Jensen of *Jyllands-Posten*; Edward Lucas of the *Economist*; Ben Brogan of the *Daily Telegraph*; and the 'Fleet Street Fox' and others who must remain anonymous because of court orders covering their work.

The lines from Wisława Szymborska's 'The Terrorist, He Watches' were translated by Robert Maguire and Magnus Jan Krynsky, and can be found in *Sounds, Feelings, Thoughts*, a 1981 collection of her poetry. I am grateful to Princeton University Press for its permission to reproduce them here.

The hospitality of Christine and Colin Clark and Mary Elford allowed me to collect my thoughts, and Anne-Marie cleared me a space to write.

Robin Harvie of Fourth Estate and Natasha Fairweather of A.P. Watt waited for a manuscript and did not flinch as deadlines whooshed by. If there were a God, he would reward them in the hereafter for their forbearance. There is no God, so my thanks must suffice.

No journalist can write without editors who will back him, and I thank John Mulholland of the *Observer* and Daniel Johnson of *Standpoint* for allowing me to develop my ideas in their pages.

As ever, all errors of taste and judgement remain the sole responsibility of the author.

NICK COHEN
*March 2013*

# NOTES

ix 'There is an all-out confrontation' *For the Sake of Argument*, Christopher Hitchens on Salman Rushdie, Verso, 1993, pp.301–2

INTRODUCTION

xii 'An old way of doing' *WikiLeaks and the Age of Transparency*, Micah L. Sifry, Yale University Press, 2011, p.42

xv 'When countries curtail' Hillary Rodham Clinton, speech at George Washington University, Washington, DC, 15 February 2011

xviii 'The great boon of the web' 'The Frontiers of Freedom', Hugo Rifkind, *Spectator*, 28 January 2012

CHAPTER 1: 'KILL THE BLASPHEMERS'

3 'It would be absurd' *Times of India*, 13 October 1988, quoted in *A Satanic Affair*, Malise Ruthven, The Hogarth Press, 1991

3 'may upset some of the faithful' *Hitch-22*, Christopher Hitchens, Atlantic Books, 2010, p.267

5 'In the film Carmen Maura' *Age of Extremes*, Eric Hobsbawm, Michael Joseph, 1994, p.320

8 'Well, what can one say?' *Does God Hate Women?*, Ophelia Benson and Jeremy Stangroom, Continuum Press, 2009, pp.29–30

13 'The thing that is most disturbing' *Guardian*, 13 February 1989, quoted in *The Rushdie Affair*, Daniel Pipes, Birch Lane Press, 1990, p.113

13 'I do not have to wade' Ruthven, p.86

18 'undermine the people's' Pipes, p.124

18 'direct involvement' Ibid., p. 131

RULES FOR CENSORS (1)

25 **'demonstrates that it is possible'** *Postmodernism, Reason and Religion*, Ernest Gellner, Routledge, 1992, p.22


CHAPTER 2: A CLASH OF CIVILISATIONS?

30 **'British thought, British society'** *Imaginary Homelands: Essays and Criticism 1981–1991*, Salman Rushdie, Granta, 1992

31 **'Abroad it was more or less OK'** *Culture of Complaint*, Robert Hughes, Oxford University Press, 1993, p.115

34 **'no law in life'** Exchange of letters in the *Guardian*, available at http://www.rjgeib.com/thoughts/burning/le-carre-vs-rushdie.html

35 **'This kind of sensationalism'** 'How One Book Ignited a Culture War', Andrew Anthony, *Observer*, 11 January 2009

37 **'Rabbis, priests and mullahs'** Pipes, p.165

38 **'The British government, the British people'** Press Association, 2 March 1989

38 **'The Embassy wishes to emphasise that the US government'** *Philadelphia Inquirer*, 14 February 1989, quoted Pipes, p.155

39 **'Rushdie is a devil!'** Ruthven, p.2

40 **'Approximately fifty women'** 'An All-Too Familiar Affair', Rahila Gupta, *Guardian*, 21 February 2009

41 **'At the heart of the fundamentalist'** *Women Against Fundamentalism Journal*, No. 1, 1990, p.12


RULES FOR CENSORS (2)

44 **'not only will they kill me'** *From Fatwa to Jihad*, Kenan Malik, Atlantic Books, 2010, pp.12–13

44 **'Months of pressure'** Salman Rushdie, *Joseph Anton*, Jonathan Cape, 2012, p. 202

46 **'Sections of the political'** 'Before and After the Norway Massacre – Symbiosis Between Anti-Muslim Extremists and Islamist Extremists', Quilliam Foundation, 28 July 2011

50 **'Artists too frightened to tackle radical Islam'** *The Times*, 19 November 2007

51 **'About one third of Muslims'** Populus poll for *Living Apart Together*, Policy Exchange, 2007

52 **'I think it has become more prevalent'** Mona Eltahawy, BBC *Newsnight*, 20 July 2010

CHAPTER 3: MANUFACTURING OFFENCE

54 'The Terrorist, He Watches', Wisława Szymborska, trans. Robert
Maguire and Magnus Jan Krynsky, in *Sounds, Feelings, Thoughts*,
Princeton University Press, 1981

55 'What I discovered' Tim Adams, unpublished interview. I am grateful
to the author for making his work available to me

56 'For me, India means a celebration of life' Interview with Shoma
Chaudhury, *Tehelka*, Vol. 5, Issue 4, 2 February 2008

56 'I used to have terrible nightmares' Ibid.

57 'You can cover up your goddess' *Offence: The Hindu Case*, Salil
Tripathi, Seagull Books, 2009, pp.17–19

60 'If Husain can step into' 'Assault on Art', *Frontline*, May 1998

62 'In India, a new puritanism' 'Only 3 Cases are Pending Against
Husain', *The Hindu*, 26 February 2010

62 'I have not intended to denigrate' *The Hindu*, 3 March 2010

63 'Whenever Hindu nationalists attack an art gallery' Tripathi,
pp.105–6

64 'We in the West know so little about' *The Jewel of Medina*, Sherry
Jones, Beaufort Books, 2008, p.358

64 'Join me on a journey' Ibid., p.vii

66 'Finally about a month after she had arrived in Mecca' *Muhammad:
A Biography of the Prophet*, Karen Armstrong, Phoenix, London, 1992,
p.157

67 'In Iran after the 1979 Islamic revolution' *Does God Hate Women?*,
Benson and Stangroom, p.59

68 'Although it would be a massive oversimplification' Ibid., p.58

68 'Thou shalt not' Leviticus 18:22, King James Bible

69 'And a man who will lie down with a male' *What Does Leviticus 18:22
Really Say?*, National Gay Pentecostal Alliance

69 'Do not sleep with a man' *Homosexuality and Torah Thought*, Rabbi
Arthur Waskow

70 'to reject literal reads' 'Get Over the Quran Burning', Asra Q.
Nomani, *The Beast*, 9 September 2010

74 'A couple of years ago' 'Our Universities Face a Radical Upheaval',
John Sutherland, *The Times*, 2 January 2010

74 'All the same' Centre for Social Cohesion press briefing, 5 January 2010

75 'When we sat down' 'Lonely Trek to Radicalism for Terror Suspect',
*New York Times*, 16 January 2010

75 **'Quite disturbing level of'** 'Freedom of Thought is All we Foment', Malcolm Grant, *Times Higher Education Supplement*, 31 December 2009

76 **'She was upset'** Ibid.

77 **'There is a very real possibility'** Ibid.

77 **'I never had this power'** 'I Didn't Kill *The Jewel of Medina*', Denise Spellberg, *Wall Street Journal*, 9 August 2008

78 **'Unlike so many other times'** 'Me and Mrs Jones', altmuslim.com, 4 September 2008

78 **'The best response to free speech'** Ibid.

79 **'We don't make a distinction between'** 'Radical Cleric Warned of Big Operation', *The Times*, 10 July 2005

80 **'Fears of Muslim Anger Over Religious Book'** Christine Toomey, *Sunday Times*, 31 May 2009

RULES FOR CENSORS (3)

83 **'Law of Social Responsibility'** In Venezuela, 'While freedoms of speech and the press are constitutionally guaranteed, the 2004 Law of Social Responsibility in Radio and Television contains vaguely worded restrictions that can be used to severely limit these freedoms. Criminal statutes assign hefty fines and long prison terms for "offending" or "denigrating" the authorities. Legal defenses in insult cases are complicated by the unpredictability of courts' rationale, often resulting in a more cautious approach on the part of the press.' Freedom House, World Report on Freedom of the Press, 2009

83 **'The official "Press Law"'** 'Bahrain's Press Law contains 17 categories of offenses and prescribes up to five years' imprisonment for publishing material that criticizes Islam or the king, inciting actions that undermine state security, or advocating a change in government.' Ibid.

83 **'organising the demonstrations'** In Belarus, 'the government subjected the independent media to systematic political intimidation, while the state media consistently glorified Lukashenko and vilified the opposition. Local reporters working for foreign services with programming aimed at Belarus – like Radio Free Europe/Radio Liberty, Deutsche Welle, and the Warsaw-based Radio Polonia – and those working for local Polish-language publications faced arbitrary arrest and aggressive harassment from the security services. A

number of reporters were detained in retaliation for unauthorized demonstrations. In January, a freelance photographer for the independent weekly *Nasha Niva*, Arseny Pakhomov, was detained and beaten by the police for covering a rally against new restrictions on small businesses. He was then sentenced to two weeks in prison on charges of organizing and participating in an unsanctioned rally.' Ibid.

83 'a tyrannical king' Mao began the terror of the Cultural Revolution when officials ignored his orders to theatres to stop showing the opera *Hai Rui Dismissed from Office*, a traditional story of a mandarin who stood up to the king on behalf of the peasants. Chinese audiences whose families had died in the Great Leap Forward did not need to have the opera's contemporary significance explained to them. See *Mao: The Unknown Story*, Jung Chang and Jon Halliday, Jonathan Cape, 2005, p.525

85 'The students killed their first' Ibid., p.537

86 'In Burma, an official' *Small Acts of Resistance*, Steve Crawshaw and John Jacks, Union Square, 2010, pp.44–5

87 'Why would you want to wear' 'Zimbabwean Man Jailed for Ten Months Hard Labour After Calling President Mugabe "Old and Wrinkly"', *Daily Mail*, 7 September 2010

87 'The police arrested a human-rights' '"Blood Diamond" Activist Kept in Zimbabwe Jail', BBC News, bbc.co.uk, 22 June 2010

89 'One must be ready to put up with' Flemming Rose, *Jyllands-Posten*, 30 September 2005

91 'free speech goes far' *The Cartoons that Shook the World*, Jytte Klausen, Yale University Press, 2009, p.186

92 'If Khader becomes minister of integration' 'Politisk Bestyrtelse over Imam-udtalelser', DR (Danmarks Radio), *Nyheder/Politik*, 23 March 2006

94 'We appreciate the incident' 'Somali Charged Over Attack on Danish Cartoonist', BBC News, 2 January 2010

96 'republication of the cartoons' 'Yale Surrenders', Christopher Hitchens, *Slate*, 17 August 2009

96 'It really is open' 'Secrets of *South Park*', Jake Tapper and Dan Morris, ABC News, 22 September 2006

97 'notoriously impertinent paper' 'Firebombed French Paper is no Free Speech Martyr', Bruce Crumley, time.com, 2 November 2011

CHAPTER 4: THE RACISM OF THE ANTI-RACISTS

99 'I was a Somali woman' *Infidel*, Ayaan Hirsi Ali, Free Press, 2007, p.72

100 'The last punishment' Al Jazeera TV, 28 January 2009

100 'Whoever finds it serving' Gay and Lesbian Humanist Association response to the Mayor of London's dossier concerning Sheikh Yusuf Al-Qaradawi, February 2005

103 'She ought to sacrifice' *A Vindication of the Rights of Woman*, Mary Wollstonecraft, London, 1791, Chapter V

104 'accepting systematic merciless abuse' Hirsi Ali, p.244

109 'My father is not' 'Yes, Hirsi Ali Lied. Wouldn't You?', Isabella Thomas, *Observer*, 21 May 2006

109 'neo-conservative wave' 'Secrets and Lies that Doomed a Radical Liberal', Jason Burke, *Observer*, 21 May 2006

112 'gentle gesture of disdain ... so closely attended to' For a full discussion of the attacks on Hirsi Ali see *The Flight of the Intellectuals*, Paul Berman, Melville House, 2010, pp.242–63

113 'A sustained attack' Ibid., p.264

114 'women are often pressured' *Sharia Law in Britain: A Threat to One Law for All and Equal Rights*, One Law for All, June 2010

114 'reformist groups' 'Panic in Whitehall', Martin Bright, *New Statesman*, 5 December 2005

116 'the paper exaggerated' *Tone Down the Shrill*, Hope Not Hate, November 2010

116 'represent mainstream Muslim' Letter to Chief Executive of Channel 4, Quilliam Foundation, November 2010

117 'Your democratically elected governments' London bomber: Text in full, BBC News, 1 September 2005

120 'Absolutely free in their' '¿Pueden convivir en paz el islam y Occidente?', John Carlin, *El País*, 20 February 2005

121 'They condemn homosexuality' 'Woman Artist Gets Death Threats Over Gay Muslim Photos', *Sunday Times*, 6 January 2008

HOW TO FIGHT BACK

135 'to make it easier for men' *Milton: Poet, Pamphleteer and Patriot*, Anna Beer, Bloomsbury, 2008, p.147

CHAPTER 5: THE CULT OF THE SUPREME MANAGER

142 'Between 2002 and 2007, 65 per cent of all income growth' Emmanuel Saez of Berkeley and Thomas Piketty of the Paris School of Economics, quoted in 'The Rise of the New Global Elite', Chrystia Freeland, *Atlantic*, January 2011

142 'In 2012 Emmanuel Saez' 'Striking it Richer: The Evolution of Top Incomes in the United States'

143 'The pre-tax income of the richest 1 per cent' 'Winner-Take-All Politics: Public Policy, Political Organization, and the Precipitous Rise of Top Incomes in the United States', Jacob S. Hacker and Paul Pierson, *Politics and Society*, June 2010

143 'stood at £98.99 billion' *Sunday Times* Rich List 2010

143 'Russia had more dollar billionaires' 'The 100 Richest Russians', *Forbes*, 23 July 2004

144 'received £37 million – 1,374 times the pay' 'Pay Gap Widens Between Executives and their Staff', *Guardian*, 16 September 2009

144 'the ratio of CEO pay to average' *St Petersburg Times*, political fact. com, 20–21 December 2010

145 'a study of wealth in America in 2004' 'The Inequality that Matters', Tyler Cowen, *The American Interest*, January 2011

146 'These are not small sums' 'The $100 Billion Question', Andrew G. Haldane, Bank of England, March 2010

146 'the rich are likely' 'Inequality and Corruption', Jong-sung You and Sanjeev Khagram, *Hauser Center for Nonprofit Organizations Working Paper No. 22, KSG Working Paper No. RWP04-001*

147 'promises all the worst features' *The Storm*, Vince Cable, Atlantic Books, 2009, p.122

147 'Of the fifty-three billionaires resident' *Sunday Times* Rich List 2010

148 'If a man is not an oligarch' Freeland

151 'her school into disrepute' '"You Deserved to be Sacked": Dinner Lady Dismissed for Exposing Bullying in School Gets Just £302.73 Compensation', *Daily Mail*, 4 February 2011

151 'his career stalled' 'Changing the Face of Whistleblowing', *British Medical Journal*, May 2009

152 'told us, rightly, that' *The End of Politics*, Chris Dillow, Harriman House, 2007, p.277

154 'Every Monday afternoon' *The God Delusion*, Richard Dawkins, Bantam, 2006, pp.283–4, cited in ibid., p.272

157 **'How a job offer'** 'Brisk and Brusque', *Forbes*, 6 March 2003

160 **'In the time that you'** 'Goodwin's Undoing', *Financial Times*, 4 February 2009

164 **'A risk manager'** 'Inside Job: How Bankers Caused the Financial Crisis', Peter Bradshaw, *Guardian*, 17 February 2011

166 **'Do you know who I am?'** 'New Witness Emerges in Libel Claim by Royal Bank's Chief', *Independent*, 27 March 2004

167 **'I warn you, don't make'** *The Choice*, BBC Radio 4, 3 November 2009

167 **'I'm doing a reorganisation'** Ibid.

168 **'Most risk professionals'** 'The RiskMinds 2009 Risk Managers' Survey: The Causes and Implications of the 2008 Banking Crisis', Cranfield University School of Management

RULES FOR CENSORS (5)

174 **'individual and collective level'** 'Freedom of Speech and the Thrash of Globalizing Cultures: Lessons from Ancient Athens for the 21st Century', Richard Landes, available at www.theaugeanstables.com

CHAPTER 6: A TOWN CALLED SUE

178 **'The Karma is'** *Polanski*, Christopher Sandford, Arrow Books, 2009

179 **'Fucking, you see'** Interview with Roman Polanski by Martin Amis, republished in the *Observer*, 6 December 2009

179 **'I was going, "No, I think I better go home"'** Transcript of evidence available at http://www.thesmokinggun.com/archive/polanskicover1.html

181 **'when he strolled outside'** Sandford, pp.321–2

182 **'Roman Polanski came over to the table'** 'Polanski Model Says he Didn't Make Advances', *Sunday Times*, 24 July 2005

185 **'each psychopath is more'** 'Crimes Against Fiction', Jessica Mann, *Standpoint*, September 2009

192 **'suffered a very serious injury'** Writ of Summons 1991 – M-6464, High Court (Queen's Bench Division)

196 **'existence of the injunction'** Inquiry into Press Standards, Privacy and Libel by Culture, Media and Sport Committee. Written evidence submitted by Guardian News and Media Ltd, 23 February 2010

197 **'The cost of libel actions in England and Wales is 140 times'** 'Comparative Study in Defamation Proceedings Across Europe,

Programme in Comparative Media Law and Policy', Centre for Socio-Legal Studies, University of Oxford, December 2008

201 **'unduly restrictive libel law'** Quoted in *Free Speech is Not for Sale*, Libel Reform Campaign, 2011, available at http://www.libelreform.org/the-report

206 **'constitutes a clear threat'** 'Libel Without Borders', Rachel Donadio, *New York Times*, 7 October 2007

206 **'When American journalists'** Office of Rory Lancman, 14 January 2008

207 **'The jury in London'** 'How I Spent my Summer Vacation in London', Graydon Carter, *Vanity Fair*, September 2005

207 **'We are not a court of morals'** 'Polanski Called "Sexual Predator"', BBC News, 21 July 2005

RULES FOR CENSORS (6)

211 **'Sorry, I can't'** *Everybody Says Freedom*, Pete Seeger and Bob Reiser, W.W. Norton, 1989, pp.7–8

212 **'Don't let anyone compare'** Ibid., p.17

214 **'It is difficult to see how Gandhi's methods'** 'Reflections on Gandhi', George Orwell, *Partisan Review*, 1949

218 **'If the libel action'** *Make No Law: The Sullivan Case and the First Amendment*, Anthony Lewis, Random House, New York, 1991, p.110

220 **'[I]t is a prized'** Mr Justice Black, *Bridges v. California*, 1941

HOW TO FIGHT BACK

230 **'reasoned that if'** *The Chiropractor's Adjuster*, Daniel David Palmer, Portland Printing House Company, 1910, p.17

231 **'I am the originator'** Ibid., p.19

236 **'ruptured vertebral artery'** *Trick or Treatment*, Simon Singh and Edzard Ernst, Bantam, 2008, pp.175–6

236 **'a 2005 study of British chiropractors'** Ibid., p.178

237 **'At the heart of science'** *The Demon-Haunted World: Science as a Candle in the Dark*, Carl Sagan, Ballantine Books, New York, 1996, pp.304–6

238 **'not a jot of evidence'** 'Beware the Spinal Trap', Simon Singh, *Guardian*, 19 April 2008

241 **'That is in my judgement'** MR JUSTICE EADY [2009] EWHC 1101 (QB), High Court, London

244 **'There was no control group'** http://www.dcscience.Net/?p=1775

245 **'that state you treat'** 'Furious Backlash from Simon Singh Libel Case Puts Chiropractors on Ropes', *Guardian*, 1 March 2010

248 **'There is nothing'** Decision of the Supreme Court in *Red Lion Broadcasting Co., Inc. v. Federal Communications Commission, June 1969*

250 **'At bottom, the Court's'** Opinion of Stevens, J., *Supreme Court of the United States, Citizens United, Appellant v. Federal Election Commission*

CHAPTER 7: THE INTERNET AND THE REVOLUTION

253 **'Out of this concourse of several hundred'** 'The Prevention of Literature', George Orwell, *Polemic*, 1946

257 **'No doubt that the punk'** Islam Online, 1 January 2008

259 **'Deadhead in Davos'** *One Market Under God*, Thomas Frank, Secker and Warburg, 2001, p.ix

260 **'universal liberation'** Parag Khanna quoted in 'The New Thinking', Leon Wieseltier, *New Republic*, 27 January 2011

260 **'foreign policy can no longer be the province'** 'Internet has Changed Foreign Policy Forever', Katherine Viner, *Guardian*, 19 June 2009

260 **'from an economic standpoint'** 'Remarks on Internet Freedom', Hillary Clinton, speech delivered at the Newseum, Washington, DC, 21 January 2010

261 **'no longer a passive'** *WikiLeaks and the Age of Transparency*, Micah L. Sifry, Yale University Press, 2011, p.48

266 **'In places like Egypt'** 'Cairo Activists Use Facebook to Rattle Regime', David Wolman, *Wired*, October 2008

268 **'The use of flash mobs'** Shirky, p.169

269 **'To speak online'** Ibid., p.171

RULES FOR CENSORS (7)

271 **'reactionary cant'** Shirky, p.69

274 **'Art Troitsky'** 'The Dangers of Satire', Emily Butselaar, *Index on Censorship*, 17 May 2011

274 **'The radio station Ekho Moskvy'** *The New Cold War*, Edward Lucas, Bloomsbury, 2009, p.78

275 **'would be commercial'** Ibid., p.80

278 **'could easily put an'** Evgeny Morozov, *The Net Delusion*, Penguin, 2011, p.73

CHAPTER 8: THE INTERNET AND THE
COUNTER-REVOLUTION

284 **'We all want one thing'** Charter 97, Speech to the judges at the Partyzansky court, 13 May 2011 http://charter97.org/en/news/2011/5/13/38527/

286 **'capitalist running dog'** 'China: Mao and the Next Generation', Kathrin Hille and Jamil Anderlini, *Financial Times*, 4 June 2011

287 **'is very much self-censoring'** *Asian Wall Street Journal*, 29 August 2000

288 **'Informants and covert'** 'Privacy as a Political Right', Gus Hosein, Privacy International, February 2010

289 **'being influenced by'** Morozov, p.11

291 **'Do you have any weapons in your car?'** 'Twitter and a Terrifying Tale of Modern Morality', Nick Cohen, *Observer*, 19 September 2010

296 **'everyone who believes'** Sifry, p.188

297 **'confirmed the existence'** 'Holocaust Denier in Charge of Handling Moscow Cables', David Leigh and Luke Harding, *Guardian*, 31 January 2011

297 **'Show the background'** Belarus *Telegraf*, 19 December 2010

298 **'Well, they're informants'** *WikiLeaks*, David Leigh and Luke Harding, Guardian Books, 2011, p.113

# INDEX

# Index